# The Rise of
# Female Kings
# in Europe,
# 1300–1800

# The Rise of
# Female Kings
# in Europe,
# 1300–1800

## William Monter

Yale UNIVERSITY PRESS  NEW HAVEN AND LONDON

Published with assistance from the foundation established in memory of
Calvin Chapin of the Class of 1788, Yale College.

Portions of chapter 2 appeared earlier in the *Journal of Interdisciplinary History*,
XLI (2011), 533–64. They are included herein with the permission of the editors
of the *Journal of Interdisciplinary History* and the MIT Press, Cambridge,
Massachusetts. Copyright 2011 by the Massachusetts Institute of Technology and
the Journal of Interdisciplinary History, Inc.

Yale University Press books may be purchased in quantity for educational, business,
or promotional use. For information, please e-mail sales.press@yale.edu (U.S. office)
or sales@yaleup.co.uk (U.K. office).

Set in Adobe Garamond type by IDS Infotech, Ltd.
Printed in the United States of America.

Library of Congress Cataloging-in-Publication Data

Monter, E. William.
  The rise of female kings in Europe, 1300–1800 / William Monter.
    p. cm.
  Includes bibliographical references and index.
  ISBN 978-0-300-17327-7 (hardcover: alk. paper)
  1. Europe—Kings and rulers—History. 2. Queens—Europe—History.
3. Empresses—Europe—History. 4. Women—Political activity—Europe—History.
5. Monarchy—Europe—History. 6. Inheritance and succession—Political
aspects—Europe—History. 7. Europe—Politics and government—476–1492.
8. Europe—Politics and government—1492–1648. 9. Europe—Politics and
government—1648–1789. 10. Europe—Politics and government—1789–1815.
I. Title.
  D217.M57 2012
  940.09'9—dc22                                                    2011014263

A catalogue record for this book is available from the British Library.

This paper meets the requirements of ANSI/NISO Z39.48–1992
(Permanence of Paper).

10 9 8 7 6 5 4 3 2 1

*For my wife, Rosellen—photographer, chauffeur, cartographer, informed critic—and my daughters, Elizabeth and Onnie*

# Contents

# Preface

When, where, and how have women exercised supreme political authority most successfully? This small book introduces a large subject, emphasizing a distinctive aspect of Western history which to the best of my knowledge has never been examined systematically: Europe's increasing accommodation to government by female sovereigns from the late Middle Ages to the French Revolution. In order to place this development within the broadest possible context, the chronological core of the book follows a global survey of reliably documented female sovereigns before uncontested women monarchs emerged in fourteenth-century Europe, and it concludes with a sketch of conditions after the modern liberal-democratic era eroded monarchical authority throughout most of Europe, so that women could still inherit thrones but no longer ruled. No woman headed any European government between the death of Catherine the Great in 1796 and the election of Margaret Thatcher as prime minister of Britain in 1979—and few do today.

Between 1300 and 1800 thirty women acquired official sovereign authority over major European states above the level of duchies. My book concentrates on women who possessed the right to govern Europe's highest-ranking states, including more than a dozen kingdoms, the Russian Empire, and the Low Countries, not only because they are the most important politically, but also because they constitute a group of female rulers that is both large enough to suggest meaningful changes over time yet small enough to be manageable. These women, arranged in chronological order by the dates on which they assumed effective sovereign power, include the following:

> 1. (1328) Jeanne II, sixteen years old and married, is invited to become monarch of Navarre; joint coronation with husband 1329; widowed 1343; dies 1349, succeeded by son.

2. (1343) Joanna I, nineteen, inherits Naples and Provence from grandfather; marries, but joint coronation canceled by husband's murder 1345; joint coronation with second husband 1352; widowed 1362; reigns alone despite two later marriages; deposed 1381; no surviving children; murdered 1382 by first of two adopted heirs.

3. (1377) Maria of Sicily, seventeen, succeeds father; kidnapped by Aragonese, married 1391 to teenage prince; joint coronation 1392; dies childless 1401, succeeded by husband.

4. (1382) Mary of Hungary, twelve, crowned king with mother as regent; deposed 1384, but usurper murdered 1385; mother also murdered 1385; fiancé crowned 1386; joint reign, dies childless 1395, succeeded by husband.

5. (1383) Beatriz of Portugal, ten, succeeds father; married but deposed 1385 by illegitimate half brother; no children; date of death (after 1420) unknown.

6. (1384) Jadwiga of Hungary, twelve, crowned in Poland and married to converted pagan Jagiello of Lithuania; joint reign until she dies 1399, a month after childbirth; succeeded by husband. Canonized 1997.

7. (1386) After her son (b. 1370) dies unmarried, Margaret of Denmark, thirty-three and widowed, is created "husband" or permanent regent of both Denmark (her father's kingdom) and Norway (her husband's kingdom); also becomes regent of Sweden 1396; with the power to name her successor, she adopts and renames a great-nephew who succeeds her in 1412.

8. (1415) Joanna II, forty-five, a childless widow, succeeds brother Ladislas as king of Naples; remarries but removes husband 1419; crowned 1421; dies 1435; succession disputed by two adopted heirs.

9. (1425) Blanca, thirty and remarried, inherits Navarre; joint coronation 1429; dies 1441; husband (who lives until 1479) prevents son (b. 1421) from claiming throne.

10. (1458) Charlotte, fourteen, inherits kingdom of Cyprus; marries 1459, joint coronation; deposed 1460 by illegitimate half brother through an Egyptian *jihad*; dies at Rome 1487.

11. (1474) Catherine Cornaro, nineteen, king's widow, legally adopted by Venetian Republic; after infant son dies, Venetians proclaim her monarch but depose her 1489; dies in Italy 1510.

12. (1474) Isabel the Catholic of Castile, twenty-three and married, claims brother's kingdom and defeats her thirteen-year-old niece Juana in lengthy civil war; reigns jointly with husband until her death in 1504; succeeded by second daughter (b. 1478).

13. (1477) Mary of Burgundy, nineteen, inherits Europe's most powerful nonroyal state; marries eighteen-year-old heir of emperor; dies in hunting accident 1482, succeeded by son (b. 1478).

14. (1494) Catalina de Foix, twenty-four and married, inherited Navarre from brother 1483; joint coronation with cousin at Pamplona; after kingdom invaded and conquered by Spain 1512, they flee to Béarn; succeeded 1516 by son (b. 1503).

15. (1504) Juana of Aragon, twenty-six, "and her legitimate husband" (the phrase used by her mother in 1474) jointly inherit Castile. Abdicates all responsibilities 1506, immediately widowed; legal status creates confusion for forty-nine years; dies 1555 as her son (b. 1500) abdicates.

16. (1553) Mary Tudor, thirty-six, inherits England, marries younger cousin (already with royal status), who becomes coruler without coronation or defined political responsibilities; dies childless 1558, succeeded by half sister.

17. (1555) Jeanne III, twenty-eight, inherits Navarre; dual coronation with husband; repudiates his authority shortly before his death in 1562; governs alone until her death in 1572; succeeded by son (b. 1553).

18. (1558) Mary Stuart, sixteen, sovereign of Scotland since birth, becomes legal adult by marrying French dauphin, giving him crown matrimonial; both her mother, who had governed her kingdom as regent, and her husband die in 1560; returns to govern Scotland 1561; remarries 1565; husband murdered 1566; remarries again but forced to abdicate in 1567 in favor of son (b. 1566); flees to England; beheaded 1587.

19. (1558) Elizabeth I of England, twenty-five, Europe's first female monarch who never married; dies 1603, succeeded by son of Mary Stuart.

20. (1598) Infanta Isabel Clara Eugenia, thirty-two, and husband jointly created sovereign archdukes of Habsburg Netherlands by her father, Philip II; childless; loses sovereign status after husband's death 1621 but remains as regional governor until her death in 1633.

21. (1644) Christina of Sweden, inherits father's kingdom at the age of six (1632) and governs by presiding over Council of State at eighteen; coronation 1650; refuses to marry but arranges succession before abdicating 1654; becomes Catholic; dies at Rome, 1690.

22. (1689) Mary II, twenty-seven, crowned as joint ruler of England with usurper husband, William III of Orange; dies childless 1694, succeeded by husband.

23. (1702) Anne, thirty-seven, Mary II's younger sister, inherits England; married to first prince consort without royal honors; no surviving children; dies 1714, succeeded by nearest Protestant relative.

24. (1718) Ulrika Eleonora, thirty and married, acquires Swedish throne over nephew; resigns in favor of husband in 1720 after kingdom refuses joint monarchy; childless; husband outlives her.

25. (1725) Catherine, forty-one, widow of Peter I, crowned 1724, Russia's first official female empress; dies 1727, naming stepgrandson (b. 1716) as heir.

26. (1730) Anna, thirty-four, childless widowed niece of Peter the Great, becomes Russian autocrat by tearing up signed constitution; dies 1740, succeeded by infant son of her niece.

27. (1741) Maria Theresa, twenty-four and married, crowned as king of Hungary under Pragmatic Sanction; also crowned king of Bohemia 1743 (husband holds no legal rank in either kingdom); dies 1780, succeeded by son (b. 1740), her official coregent after husband's death in 1765.

28. (1741) Elisabeth, thirty-two, daughter of Peter I and Catherine (see no. 25 above), becomes Russian autocrat after coup d'état; never marries; dies 1762, succeeded by nephew (b. 1728).

29. (1762) Catherine II, thirty-three, becomes Russian autocrat after overthrowing husband in coup d'état; dies 1796, succeeded by son (b. 1754).

30. (1777) Maria I, forty-two, inherits Portuguese throne; husband (her paternal uncle) receives auxiliary coronation; widowed 1786; incapacitated by illness 1792; son (b. 1766) becomes regent 1799; taken to Brazil, where she dies in 1816.

Geographically, outside of a large core zone composed of France, the Holy Roman Empire, and the Papal States, all of which explicitly excluded female rulers, female monarchs were distributed extremely widely across the European continent, as the locations of their official coronation ceremonies demonstrate.

The history of female sovereignty, including the phrases one must use to describe it, involves so many transgressions of prescribed female roles that it seems unwise to impose more theory than the material can support comfortably. Therefore my basic arrangement is organized primarily around the dominant solutions adopted in different eras to the weighty political problems that inevitably resulted from the expectation that all female monarchs would marry. Two caveats must also be entered at the outset. First, as far as

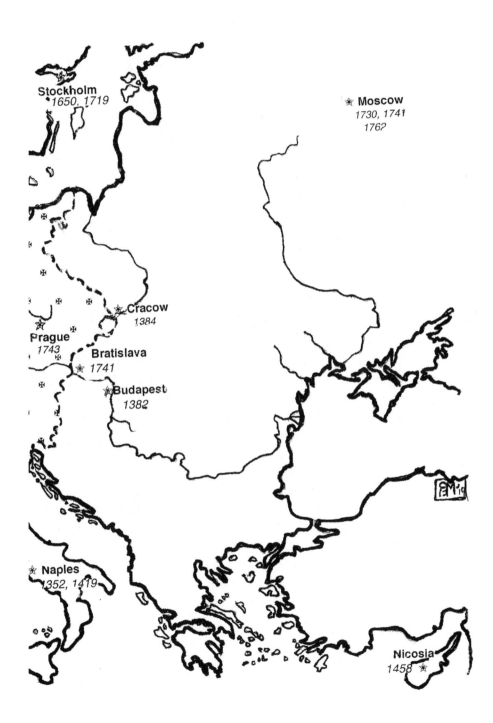

possible this book deliberately avoids using the confusing English noun *queen* to describe female sovereigns. Derived from Old English *cwen*, meaning "wife of a king," it collapses the huge difference between its original and primary meaning and a woman who wields supreme monarchical authority with divine approval in her own right. English, like Latin and other major European vernaculars, has no feminine form of *king*. However, England and many other parts of Europe were ruled by several women who exercised precisely the same authority as male kings and deserve to be called kings. Compounding the confusion, the vast majority of these female kings (except for Elizabeth I of England and two others) also functioned as queens in the original sense because legitimate dynastic reproduction formed a vital part of their responsibilities.

Second, this is not a survey of the history of every type of female authority in every major European state before 1800. That subject is enormous. Aside from so-called soft power, i.e., the informal exercise of influence by women at royal courts, the history of any autonomous hereditary state that lasted more than a century includes at least one wife or close female kin (mother, sister) who exercised formal authority on an interim basis as regents substituting for underaged, absent, or incompetent male rulers. Because the authority of female regents was always delegated and temporary, I do not attempt to survey them en bloc. However, because both the most innovative printed arguments for women's right to exercise political authority and the most extreme pictorial representations glorifying female rule produced in early modern Europe were sponsored by long-serving female regents rather than by women claiming to govern by divine right, I include a chapter profiling the careers and patronage of several culturally innovative female regents who served in major European states between 1500 and 1650: six Habsburg princesses in the Low Countries and Iberian kingdoms and two widows from the grand duchy of Tuscany in France.

My search for pertinent information was made possible largely by the generosity of the Mellon Foundation, which awarded an Emeritus Fellowship in 2008–09 to a septuagenarian who had abandoned this area of scholarship decades ago. The foundation's financial assistance has let me explore places connected with these bygone female rulers, including their palaces; many of the most splendid examples are now museums, although part of the oldest palace, in the small Navarrese town of Olite, is a luxury hotel, or *parador*. It also took me to many well-stocked national libraries from Lisbon to St. Petersburg (this last founded by a female monarch) and into a few archives, among which the manuscript collection of the venerable medical faculty of the University of Montpellier proved the most useful. Finally, a search for visual representations of women sovereigns has introduced me to such auxiliary disciplines as numismatics and film studies.

My largest debts of gratitude are connected with Northwestern University, my employer for forty years. First and foremost, they go to a former graduate student, Sarah Ross, now at Boston College, who collaborated enthusiastically in an ill-fated joint venture which never saw publication but alerted both of us to the posthumous manipulations of fathers by some of Europe's most ambitious female rulers—a subject that probably deserves a full-length separate study. Other former graduate students have also provided invaluable assistance, especially Peter Mazur and Elizabeth Casteen, whose thesis on Europe's first successful female sovereign breaks fresh ground. Departmental colleagues of long acquaintance have also offered precious guidance. Both Ed Muir and Robert Lerner read and commented most helpfully on early draft chapters; Carl Petry happily translated some Arabic sources concerning fifteenth-century Cyprus, and John Bushnell reassured me that I had not grievously misrepresented eighteenth-century Russia. At Northwestern's University Library, Harriet Lightman, an expert on French regencies turned bibliographer, identified and purchased several invaluable items. Input from the early modern graduate seminar at the University of Chicago has also proved extremely helpful.

Friends living far from Chicago have also helped to shape this essay. Colleagues abroad have provided indispensable assistance and much-needed encouragement: in England, Mark Greengrass; in Paris, Isa and Josef Konvitz, Francine Lichtenhahn, Aleksandr

Lavrov, and Robert Muchembled; in Spain, Gustav and Marisa Henningsen and James Amelang; in Portugal, José Paiva; in Austria, Karl Vocelka and his young colleague Karin Moser of the Austrian Film Institute. This work frequently foregrounds numismatic evidence, and it is a real pleasure to thank many unfailingly courteous numismatists, most notably Robert Hoge of the American Numismatic Society in New York, his counterparts at the British Museum and elsewhere in western Europe, and Evgenia Shchukina in St. Petersburg, all of whom tried their best to help an elderly novice with an odd agenda. All erroneous information and unsustainable opinions in this book remain the sole responsibility of the author.

# The Rise of
# Female Kings
# in Europe,
# 1300–1800

# 1

# Early Female Sovereigns in Global Perspective

A woman will be king.
—medieval Zoroastrian (retro)prophecy, from C. G. Cereti,
*A Zoroastrian Apocalypse*

Officially acknowledged female sovereigns have been extremely rare throughout most of recorded history. As recently as 1980 a cross-cultural survey found women as heads of government in only 0.5 percent of all organized states.[1] At the same time, women rulers seem ubiquitous if one looks carefully enough. Regardless of how rigidly any highly organized monarchical state or empire tried to prohibit female government, officially acknowledged women rulers will appear in its history if it endured for more than a few centuries. Because of its extreme rarity, official female rule has yet to be studied as a distinctive historical phenomenon; and for the same reason, studying it adequately requires an extremely long chronological frame. Officially acknowledged female rule can and did occur almost anywhere—even where it was supposedly prohibited—so studying its early history, before Latin Europe began producing several female sovereigns about seven centuries ago, also requires a global perspective. Only in this way can one accumulate a critical mass of trustworthy evidence about early experiences of official female rule in highly organized states that will help identify both long-term continuities and changes in its exercise.

Such a global reconnaissance yields reliable historical evidence about approximately two dozen women who were acknowledged as sovereigns of important monarchies or empires in various parts of the world (primarily in Asia) before A.D. 1300. Almost none of the women in this sample exercised sovereignty more than two thousand years ago because, except for the many reconstructed statues and frescos depicting the female Egyptian pharaoh Hatshepsut (r. 1479–1458 B.C.), contemporary sources offer almost no trustworthy information about them. However, starting with another female ruler of Egypt, Cleopatra VII (r. 51–30 B.C.), reliable contemporary historical evidence survives about several women who became official sovereigns of important states in various parts of Asia, Europe, and north Africa during the next thirteen centuries. This hard evidence is first and foremost numismatic. For over two thousand years the issuing of coins has been a universally recognized method for both male and female sovereigns to proclaim their official status. In combination with more conventional kinds of historical evidence from contemporary chronicles and charters (both of which become more abundant about a thousand years ago), this information enables one to identify two principal paths— inheritance from fathers and usurpation by regents—through which ambitious women could become officially acknowledged sovereigns. It also suggests that, like male rulers who ordinarily claimed divine approval and support, these extraordinarily rare and widely separated female rulers required supernatural doubles in order to explain and legitimate their authority.

## The Problem of Evidence

In attempting to analyze early historical experiences of formal female rule, it seems prudent to avoid not only a priori assumptions about women's capacities as rulers, but also any written testimony that was not recorded until centuries after the ruler's death. Supposedly historical evidence about very early female sovereigns is often intertwined with legendary elements that sometimes overwhelm it. For example,

Jewish and Muslim scholars have produced a rich exegetical literature about a female monarch who is mentioned in both the Bible and the Koran, and Christians have also commemorated her: a medieval Ethiopian fresco depicts her en route to Jerusalem, riding with a man's sword under her saddle and a lance in her hand.[2] For all three monotheistic religious communities, unassailable authority identifies this woman's royal rank (accepting the historical existence of a female monarch thus becomes an act of faith); unfortunately that same unquestionable authority never provides her name, making corroborative evidence about her almost impossible to obtain. Muslim scholars later named her Bilqis, and expeditions still try to locate her royal palace in Yemen, so far unsuccessfully.

Until the past two millennia, what is claimed to be known about female rulers usually contains more disinformation than information. With her numerous statues and temple inscriptions now restored (see fig. 1), Pharaoh Hatshepsut is the exception that confirms the rule. However, Hatshepsut's existence remained unknown to educated Europeans until after 1800. Instead, mythical (or at any rate, unverifiable) early female rulers still crowd people's cultural baggage, as they did a few centuries ago. Like the unnamed Queen of Sheba, some of the early female rulers most familiar to classically educated Westerners, such as the Amazons or Dido of Carthage, lack any corroborative historical evidence. With Semiramis, Europe's second most often mentioned early female ruler behind Cleopatra, the situation improves only slightly. The abundant tales about her recorded by Greeks many centuries later can be corroborated by one or two inscriptions on stelae that link to a similarly named Assyrian woman (r. 812–790 B.C.) who may have served as regent.

Greek legends about Semiramis "invariably stress two things: the 'extraordinary' nature of everything about her, and also her use of trickery to attain political supremacy, censuring in more or less veiled terms, behavior stigmatized as luxurious, corrupt, and especially, without limits."[3] They depict an Assyrian woman whose spectacular transgressions, particularly her usurpation of power literally in male disguise and her subsequent marriage to her son, run systematically counter to normative female behavior in Greco-Roman sources (when Jocasta marries Oedipus, neither is aware of their kinship, and she does not rule). But the Assyrian woman's reported behavior fits well with even earlier evidence from Hatshepsut, who often appears with a false beard and who seized power from her stepson. Despite or perhaps because of such transgressive behavior, these same tales also insist that Semiramis, like Hatshepsut, ruled successfully for many years, as her stelae appear to confirm.

A millennium after Semiramis, Japan records a parallel instance of successful transgressive female rule. Its earliest chronicle, the *Nihon shoki*, or *Annals of Japan*, composed by order of a later female ruler, named as Japan's fifteenth ruler Jingu, de facto head of state from her husband's death in A.D. 209 until her son ascended the throne many years later. Jingu reportedly led an army into Korea and returned victoriously three years later; more remarkably, her son, conceived before Jingu's husband died, was not born until after her return. The only evidence of an early Japanese presence in Korea around this time is a stele discovered in the late nineteenth century on the Yalu River between Korea and China, the interpretation of which is even more hotly disputed than that of the Assyrian stele mentioning Semiramis. Modern Japan remains unsure of how to commemorate Jingu. In 1881 she became the first woman featured on a Japanese banknote, but after the Meiji restoration officially prohibited female rule in 1889 she was reclassified as legendary. Nevertheless, tourists can still visit her officially designated *misasagi*, or tomb, in Nara, an old capital founded by a later female ruler.

Misogyny has a long history, and much undisguised hostility to female rule can be found in early texts from diverse cultural traditions. In Confucian China an early Han dynasty chronicler wrote, "Where women conduct government, peace will not reign." The rebellion of Zenobia of Palmyra (r. A.D. 270–72) lasted barely a year, but a Roman source complained that "she ruled longer than could be endured from one of the female sex." An early Muslim *hadith* predicted that "those who entrust power to a woman will never enjoy prosperity." The great epic poem of Persia, the *Shahnameh*, or "Book of Kings" (c. A.D. 1000), introduced the first historical female ruler of Persia by asserting that "affairs go badly under the domination of a woman" but then praised her achievements.[4]

If a woman had ruled shrewdly, her circumstances were transformed. Another epic poem, composed shortly after the death of a Muslim woman ruler in thirteenth-century Cairo and still widely read today, reverses the Cinderella story. Its heroine, a real-life servant, purchased as a concubine by a future Egyptian sultan, became the spoiled daughter of a great caliph of Baghdad, who gave her a dress made entirely of pearls (her nickname translates as 'tree of pearls') and granted her Egypt to rule. Ironically, the real-life caliph ridiculed the Egyptians for choosing a woman as their ruler and refused to recognize her as sultan.[5]

Surviving physical evidence should offer invaluable assistance in cutting away such luxuriant fictional overgrowth about early historical female rulers. Yet it is difficult, for example, to find an authentic tomb of any early female monarch that provides useful evidence about her. The ruins of the elaborate mausoleum built by Cleopatra VII, where she was presumably buried with her famous Roman ally Marc Antony, remain underwater in the harbor at Alexandria. On the other hand, an almost equally famous female emperor of ancient China, Wu Ze-tian (r. 690–705), is buried in a fairly well preserved but still unexcavated mausoleum. It is China's only joint imperial tomb, holding both her and her husband, Gaizong. She wrote his epitaph, but none of her successors dared to compose one for her: it remains the only imperial tomb in the country with a blank inscription space. No one has yet located the tomb of Tamar (r. 1191–1213), who ruled Georgia in its Golden Age.

Authentic portraits of early women rulers are similarly elusive. Official statues and paintings of Hatshepsut survive in abundance, but all were stylized and most were defaced or smashed to pieces not long after her death. Much later, her Egyptian successor Cleopatra VII had herself depicted in similarly stylized fashion on a temple wall, together with her young son by Julius Caesar (see fig. 2). Where the appropriate religious edifices survive, the few near-contemporary portraits of early female rulers portray them, unlike

Hatshepsut, who is often shown with a false beard, as clearly female. One of the two earliest portraits of Wu Ze-tian, both preserved in a Buddhist temple outside her capital, shows her as a frail, white-haired old lady. The largest number of surviving near-contemporary portraits—five, all in her kingdom's monasteries—depict Tamar of Georgia. Only one, located in a Spanish cathedral, depicts an early European female monarch, Urraca of León-Castile (r. 1109–26).

The most politically useful physical evidence left by early female monarchs comes from their coins. Cleopatra VII was the first woman ruler who put both her image and her titles on numerous coins struck both in Egypt and in several parts of the eastern Mediterranean. Just as her Egyptian predecessor Hatshepsut provides by far the largest collection of statues left by any early female ruler, Cleopatra VII provides by far the richest trail of numismatic evidence left by any female ruler during the next thirteen centuries. While Cleopatra's posthumous reputation rests overwhelmingly on much uniformly hostile Roman propaganda, and few papyrus documents survive from her reign, Cleopatra's coins constitute the best contemporary source for studying her as a ruler, offering an antidote to the legends transmitted by her Roman enemies and by the Jewish historian Josephus. She had four children, all by Roman fathers, but none had Roman citizenship because they lacked a Roman mother, and she never officially ruled alone. However, her theoretical corulers, two younger brother-husbands, at least one of whom she had murdered, never appear on her coins, while her oldest son appears only as an infant on a Cypriot coin from 46 B.C. A decade later her head appears opposite Marc Antony's on a series of coins from Phoenician cities. The most remarkable of these, a silver Roman *denarius* of 34 B.C., celebrates one of his victories with a bust of Cleopatra on the reverse, accompanied by the Latin inscription *Cleopatrae reginae regum filorum regum* (of Cleopatra, Queen of Kings, and her sons who are Kings).[6]

After Cleopatra, imperial Rome encountered one other female ruler, Zenobia of Palmyra, and defeated her also. Zenobia had coins struck in her name only in Egypt, from whose rulers she claimed descent and where female monarchs were well known. Her kingdom was a Roman satellite; in 270 its coins depicted her son jointly with the emperor Aurelian, but the following year Egyptian coins portrayed "Zenobia Augusta." A year later she was captured by Aurelian and paraded in triumph at Rome.[7]

During the next thousand years coins became essential markers for legitimate rulers, spreading from the Roman Empire and its successor states throughout much of the ancient world. As with Cleopatra VII and Zenobia, the political messages later female rulers engraved on their coins can be compared with what chroniclers later recorded about them. By A.D. 1300 ten more female rulers of monarchical states with various official religions, including Zoroastrian, Greek Christian, Latin Christian, and Muslim, had issued coins in Persia, Byzantium, northern India, the Caucasus, and, once again, Egypt. Only one identified herself as the ruler of a European kingdom.

## A Political Trace Element in Great States

In major states, periods of official rule by autonomous women, reflected most accurately through their coins and their titles on state decrees, have not only been extremely rare but also generally brief. The records of the world's three longest-lasting empires—Egypt, China, and Byzantium—reveal officially acknowledged female rulers as a political "trace element," governing each of them less than 1 percent of the time. Ancient Egypt possesses the earliest and longest set of official dynastic records; they cover three thousand years, divided into thirty-one dynasties in the Old, Middle, and New Kingdoms, and include approximately three hundred acknowledged pharaohs. Three of them are women; but although Hatshepsut governed both Upper and Lower Egypt for about twenty years around the middle of these thirty-one recorded dynasties, the combined reigns of its three female pharaohs cover less than 1 percent of ancient Egyptian history.

Much the same can be said of the political history of imperial China, which lasted for almost two thousand years. Like Egypt, it contains many politically active female regents, including a very important one barely a century ago; its early history includes at least

eight Han-era dowagers between 206 B.C. and A.D. 220 who were so
politically prominent that official chroniclers subsequently invented
the euphemism "appear in court and pronounce decrees" in order to
describe their actions without acknowledging them as official rulers.
However, China had only one female emperor, Wu Ze-tian. She had
spent almost thirty years as a regent, first for her incapacitated
husband and then for two of her sons, before declaring herself
the sovereign at the age of sixty-five. Wu Ze-tian created what is
arguably the greatest political success story of any woman ruler
anywhere, and perhaps the ugliest as well; there is plenty of blood
on her hands. A low-level palace concubine, she rose to become
the principal wife of the emperor Gaozong after arranging the deposition and sadistic deaths of her two most highly placed female
rivals. In 667 Wu became her husband's official spokesman when he
suffered a debilitating stroke. After he died in 683 Wu suppressed a
rebellion and instituted a lengthy reign of terror, directed primarily
against traditional supporters of the Tang. She remained at the
center of power, deposing her older son in favor of his younger
brother before deposing him also and making herself emperor.

Wu enjoyed considerable support among Confucians by
greatly strengthening the meritocratic examination system for
choosing officials. She promulgated her most daring and imaginative
reforms—making the official mourning period for mothers equal to
that for fathers and reforming the way several characters of the
Chinese alphabet were written—even before she became official
head of state.[8] There was no organized opposition even when Wu
announced that her reign had begun a new dynasty; but it ranks
among the shortest in Chinese history, ending with her deposition
shortly before her death. As in the case of Egypt's three female
pharaohs, the fifteen years of Wu's official rule occupy less than
1 percent of China's imperial history.

From its foundation by the first Christian Roman emperor until
the Ottoman conquest eleven centuries later, Byzantium offers a third
long-lasting major empire with a trace element of official female rule.
Several female regents also governed it for lengthy periods. As Judith
Herrin has emphasized, two of them exercised crucial influence on

Byzantine religious policy by officially overturning the iconoclastic policies of seventh- and eighth-century emperors and restoring image worship.[9] Only one Byzantine woman, Irene of Athens, eventually deposed an allegedly unworthy son and replaced him on the throne, as her coins confirm. After five years in power, a period during which Charlemagne, Latin Europe's greatest monarch, declared that the imperial throne was vacant and had himself crowned at Rome by the pope, Irene was deposed by a bloodless coup in 802. Subsequently, Byzantium was officially ruled by two sisters, Zoe and Theodora, for two months in 1042. This unique situation in the recorded history of a major state lasted just long enough to produce a gold coin with the heads of both sisters on the front. In 1055 the seventy-year-old younger sister, Theodora, emerged from her monastery to govern the Byzantine Empire for eighteen months. Together, these three episodes of official female rule occupy less than seven years during the eleven centuries of Byzantine history, thus placing this empire also below the 1 percent threshold of official female rule.

Some less durable major early states, such as Sassanid Persia (A.D. 205–651), also replicated the trace element pattern of official female rule. Its twenty-sixth and twenty-seventh rulers, shortly before it was overthrown by Arab caliphs and converted to Islam, were daughters of a famous shah, Khusrau II Parvez (r. 590–628). In her sixteen-month reign, the older sister, Boran, attempted to revive her father's glorious memory and prestige. After executing the murderer of her nephew, Boran negotiated a peace treaty with the Byzantine Empire. She also made a golden *dinar* on which her image resembled her father's, but she never completely restored central authority. Her younger sister, Azarmidokht, became the next Sassanid monarch. Ambitious to "make herself mistress of the world" and promising to be a "benevolent father" to loyal followers, she ruled about six months, making coins closely imitating those of her father. Later chroniclers report that when a Sassanid general proposed to marry her she had him murdered; his son then captured the capital and ordered that Azarmidokht be raped, blinded, and then killed.[10] Ancient Iran's two female rulers also accounted for under 1 percent of Sassanid history.

Mohammed considered female rulers an indication of Persian weakness, but the Islamic world has never been completely impervious to this phenomenon. Like the popes, their analogues in Latin Christendom, its supreme religious leaders, the caliphs, were exclusively male; yet much like early medieval Christian states, early Muslim states included a few acknowledged women rulers. The first to have their names and titles pronounced as lawful rulers jointly with their husbands in *khutbas* at Friday noon prayers governed Shi'ite Yemen (the home of the Queen of Sheba) around A.D. 1100.[11]

## Female Rule in East Asia, A.D. 500–900

From the sixth through the tenth centuries of the Christian era the region where major states seemed least resistant to officially acknowledged female rulers was East Asia. Two special problems complicate this picture. The first is that regional coinage offers no assistance for the study of early female rulers. Although coins have been abundant in the Far East for over two thousand years, unlike coins from other regions they did not carry the names and titles of the rulers who issued them. The other problem is ideological. Confucianism, the region's most important governmental philosophy, has a well-deserved reputation for being deeply opposed to the idea of female rule. Soon after the creation of a durable empire in China over two thousand years ago, an edict specifically forbade women from involving themselves in politics. Nevertheless, Tang China (618–907) saw a female emperor, while between 590 and 900 no fewer than nine other women became paramount sovereigns in Japan and Korea, two East Asian neighbors both heavily dependent on classical Chinese culture. Before the Heian era (794–1180) Japan avoided naming immature boys as monarchs, and six of their adult female relatives, women who in other parts of the world would have been considered regents, ruled here as *tennos* (a noun with no specific gender, usually translated as "heavenly sovereign"). Pre-Heian female reigns actually include eight tennos because two women each ruled twice for several years under a different official name. The first female tenno, Suiko (r. 593–628), reigned longer than any other Japanese sovereign for the next twelve centuries. In combination, their reigns cover 30 percent of the two centuries before the Heian era, a ratio never approached by any other early major state.[12]

Why did early Japan, unlike the early Chinese empire from which much of its culture derived, produce so many female tennos? One possible explanation involves religion. Although various major religions have accepted official rule by women, Buddhism seems the most accommodating, and its early record in East Asia, especially in Japan, is remarkable. Suiko, Japan's first undeniably historical female tenno, had taken vows as a Buddhist nun before becoming a heavenly sovereign. During the decade after Japan's official recognition of Buddhism in 594, her rule saw such major achievements as the opening of diplomatic relations with China and the adoption of an official rank system. Female tennos who ruled during Wu Ze-tian's Buddhist-supported personal reign in China built Japan's first true royal palace in 694 and promulgated a law code in 702, while later female tennos moved Japan's capital, sponsored its first official chronicle, and introduced silver and copper coins. Only the last of these six women, Koken, was never a regent; as she later noted, she became her father's heir "even though a woman." Forced to abdicate in 758 after nine years on the throne, she shaved her head and dressed as a Buddhist nun. Six years later she was restored under a new name, and she made a Buddhist monk her chief minister.[13] Her second term ended in confusion, and her successor, a distant relative, moved Japan's capital.

In Korea, the Silla dynasty also adopted Buddhism before unifying the peninsula from the seventh to the tenth century. It produced three female sovereigns. The first, Seondeok (r. 632–47), was the eldest of three daughters of a king with no sons. Although rebellions and wars marked her reign, she sent scholars to Tang China and built the first known observatory in the Far East.[14] A female cousin, Jindeok, succeeded her for seven years. The third woman, Jinseong (r. 887–97), followed two childless brothers as the final ruler of a unified Silla. During her reign domestic government collapsed; Jinseong died shortly after abdicating, as independent kingdoms arose in other parts of Korea.[15] Overall, Silla-dynasty women ruled Korea nearly 10 percent of the time, well below women's official share of rule in pre-Heian Japan but far above that anywhere outside of eastern Asia during these centuries.

## Female Monarchs Outside of Europe, 1000–1300

In the first three centuries of the second Christian millennium, no female rulers appeared in East Asia, while the most prominent women monarchs governed either Orthodox Christian or Islamic states. After 1170 a mother and daughter, Tamar and Rusudan, governed Georgia for over fifty years. Between 1236 and 1258 two women issued coins as rulers of major Muslim states in India and Egypt; afterward, other Muslim women holding minor titles in thirteenth-century Iran also issued coins. Meanwhile, Latin Europe, which would dominate the global history of female sovereignty after 1300, remained unimportant: from 1150 to 1300 none of the half dozen female monarchs who issued coins ruled a Latin Christian kingdom.

Female rule flourished even in the unlikely atmosphere of a medieval warrior-state like Georgia. In this small Orthodox Christian kingdom of central Asia, where Byzantine, Muslim, and Persian cultures converged, both Tamar and Rusudan described themselves on their coins as "Queen of Kings and Queens, Glory of the World, Kingdom and Faith, Champion of the Messiah, [may] God increase her victories." Both women were married, but their coins clearly illustrate their political predominance. Tamar's coins displayed her monogram (a theta) on top of her husband's (see fig. 3), while her daughter's coins simply omit her husband's name.[16]

Tamar, who ruled jointly with her father in 1178–84 and in her own name until her death in 1213, remains locally famous as the monarch presiding over Georgia's Golden Age, when her kingdom reached its maximum territorial boundaries and produced its greatest epic poetry. Shota Rustaveli, Georgia's premier poet, described an aging king crowning his daughter and commented that "a lion cub is just as good, whether female or male." An Arab chronicler noted that Tamar sent envoys to Saladin after the capture of Jerusalem in 1187 and claims that she outbid the Byzantine emperor to obtain the relics of the True Cross.[17] Many centuries later Georgia's Orthodox church would canonize her, and she remains locally popular; in 2008 Tamar was the second most common name given to girls born in Georgia.

Tamar was exceptionally fortunate politically in two ways. First, she had an early apprenticeship, not only being proclaimed as official heir by her father but also crowned and employed for six years as his surrogate. But Georgia had never had a female ruler, and both her influential aunt Rusudan and Georgia's patriarch, or *cathol- icos*, intervened to have Tamar crowned a second time after his death. Second, her kingdom enjoyed unusually favorable political circumstances—that is, if she could find a suitable husband to command its army and assure dynastic succession. Once she did this Tamar expanded Georgia's borders while both of its great neighbors, Persia and Byzantium, encountered political turmoil. But this window of political opportunity soon closed, and a quarter century after Tamar's death her unfortunate daughter Rusudan could not prevent Georgia from collapsing under Mongol attacks.

Tamar faced considerable opposition during her first years on the throne. Georgia's nobles chose the queen's first husband, Yuri, an exiled Russian prince living among Georgia's neighbors. Although a capable soldier, Yuri proved to be an impossible husband and soon quarreled violently with his wife. Three years after her accession the patriarch and chancellor died, and Tamar persuaded her council to approve a divorce, accusing Yuri of chronic drunkenness and sodomy. Removing an inconvenient royal husband was extremely difficult. Assisted by several Georgian aristocrats, Yuri made two unsuccessful attempts to overthrow Tamar before disappearing into obscurity after 1191. Tamar herself now chose a second husband, David Soslan, a minor prince and capable military commander who had defeated Yuri's supporters. They had two children, a son, born in 1191 amidst great celebrations, and a daughter born a few years later.

Ten years after Tamar's death, her daughter Rusudan succeeded her childless brother. Her reign began well; a year after her accession Rusudan married a Seljuk prince who agreed to accept Christian baptism. They had a son, David, and a daughter, Tamar, who eventually married a Seljuk cousin, a sultan. In 1230 Rusudan issued a coin with a Georgian inscription reading, "In the name of God, struck in the K'oronikon year 450" and an Arabic text translated as "Queen of Queens, Glory of the World and the Faith, Rusudan daughter of Tamar, champion of the Messiah"; its central cartouche contains her abbreviation, RSN. Yet she enjoyed little of her mother's good political fortune, and military setbacks undermined her reign. The Mongols invaded Georgia and conquered it within five years. In 1242 Rusudan became a vassal of the Mongol khan, paying him an annual tribute of fifty thousand gold pieces. When she died three years later the remnants of her kingdom were divided between her son and her nephew.

During Rusudan's lifetime another woman, Razia-ad-Din, ruled a major Muslim state in north India from 1236 to 1240. Like Tamar, Razia had been named as successor and employed as a surrogate by her father, but before obtaining her inheritance she had to overcome even greater obstacles than Tamar. Minhaj, a relatively dispassionate chronicler writing in Persian, experienced Razia's reign as sultan of Delhi. He began his account by remarking that the first woman to rule a major Muslim state, "may she rest in peace, was a great sovereign, and sagacious, just, beneficent, a patron of the learned [Minhaj notes that Razia named him to head a college], a dispenser of justice, the cherisher of her subjects, and of warlike talent, and was endowed with all the attributes and qualities necessary for kings. But," he then asked with exquisite irony, "as she did not attain the destiny of being counted as a man, of what advantage were all these excellent qualifications to her?"[18]

Like a few Turkish Seljuk princesses of that era, Razia ignored customary female behavior and showed aptitude for public business. However, in India opposition to acknowledging a politically experienced but unmarried heiress exceeded even that in Georgia. After her highly respected father, Sultan Iltutmish, died, northern India's Muslim political elite ignored his wishes and elevated Razia's young half brother Ruknuddin to the throne while his mother, Shah Turkan, dominated public business. After six months, Razia staged a coup d'état. She appealed for public support against her stepmother and brother at Friday noon prayers, provoking a riot which first slaughtered Ruknuddin's mother and then Ruknuddin himself. In the aftermath, local notables reluctantly agreed to make Razia ruler of Delhi, although Minhaj notes that the *wazir* refused to acknowledge her, "and this opposition continued for a considerable time."

Razia preferred to be called sultan and behaved like one. Minhaj assures his readers that she "donned the tunic and assumed the headdress of a man" and subsequently kept her face unveiled when riding an elephant into battle at the head of her army. She reportedly patronized schools and libraries that included ancient philosophers and some Hindu works alongside Muslim classics. Minhaj considered her a shrewd, broad-minded politician who tried to divide the hostile emirs and sought local support by appointing a converted Hindu to an official position. Her confirming of Yaqut, a former Ethiopian slave, in the important office of superintendent of the stables provoked a rebellion by several provincial governors, including a childhood friend named Altunia. In the ensuing battle Yaqut was killed and Razia taken prisoner; her youngest half brother, Bahram Shah, was proclaimed sultan. To escape death Razia married Altunia. When they tried to recover power in October 1240 both were killed after being defeated in battle.

The other woman to govern a major thirteenth-century Muslim state remains incredibly mysterious. We know neither the personal name nor the ethnic origin (probably Armenian) of the beautiful, clever, and ambitious servant known as Shajar al-Durr, or "tree of pearls," a name taken from #958–62 of the *Thousand and One Nights*. After an Egyptian crown prince purchased her in 1239, her rise to power, like the name by which she is known, also reads like something from the *Thousand and One Nights*. When her owner, Ayyub, became sultan of Egypt in 1240, Shajar al-Durr followed him to Cairo, where she became not only his sole wife, a remarkable development for a Muslim sultan, but also his most trusted adviser. Although their son died in 1246, later documents, including Ayyub's testament, continue to call her *Umm Khalil*, or Khalil's mother. She was Egypt's official ruler for three months in

1250, during which she became the only Muslim ruler ever to ransom a Christian saint. Afterward, as the second wife of her second husband, she may actually have governed Egypt even longer than Razia ruled the sultanate of Delhi. Early Arab sources uniformly describe her as Egypt's real ruler during this period, during which she made her only recorded royal decision.[19]

Umm Khalil's fairy-tale political rise includes several Machiavellian twists. Her political preeminence began in 1249, when Ayyub fell gravely ill as Louis IX, the Frankish crusader-king and future saint, attacked Egypt.[20] His crusaders captured Damietta at the mouth of the Nile and advanced upstream. When Ayyub died in late November, Umm Khalil concealed his coffin and summoned her stepson Turanshah from exile, while the chief eunuch forged orders from his dead master. However, the Franks learned of the sultan's death and attacked the Egyptian camp, killing its commander. When her stepson reached Egypt in February 1250, Umm Khalil announced Ayyub's death and had Turanshah proclaimed sultan. Proceeding to Al-Mansurah, where the crusaders were besieged, he crushed them in April 1250 and captured their king.

Immediately after this splendid success, the new sultan began replacing his father's officials and ordered Shajar al-Durr to hand over his father's treasure and jewels. Complaining about ingratitude, she fled to Jerusalem, and some equally angry Mamluks soon assassinated Turanshah. When Ayyub's widow returned to Cairo, the political elite, unable to agree on a new ruler, finally proposed her. An eyewitness, the chronicler Ibn Wasil, noted that "all the business of state began to be attributed to her and documents began to be issued in her own name and to bear her own signature in the form "Khalil's mother"; the *khutba* was read throughout Egypt in her name as Sultan. "An event like this," he concluded erroneously, "was not known to have occurred previously in Islam."[21]

Her rule was brief but eventful. An old emir negotiated with their royal captive, and Louis IX agreed to pay half the ransom originally proposed. When the money was rapidly raised, the king and his crusaders departed, unaware that they had been dealing with a woman. However, an emissary of the caliph of Baghdad rejected her title because women could not govern Muslim states, and Syrian rebels took advantage of the unconventional situation by invading Egypt. Ibn Wasil reported that Egypt's emirs "said that it was impossible to defend the country when the ruler was a woman";[22] she then abdicated and they chose a Mamluk named Aybak as their commander. The caliph endorsed him as sultan, beginning a period of Mamluk rule that would last over 250 years. Not long afterward Shajar al-Durr became the second wife of Egypt's new sultan, and they governed Egypt jointly.

Shajar al-Durr's story ends badly. By 1257 she was concealing public business from Aybak and insisted that he divorce his original wife; instead, he took a third wife from a clan hostile to Shajar al-Durr. She then had her servants murder Aybak in his bath, claiming he had died accidentally. Suspicious Mamluks arrested her servants, who soon confessed under torture. While Aybak's teenage son became the new sultan, his mother's house servants beat Shajar al-Durr to death. Their victim had already erected a superb tomb for herself, which still stands inside a school for girls that she had reportedly founded.

One year later (1258), the Mongols deposed and murdered the caliph who had refused to recognize Shajar al-Durr. Mongol leaders soon accepted Islam and proved vastly more accommodating than caliphs toward women rulers; as Gavin Hambly noted, they assumed that "sovereignty could be exercised by a woman as well as by a man, without any of the constraints which seem to have inhibited Muslim women at other times and places from participating in active politics." For example, Absh Khatun enjoyed a long reign (1263–87) and had coins struck as a Mongol client-ruler of Shiraz, a Persian province. The Mongols even allowed Padishah Khatun — who was reportedly raised as a boy, composed poetry, and had originally married a Buddhist — to govern another Persian province, Kirman. She remarried a former stepson and intimidated him into naming her as official ruler. Her gold coins were inscribed *Khadawand 'Alam*. Since *Khadawan* means "sovereign" in Turkish and *'Alam* means "world" in Arabic, the ruler of this obscure province described herself as "sovereign of the world." Padishah Khatun, after ruling for four years, was murdered in 1295.[23]

## Female Monarchs in Europe, 1100–1300

Medieval Muslim women rulers could lead an army on a war elephant or ransom a crusading king, but their female counterparts in Latin Europe boasted no such accomplishments. Not because its queens were overly modest or passive; for example, a chronicler described Sarolt, a tenth-century Hungarian queen and mother of St. Stephen, as a woman who "drank excessively, mounted horses like a man, and even killed a person in a fit of rage." After 1000, queens in Latin Europe possessed one privilege their Muslim and Orthodox Christian counterparts lacked, but it was an abstract one: they became represented on chessboards as the second most valuable piece alongside the king—although these pieces lacked the remarkable powers of Europe's modern chess queens, first described in the Spain of Isabel "the Catholic" in 1496.[24]

Before 1300, women affected the political history of Latin European monarchies only as wives and mothers of kings; very few ruled important states in their own names, and only a handful claimed to govern kingdoms. The architectural historian Therese Martin sums it up best: "In the central Middle Ages, reigning queens were a brief anomaly of the twelfth century, a not altogether successful experiment." Her three examples, from England, Spain, and the crusader kingdom of Jerusalem, "all had turbulent reigns, brought on by parallel situations" when "powerful opposition to the new queens arose after their fathers' deaths." All three were succeeded by their sons, but only the Spanish queen remained on her throne throughout her lifetime.[25]

Coins and charters suggest that Europe's most successful female monarch of the high Middle Ages was Urraca, who ruled the united kingdoms of León and Castile in 1109–26. She was the oldest legitimate daughter of Alfonso VI, a famous king who had ruled León and Castile since 1072 and conquered Toledo in 1085. Urraca claimed her father's throne because (after six marriages!) his only acknowledged son had predeceased him. A twelfth-century Galician chronicle remarked, "She governed tyrannically and like a woman [*tirannice et muliebriter*] for seventeen years." As ruler of what was then Spain's largest Christian state, she issued eighty-eight charters in her own name as "Queen of Spain" and three more as "Empress of Spain"; a few of them claimed she ruled "by the grace of God" (*Dei gratia regina*). The first Latin Christian woman ever depicted on coins with a royal title, Urraca also made adroit use of ecclesiastical patronage. Martin has established her as the principal builder of the great Romanesque monastic church of San Isidoro in León, which she greatly expanded "precisely because her precarious position required a monumental declaration of her legitimacy."[26]

Urraca provides the first (and for a long time the only) evidence from Latin Europe that a daughter could not only inherit a kingdom but also govern it, even in opposition to a husband. During her father's lifetime Urraca married a minor ruler in Galicia and in 1105 bore a son who would eventually succeed her. After her husband's death two years later, she became regent of Galicia. Shortly after her father's death in 1109 Spanish nobles arranged her disastrous remarriage to an exceptionally bellicose and brutally misogynistic king of Aragon and Navarre nicknamed "the Battler." It rapidly degenerated into prolonged civil war as Urraca claimed sole rule over her father's kingdoms. But it took her until 1114 to obtain a legal annulment of her marriage from the pope—an even more cumbersome process than Tamar's dissolution of her first marriage in Orthodox Georgia eighty years later.

After three more years Urraca had reclaimed most of her inheritance from her husband before negotiating a durable truce with him in 1117. During these struggles Urraca maintained a liaison with a prominent noble, Count Pedro Gonzalez de Lara, who witnessed most of her charters and fathered her last children. Although she never married Lara, Urraca discreetly acknowledged their illegitimate son in 1123; like Catherine the Great's illegitimate son over six centuries later, he would play no significant political role. Urraca's oldest son, knighted in 1124, inherited León and Castile two years later when she "concluded her unhappy life," according to a contemporary chronicler, "in giving adulterous birth" at the age of forty-four.

In addition to prolonged conflict with her second husband, Urraca waged war against her younger half sister Teresa in 1116 and

1120–21 over their mutual claims to Galicia. Widowed at the age of eighteen with a young son, Teresa began governing the frontier country of Portugal in 1112. Her inheritance, recently expanded southward by conquests from Muslims, became as large as many other Iberian kingdoms, and after 1117 she issued several documents as queen. After her conflicts with Urraca were finally resolved Teresa held Portugal as a fief from her sister; in 1139 Teresa's son Afonso would make it an independent kingdom.[27]

From 1139 until 1148 Matilda, the lone surviving legitimate child of King Henry I of England, attempted to occupy her father's throne. He had twice made his vassals acknowledge her as his heir, and England's major contemporary chronicler supported her claim. Matilda's coins boasted an imperial title from her first marriage; her state seal, copied from those of German empresses, depicted her enthroned with crown and scepter; after 1141 her charters ended with the formula *et Anglorum Domina*. Nevertheless, her nephew Stephen managed to seize power while Matilda delayed her arrival in England in order to bear her children; and when she finally entered without either husband or children she was unable to depose Stephen or stage a coronation. After governing parts of England for several years she finally returned to Normandy.[28]

Urraca enjoyed greater political success than Matilda, but each heiress experienced serious obstacles in attempting to govern a kingdom. Both had legitimate sons (Matilda's came from a second marriage to a much younger man) who assumed power unopposed after their mother's death. Urraca's ambitious sister Teresa had far worse luck. During their conflict over Galicia in 1120 Teresa became allied to a powerful Galician nobleman, the count of Trava, who abandoned his wife for her. Like her rival Urraca, Teresa had an illegitimate child, and the scandal ruined her political authority. In 1128 Teresa's legitimate son deposed his mother, forcing her into exile with the count of Trava in Galicia, where she died two years later.

High-medieval Latin Europe saw several dowager regents governing major kingdoms for their sons, while several women who governed nonroyal states issued coins. In the Low Countries, the wealthy County of Flanders was officially ruled by two sisters for over seventy years after 1205. However, royal heiresses remained extremely rare. By 1300 female rule seemed in retreat in Europe's most prestigious states: women could no longer become regents in the Holy Roman Empire (as they had been when chess queens were invented), and they would soon be formally excluded from inheriting its largest kingdom, France.

## Patterns of Female Rule

Until fairly recently women had only two ways to become the official rulers of any monarchy. The more common way, as it would also be in Europe after 1300, was through inheritance from fathers. Although royal or imperial daughters rarely inherited directly, one encounters such heiresses in places that were widely scattered both geographically and chronologically. The most prominent early example is Cleopatra VII of Egypt, who always called herself Philopatro, "father-loving." From 600 to 1300, daughters succeeded their fathers to rule monarchies which were officially Zoroastrian, Buddhist, Orthodox Christian, and Muslim—and once in Latin Christendom. Two sisters successively inherited Sassanid Persia in order of seniority. In East Asia, daughters inherited once in both Japan and Korea. Eleventh-century Byzantium experienced a brief joint official rule by two "purple-born" sisters, and medieval Georgia even had a mother–daughter succession.

But even when powerful monarchs chose daughters as their heirs, they were never formally installed without considerable opposition from all-male governing elites. Cleopatra VII was deposed early in her reign and returned from exile to be restored, largely by seducing Julius Caesar. Subsequently, Tamar needed a second coronation in Georgia. In the Muslim world, Razia's father had similarly made her his deputy, but Delhi's emirs chose a younger male instead. She had to foment an uprising that killed her half brother and his mother before being reluctantly accepted as ruler, but then she managed the almost impossible achievement of ruling without needing to marry.

For royal heiresses, marriage seemed almost inevitable, but at the same time it posed almost insoluble problems. Following

Ptolemaic tradition, Cleopatra VII was married to two younger half brothers, both of whom she had murdered. In Sassanid Persia, Azarmidokht's refusal to marry a prominent general soon led to her rape and murder. Both Urraca of León-Castile and Tamar of Georgia experienced huge difficulties trying to dissolve marriages imposed on them by the political elites of their kingdoms. Even Razia-ad-Din accepted marriage to a subordinate prince in order to regain power after being defeated in battle. Thirteen centuries after Cleopatra VII, Shajar-al-Durr also arranged the murder of her coruler and husband when he threatened to repudiate her.

Women's alternative path to sovereignty was to become guardian for a young male heir and eventually usurp his place. Although far less common than inheritance by daughters, this tactic is nevertheless important because it describes the only women who exercised supreme authority in their own names for at least five years in three long-lived major empires: Egypt, China, and Byzantium. All three women had been longtime guardians of young male heirs, accustoming public opinion to their de facto authority before they proclaimed themselves de jure rulers. Hatshepsut had governed as her stepson's regent for at least seven years; Wu Ze-tian and Irene of Athens, who had no royal blood and thus no claim to govern except through their sons, waited much longer before taking supreme sovereignty themselves. Both were forcibly deposed although not physically harmed. Hatshepsut also died a natural death, but her stepson Thutmose III later erased all of her titles and images that had been visible to the general public.

Successful female usurpers occurred only in major empires, and only Hatshepsut had royal ancestry. The closest approximation elsewhere occurred when a sizable state, including modern Egypt and Syria, was briefly ruled by a female sultan with neither royal blood nor a living son. If inheritance by daughters was never unproblematic, any woman who usurped sovereignty successfully needed a rare blend of shrewd judgment, extreme ambition, and ruthlessness at decisive moments—a combination that also describes the greatest female usurper in Western history, Catherine II of Russia (r. 1762–96). The most important historical counterexample to such female regent-usurpers is pre-Heian Japan, where numerous female tennos generally promoted quasi-maternal patterns of female rule; one Japanese mother–daughter succession served a combined seventeen years while their son and younger brother grew to maturity. Once their wards had become adults, these female tennos almost always abdicated into dignified retirement—but one should not forget that Japan's male tennos also seem far likelier than their counterparts elsewhere to abdicate voluntarily.

The extreme rarity of women rulers in major states required some extraordinary forms of self-presentation in order to justify their rule and facilitate acceptance among officials who were exclusively male. One significant tactic was to endow a female ruler with a metaphysical 'body' to complement her physical body. This practice can be glimpsed as far back as ancient Egypt, where the divine aspect of royal identity was called the royal *ka*. Describing a cycle of divine birth scenes commissioned for a temple about thirty-five hundred years ago by Egypt's first major female pharaoh, Joyce Tyldesley noted that it closely resembles the only other elaborate royal birth cycle, made a few centuries later for an unusually young male pharaoh: "We . . . see the royal baby and her identical soul or Ka being fashioned on the potter's wheel by the ram-headed god Khnum. The creation of the royal Ka alongside the mortal body is of great importance; the royal Ka was understood to be the personification of the office of kingship. . . . At the climax of her coronation ceremony, she would become united with the Ka which would have been shared by all the kings of Egypt, and would lose her human identity to become one of a long line of divine office holders. Hatshepsut consistently placed considerable emphasis on the existence of her royal Ka, even including it in her throne name Maat-*ka*-re."[29]

More than two thousand years later in Tang China, Buddhists offered a related metaphysical explanation for female rule. Wu Ze-tian's propagandists faced a far more daunting task than those justifying the authority of Hatshepsut, who was the daughter of semidivine rulers; this woman, as everyone knew, had begun as a low-ranking palace concubine. In 688, shortly before Wu claimed the throne, her nephew conveniently discovered a mysteriously inscribed stone tablet prophesying that "the Sage Mother comes among men—an imperium of eternal prosperity." However, an obscure Buddhist sutra served even better to convince Wu's subjects that a woman could obtain the Confucian Mandate of Heaven. The doctrine of reincarnation had sufficient flexibility to suppose that a divine being could manifest itself at some point in a woman's body. Where the Great Cloud sutra said, "You will in reality be a Bodhisattva who will show and receive a female body in order to convert beings," Wu's supporters drew the conclusion that "we humbly believe that what is said in the *Prophecy of Confucius*, 'Heaven generates the Saint [who comes] from grass' does not refer to a man; here in fact with obscure words it is predicted that *Shen-huang* [Wu's current title] would govern the world." Ultimately, a reincarnated Buddha must be male. Later in this sutra the disciple asks when she will "be able to change this female body" and Buddha explains, "You must know that it is an instrumental body and not a real female body." Like the Egyptian pictorial description of the royal *ka*, Buddha's remark about an "instrumental body" assumes that a female ruler's physical body requires some form of metaphysical double in order to establish its legitimacy. A grateful Wu promptly rewarded her exegetes by creating special temples to expound their doctrine, and two of the master texts used in them have been preserved.[30]

Almost nine centuries later an unmarried European female monarch still found it politically convenient to possess a doppel-gänger. In tracing the origins of an obscure British legal doctrine known as the king's two bodies, which distinguished between the physical and metaphysical aspects of royal authority, the great medievalist Ernst Kantorowicz overlooked the significance of the ruler's gender. Kantorowicz knew that it first emerged in print in 1562, early in the reign of Elizabeth I; but like every other medievalist of his generation he considered kings as necessarily male (which the overwhelming majority of them certainly were), and his research agenda thus ignored the peculiarity of the monarch's physical body. However, the circumstances of its formulation suggest that the doctrine emerged when it did precisely because this king was a woman; it coincided with the first time any major west European kingdom had a crowned but unmarried adult female monarch, and it was applied most often during her long reign.[31]

What links Hatshepsut's Egyptian temple artists and Wu Ze-tian's Buddhist acolytes to crown lawyers explaining the queen's two bodies in Elizabethan England is that all three types of propagandists used considerable ingenuity to adapt variants of a common enterprise to their particular time and place. All three were projecting some form of supernatural double on a royal body whose political authority was unusually problematic precisely because it was a *female* body. Each age leaves its own forms of historical evidence, and these three instances span three thousand years, but they all had to explain unprecedented, yet divinely ordained, female monarchs.

# 2

# Europe's Female Sovereigns, 1300–1800

## An Overview

If women had been universally excluded from exercising the sovereign authority, Elizabeth, Joanna of Naples, Christina, the two Catherines, and many others which might be named, would not have . . . obtained from their grateful country and the world at large, the title of great men.

—Alexandre-Joseph-Pierre de Ségur,
*Women, Their Condition and Influence in Society* (1803)

After 1300, female sovereignty in highly organized states became centered in Christian Europe and remained there for many centuries. With Confucius now the master text of East Asian courts, officially acknowledged women rulers vanished from Chinese and Korean history for a thousand years and almost disappeared from Japanese history: in the eleven centuries from the Heian era until women were officially prohibited from ruling Japan, only two more women became tennos and both abdicated as soon as adult male replacements became available. In the Muslim world Sati Beg (r. 1338–39) issued numerous coins in Iran, mainly using masculine language (*sultan* but sometimes *sultana*). She evoked praise from Ahmadi, a fourteenth-century Ottoman poet; "Although she was a woman," he began, "she was wise / She was experienced, and she had good judgment. / Whatever she undertook, she accomplished. / She succeeded at the exercise of sovereignty." But she did not succeed at exercising it for very long; after a year Sati Beg was deposed and forced to marry her successor. Afterward, a Turkish scholar, Badriye Uçok Un, identified seven women who were named as rulers at Friday noon prayers and also had their names on coins. However, they governed only two minor states: three ruled the Maldive Islands for forty years after 1347, and four ruled consecutively in northern Sumatra from 1641 to 1699, despite a *fatwa* from Mecca declaring that it was forbidden by law for a woman to rule.[1]

The contrast with Europe's increasing accommodation to rule by women monarchs during these same centuries is truly remarkable. From the late Middle Ages to the French Revolution both the numbers of female monarchs and the length of their effective government reached unprecedented levels. Two dozen women were officially acknowledged as sovereigns in kingdoms scattered throughout Latin Christendom, and four more governed the Westernizing Russian Empire in the eighteenth century (see preface). A comprehensive overview suggests an improving record between 1328, when a young heiress was invited by her subjects to rule Europe's smallest kingdom, and 1796, when the last female Russian autocrat died. Several of these women, like the first one, shared sovereignty with their husbands; but most, like the last one, ruled alone.

Unlike almost all of their female predecessors, several of Europe's female monarchs enjoyed lengthy reigns in very important states. Previously, documented women rulers since the time of Cleopatra VII had rarely governed officially anywhere for as long as twenty years; no female tenno except the very first remained on Japan's throne for ten consecutive years. The longest recorded medieval female reign, almost thirty years, occurred in the relatively small kingdom of Georgia. But after 1300 Latin Europe produced four female monarchs (one in seven, a lower proportion than among male kings) who governed major states for at least thirty years: Isabel the Catholic in Castile (1474–1504), Elizabeth I in England (1558–1603), Maria Theresa in both Hungary (1741–80) and Bohemia (1743–80), and Catherine II in Russia (1762–96). Only Isabel ruled jointly with her husband; the others ruled alone. In addition to them, four women ruled important European monarchies by themselves for at least twenty years, while five governed alone for at least ten years and another five ruled jointly with their husbands for over a decade.

In Christian Europe, by contrast with the greatest empires of antiquity, no female guardian ever seized power officially from a young male. The closest approximation occurred in Russia in 1686, when the regent Sofia Alekseevna attempted, via both state decrees and coins, to promote herself to coruler alongside her younger brother and half brother; three years later, her half brother forced her to enter a convent. The sharpest mother–son conflict in Latin Europe ended in 1617, when Louis XIII of France overthrew the government of his mother, Marie de Medici, after seven years of her rule; yet she would remain influential for at least another decade. European regencies produced such bizarre arrangements as France's double state correspondence during fourteen years of nominal rule by young king but de facto government by his mother, Catherine de Medici. Nevertheless, the formal illusion that the male heir ruled was never erased—at least not until 1762, when Catherine II of Russia immediately disabused those supporters who expected her to govern temporarily as a regent for her eight-year-old son.

## Numismatics as a Litmus Test for Sovereignty

Ever since the time of Cleopatra VII numismatic evidence has offered admirably clear and precise guidance for deciding whether or not to consider a woman as the reigning sovereign of a particular kingdom or major independent state, either alone or jointly with a man (two female co-sovereigns appear on the same coin only once, in eleventh-century Byzantium, and the arrangement lasted less than two months).[2] Minting coins had become a prerogative of legitimate sovereigns throughout Europe long before women began acquiring thrones in significant numbers. As female sovereigns became less uncommon in late medieval Europe, their coins express their claims to possess exactly the same divine right status as their male counterparts; immediately following the ruler's name on the coin's face comes the phrase *Dei Gratia Regina*, "Monarch by the Grace of God." The custom spread quickly to autonomous subroyal women rulers like Joanna of Brabant, who ruled a major duchy in the Low

Countries for half a century after 1355; she even issued coins during her husband's lifetime calling her Duke (*Dux*) of Brabant by the Grace of God.[3]

Between 1350 and 1800 almost two dozen European women, including several named jointly with their husbands, issued coins with some form of *D.G. Reg.* after their names. The small size of many of these coins required other abbreviations, particularly for joint reigns that used both names. One from early fifteenth-century Navarre used "*J*(uan) + *B*(lanca) *Dei Gra*(tia) *Rex* + *R*(e)*g*(in)*a Navarra*"; only the name of their kingdom was spelled in full. Of course, a woman ruling alone also needed abbreviations if she held many possessions. Some small coins from the eighteenth-century Habsburg Netherlands are inscribed *M.T.D.G.R.IMP.G.H.B.REG. A.A.D.BURG*, for "Maria Theresa by the Grace of God Roman Empress in Germany, Queen of Hungary and Bohemia, Archduchess of Austria and Duchess of Burgundy" (those minted for use in Luxembourg end with *D.LUX.*). The only words even partially spelled out are "Empress," "Queen," and the location of her local mint, in this case "Burgundy."

In addition to providing thousands of pieces of evidence from many parts of Europe affirming that women sovereigns governed by divine right, coins offer both iconographic and diachronic advantages to political historians. Those made of noble metals, gold or silver, often provide metallic portraits of female rulers. Until the very end of the fifteenth century few of Europe's female monarchs put their effigies on their coins, and none seem as realistic as some of Cleopatra VII's effigies. Afterward, every European female sovereign did so, sometimes with husbands but more often alone. After 1550 coins usually carry dates, making it possible to pinpoint changes in the official status of such sovereigns as Mary Tudor and Mary of Scotland when they married during their reigns; in the case of Mary of Scotland they reveal even changes in her husband's legal status during their marriage.

Even the most obscure and unfortunate late medieval royal heiresses, including very young women who were rapidly over-thrown, have left numismatic testimony to the legitimacy of their claims. Only three known silver coins bear the name and effigy of the unfortunate princess Beatriz, a preadolescent Portuguese heiress totally dependent on Castilian aid who rarely saw her father's kingdom after his death in 1383. Ninety years later, more surviving coins bear the name of the equally unfortunate princess Juana, a juvenile Castilian heiress heavily dependent on Portuguese aid in her unsuccessful struggle against her now-famous aunt Isabel of Castile. Because coins faithfully reflect the official, but not necessarily the real, sovereigns, they occasionally send misleading messages. The most extreme example is Isabel's successor Juana the Mad, who never functioned as Castile's ruler during her last forty-nine years; however, because she remained Spain's official or 'proprietary' monarch, her name and titles and sometimes her effigy appeared on millions of Spanish coins. Since Juana's oldest son was Spain's de facto ruler for almost forty years, she also became the only female monarch in Europe whose name appears on millions of coins together with that of a man other than her husband.

Numismatic evidence also helps clarify the complex status of two women in this sample, Mary of Burgundy and her great-great-granddaughter Isabel Clara Eugenia, who became sovereigns in the Low Countries, western Europe's most important nonroyal state. Through their marriages both women were archduchesses of Austria; but the first had inherited these possessions and governed them in 1477–82 as a duchess of Burgundy, while the second ruled from 1598 to 1621 as a Spanish infanta. In population and certainly in wealth, Mary's legacy in fifteenth-century Burgundy outranked all but the very greatest monarchies of the time. Her father had narrowly missed becoming a king in 1473; four years later his only child, a daughter, still unmarried at nineteen, inherited his vast possessions. His heiress soon married the son and heir of the Holy Roman emperor, but her numismatic privileges remained intact. One day after their wedding all provincial mintmasters were instructed to omit his name from her coins, and these guidelines were scrupulously observed until her death.[4]

The other female sovereign of the Low Countries suffered from three major disadvantages compared to her great-great-grandmother.

First, under the terms of her father's will, Isabel Clara Eugenia had to marry her Austrian archduke before claiming her inheritance in the Low Countries, and he could claim sovereign status only after marrying her; thus, as their coins confirm, they had to reign jointly. Second, the Archdukes, as they are still popularly known, governed barely half of Mary of Burgundy's possessions, essentially only present-day Belgium and Luxemburg. Third, both would lose sovereign status if either of them died childless. Numismatic evidence confirms that their names and images disappeared abruptly from regional coins after Isabel's husband died in 1621, although she continued to serve for twelve years as its governor general.[5]

Not all of Europe's major female sovereigns between 1300 and 1800 who are listed in the preface were monarchs. If both archduchesses who issued coins in the Low Countries were one formal rank lower, four other women were one rank higher. Emperors of either sex outranked kings, and these eighteenth-century Russian women issued coins proclaiming them *Imperatritsas*, empresses, and autocrats. Numismatics thus offers a uniform criterion for identifying a total of thirty female sovereigns, including empresses and archduchesses, whose coins claimed that they ruled major European states "by the grace of God" between 1300 and 1800. Coins by themselves obviously reveal little about how or even if a sovereign actually governed, but the sample they provide seems sufficiently large to permit some meaningful observations about the evolution of female rule throughout Europe across these five centuries.

There is even an exception to confirm the general usefulness of numismatic criteria for identifying de jure women sovereigns. Margaret of Denmark, who is generally accepted as having been monarch of two late medieval kingdoms, Denmark and Norway, for over a quarter century (1386–1412), never issued any coins bearing her name, although her adopted male successor was issuing coins even before her death.[6] While it is always difficult to explain something that did not happen, it seems pertinent to note that Margaret, the younger daughter of a Danish king and the wife (and later, widow) of a Norwegian king, had no hereditary claim to either kingdom. In Denmark she usually referred to herself as "the king's

daughter" or as the only living child of its previous king and thus the
"rightful heir" instead of the son of her deceased older sister. After
1376 she became regent of Denmark for her young son, adding
Norway after her husband, the boy's father, died in 1380. When her
son died unmarried in 1386, Margaret received authority to continue
governing both kingdoms alone, indefinitely, as a sort of permanent
regent with the right to designate her successor. She neither called
herself a monarch nor claimed to rule by divine right: thus, although
functioning as a monarch for all practical purposes, she lacked the
right to strike coins. Another peculiar late medieval female
monarch—Catherine Cornaro, a Venetian noblewoman and widow
of the previous king, nominally sovereign of the kingdom of Cyprus
in 1474–89—had pseudodynastic silver coins calling her Catherine
of Venice, with the usual *D. G. Reg.*

Neither queens nor female regents—not even Margaret of
Denmark—possessed this essential privilege of sovereignty. Unlike
some Roman emperors, European kings never named their wives on
their coins. Even Isabel of Castile, who enjoyed some unusual privileges in her husband Ferdinand's kingdom, is not named on coins
from Aragon, while his name always appears on hers in Castile. As
this example illustrates, joint rule posed numismatic problems for
any married royal heiress. Only once, in mid-fifteenth-century
Cyprus, did both the heiress and her husband issue separate silver
coins after his coronation, and many more survive with his name
than with hers. Joint effigies of husbands and wives rarely appear on
the same coin before 1497, when Castile's new high-value *excelentes*
depicted both Isabel and Ferdinand crowned and facing each other.
This motif was copied immediately by the less famous joint
monarchs of a small neighboring kingdom, Navarre. Until the eighteenth century, high-value coins of married female sovereigns
provide many similar examples of joint effigies, always with the
husband's name first and his face on the left. As late as 1689–94
England's high-value coins even half-conceal the face of Mary II
behind that of her husband, William III.

At the same time, numismatic evidence suggests an increasing
degree of personal autonomy among early modern female monarchs,

who as early as 1553 were shown enthroned majestically on gold coins called sovereigns. Thirteen years later, another woman put her name ahead of her husband's on coins called royals. In the mid-seventeenth century Christina of Sweden wore a laurel wreath instead of a crown on her coins. After 1700, starting with Mary II's younger sister Anne, the coins of European married royal heiresses no longer depict or name their husbands—except the last one. D. Pedro III of Portugal was a paternal uncle of his wife, Maria I, and had received an auxiliary coronation; they were thereafter depicted on Portugal's high-value coins, but, in an exact reversal of William III and Mary II, her profile overshadows his. Numismatic evidence illustrates how the role of prince consort became a royal institution, one which has lasted until the present.

## Female Sovereigns: When and Where?

If one divides the list of Europe's thirty female sovereigns given in the preface at the chronological midpoint of these five centuries, 1550, it splits them into equal halves and reveals some significant differences between the earlier and later groups. Most of the first group were younger women who generally ruled in close association with and often politically subordinated to their husbands. Fourteenth- and fifteenth-century Europe contained approximately twenty autonomous kingdoms, although their numbers were gradually contracting. Female inheritance, previously rare in Latin Christendom, occurred frequently as fifteen women acquired sovereignty in twelve kingdoms. Most of them were youthful: two-thirds inherited before their twentieth birthday. Many had husbands who received joint coronations and inherited if their wives died childless, which happened on four occasions. However, by the late fourteenth century an older woman ruled a large kingdom alone for twenty years, while Margaret of Denmark governed two kingdoms even longer and became regent of a third. A century later the very active Isabel of Castile ruled a major European kingdom jointly with her husband for thirty years.

In the second half of this period (1550–1800) relatively few monarchies that permitted female inheritance remained. The last small kingdoms in western Europe, Scotland and Navarre, lost their autonomy after a son of their final heiress also inherited a major neighboring kingdom. By 1620 Europe contained few separate kingdoms: England-Scotland, France-Navarre (which prohibited female inheritance), Denmark-Norway, Sweden (which prohibited female inheritance from 1654 until 1683 and after 1720), Poland-Lithuania (elective after 1572), Hungary, Bohemia (also theoretically elective), and Spain (Castile-Aragon, which also prohibited female succession after its acquisition by a French prince in 1700). Portugal lost its autonomy in 1580 but regained it in 1640. In 1713 Prussia, a Germanic state that excluded female rulers, became the first new monarchy in Europe since the Middle Ages.

Despite such restrictions, after the midpoint of these five centuries eleven women claimed thrones in eight kingdoms (Maria Theresa had coronations in two kingdoms), and four more ruled the Russian Empire. Few women in this group inherited before the age of twenty, but they generally governed for longer periods than the previous group. After 1550 Europe saw fewer female figureheads than before, and each of its nine genuine royal heiresses governed her kingdom autonomously for at least part of her reign. After 1566 few of them had husbands as joint rulers, although it was still possible for a husband to succeed his wife as sole ruler as late as 1694. Three of them, including the last to inherit as a young girl (in 1632), preferred to avoid marriage.

These examples reinforce clues from numismatic evidence that the political autonomy of Europe's royal heiresses increased between the late Middle Ages and the eighteenth century. At first, most of them inherited very young, married very early, and frequently played only minor roles in governmental records; by the end of the old regime, husbands played subordinate roles in western Europe and were completely absent in the Russian Empire. Even the styles of overthrowing an established ruler changed. In the late Middle Ages it was occasionally possible for illegitimate males to oust royal heiresses (Portugal 1385, Cyprus 1463); by the mid-eighteenth century it became possible for female usurpers to overthrow officially proclaimed male heirs (Russia 1741, 1762).

Geographically, as the map of Europe circa 1400 shows (see preface), female monarchs were scattered very widely around today's European Union, from Scotland in the northwest to Cyprus in the southeast, and they even extended to Europe's eastern geographical limit in Russia. At the same time, despite the vast geographical area that acknowledged female monarchs, this map reveals that a large core zone of old Europe remained impermeable to female sovereignty. It included the three most prestigious parts of Latin Christendom: the temporal lands of the papacy, an elective office which claimed superiority over all secular powers; the equally elective Holy Roman Empire of the German Nation, the only secular power in Christendom capable of creating new kingdoms, which it never did until 1713; and the kingdom of France, which by 1300 claimed preeminence over other kingdoms after acquiring the title of Very Christian King from the papacy. Curiously, while France remained the outstanding example of female exclusion from a hereditary monarchy, French remained the language most widely shared among Europe's female monarchs from the fourteenth century through the eighteenth.

The corner of Europe with the richest tradition of women rulers before 1800 does not appear on this map because it never reached the formal status of a kingdom until 1815. Conventionally known as the Low Countries or Netherlands, it was located along the frontier between Europe's two most important female-exclusionist states, where the northernmost edges of France encountered the northwestern boundary of the Holy Roman Empire. In this region a series of fourteenth- and fifteenth-century Burgundian dukes eventually shaped a network of duchies, counties, and minor polities into the richest and most important subroyal hereditary state of Europe. Some of these territories were vassals of the empire, others of France; parts of Flanders, its single richest unit, belonged to each. Although both overlords prohibited female inheritance themselves, women frequently governed the borderlands between them. When Mary of Burgundy inherited a vast collection of provinces in 1477, nearly all of those acknowledging French suzerainty were reclaimed by the French crown, but the rest remained loyal to her.

After the Burgundian Netherlands became the Habsburg Netherlands, a tradition of female rule persisted in the region, beginning with Mary's daughter and continuing through five generations of female Habsburgs descending from Mary's son. Between 1507 and 1793, present-day Belgium and Luxemburg were governed for a total of 115 years by no fewer than six female regents, all appointed for indefinite terms because of their presumed governmental skills.[7] Most of them died in office; the first to govern jointly with her husband outlived him and served alone until her death twelve years later. Only one, Margaret of Parma, who resigned in 1567, was not politically successful, but she was also the only one with male descendants, and her son soon governed the region extremely successfully for fourteen years. However, selective amnesia about previous experience of female rule seems far from uncommon in European history. Although no other region of Europe could match this long-term record, in 1831 the new kingdom of Belgium excluded women rulers by adopting France's Salic law.

## Female Inheritance and Its Discontents

How did women establish legitimate claims to govern so many European kingdoms between 1300 and 1800? Regardless of their actual size, kingdoms outranked everything except empires in prestige; and, with the notable exception of France, they usually followed rules of dynastic succession that opened possibilities for women to become monarchs "by the Grace of God." In reality, only four general principles governed dynastic successions to major states almost everywhere in Christian Europe. In order of descending importance, they were (1) legitimate birth, (2) masculine priority, (3) direct over collateral descent, and (4) primogeniture. All but the last came directly from Roman law. These fundamental guidelines seemed so obvious and uncontroversial that contemporaries rarely bothered to put them in writing. The most comprehensive discussion of female rule fills only a few pages of an obscure treatise, written in French by a Protestant Scot named David Chambers and printed at Paris in 1579. It asserts that in kingdoms and lesser hereditary governments "it is a general rule that women succeed in the absence of males," adding with some exaggeration that "their government in such cases is universally received at all times and approved by all nations"—unless, as was the case in the place it was printed, "some great consideration by a special positive law orders the contrary."[8]

Useful information about how the rules of dynastic succession were actually applied must therefore be sought in evidence from a few unusually complex situations. These include royal prenuptial contracts involving succession rights of future children born to spouses from states with differing customs, for example, Elizabeth I's premarital agreement with a French crown prince; final testaments of monarchs with children from different marriages, especially Henry VIII of England, who had successively delegitimized and rele-gitimized his daughters; disputed successions like that of Portugal in 1580, where the three leading claimants were the son of an elder royal daughter, the daughter of a younger royal son, and an illegiti-mate son of a younger royal son; England's Glorious Revolution of 1688, when a legitimate royal son had to be bastardized and a usurping foreign prince learned that a royal daughter took prece-dence over a royal nephew; and Habsburg family compacts, among which the Pragmatic Sanction of 1713 became exceptionally impor-tant because, by placing territorial unity above everything else, including gender, it made possible the amazing inheritance of the then-unborn Maria Theresa.

Moreover, if legitimate female inheritance is the dominant part of this story, it is far from being the only part. Europe's female regents never usurped thrones, but European political history between 1300 and 1800 includes several ambitious women who successfully pushed aside either female or male rivals with better dynastic claims. At least eight of the thirty women in this sample, including Isabel the Catholic in Spain and all four Russian empresses, were technically not legitimate heiresses. Three of the eight women boasting the longest reigns between 1300 and 1800 had seized power through either coups d'état or civil war.

For such reasons conventional political theory provides little guidance to a historian of female sovereignty. Even the first and most

important feminist author of the old regime, Christine de Pizan
(1365–c. 1434), had a blind spot about female sovereignty. She
explained why women were capable of governing and pointed out
that they had done so in antiquity; she also offered modern examples
of women who exercised authority temporarily as regents. But for all
of her intellectual daring, she never raised the possibility of modern
women governing as monarchs. Two reasons probably lurk behind
de Pizan's prudent silence on this topic. First, she was writing in
France, where female exclusion was already so well entrenched by
1400 as to be beyond criticism by anyone with connections at its
court. Second, she loathed the most famous European female sovereign of her lifetime, Joanna I of Naples, and excluded her from the
*City of Ladies* because she believed that Joanna had arranged her first
husband's murder. Male authors did no better in explaining either de
jure or de facto female sovereignty. If one can infer a few basic rules
affecting female inheritance, only Machiavelli's *The Prince* dared to
propose guidelines for usurpers—but the author's republican background prevented him from seeing that a woman like his famous
contemporary Isabel the Catholic would fit his description of a new
prince better than her husband.

Europe's most successful female usurper, Catherine the Great,
offers an especially illuminating example of the practical difficulties
involved in codifying rules of succession. In composing her guidelines for Russia's legislative assembly of 1767, she wanted to replace
Peter the Great's precedent that each dying emperor name a
successor. The question seemed extremely important because
Montesquieu, her principal guide, considered a law of succession to
be the most fundamental of all laws. Catherine therefore wrestled
with a problem that defeated even a clever, well read, and usually
resourceful empress. An undated, unfinished draft, notes her greatest
modern expert, Isabel de Madariaga, shows that Catherine II was
unable to write a law of succession that would legalize her own position. She began by paraphrasing Montesquieu: "The first principal
law of this sovereign realm is the stability of the throne and a fixed
succession," adding, "The throne can never be vacant," the venerable doctrine that the king never dies. "On my death," Catherine

continued, "my son will inherit"; then, "after my son, if his son is already 21 years old, then his eldest son will inherit; *if he is less than 21 years old, then his mother should be concerned, and let her reign for the rest of her life, for a minority of the sovereign would be dangerous for the empire*; if there is no male heir, then let the eldest daughter [inherit] . . ." Catherine abandoned the attempt.[9] Her forty-two-year-old son, Paul, did indeed follow her and promptly decreed a far simpler rule of succession: no woman could ever again occupy the throne of Russia. It was his most important piece of legislation, lasting until the Bolshevik Revolution.

The most basic general principle of royal succession throughout Europe, so fundamental that neither Chambers nor Catherine II bothered to mention it, was legitimate birth. Once marriage had become generally recognized as the seventh sacrament in the high Middle Ages, the heir to a major Christian polity had to be born to parents who were legally married; Catherine II, who also had an illegitimate son, ignored him when discussing her order of succession. The next most important principle of monarchical succession, acknowledged by both Chambers and Catherine II, was that male children of any age preceded females of any age—but this principle came second because legitimate females preceded illegitimate males. Several illegitimate sons attempted to seize royal thrones until the eighteenth century, but only two were successful, both of them relatively early and under truly exceptional circumstances. The last such instance, in 1460, required the assistance of a Muslim *jihad* (see chapter 3); after this usurper's death ten years later, a Venetian fleet commander rebuffed a plea from the dispossessed heiress that it was his Christian duty to restore her, retorting that the previous king was legitimate because the Egyptian sultan (although not the pope) had recognized him.[10]

The four general principles applied to both sexes almost everywhere except France, which shortly after 1300 consistently barred any claim involving female succession rights. As Chambers said in 1579—in French and at Paris—if a deceased king anywhere else left legitimate daughters but no legitimate sons, the oldest surviving daughter took precedence over more distantly related males. The most troublesome problems usually occurred if a dying king left only very young daughters but had younger brothers who were already adults. This was precisely the situation in 1316 when Capetian France infringed the third general rule and began a progressively more strident insistence on female exclusion. However, when a similar situation arose only fourteen years later in a large kingdom ruled by a French dynasty, Robert the Wise of Naples awarded his entire inheritance to a four-year-old granddaughter and excluded his two younger brothers from a regency council.

The second outcome proved typical. Although various major French thinkers of later centuries, men as original and as different as Jean Bodin, Michel de Montaigne, and Montesquieu, claimed that France's Salic law was eminently reasonable and deserved universal application, the overall record of the rest of Latin Christendom presents a very different picture. Outside of a few French satellites like eighteenth-century Bourbon Spain, Chambers's assertion of 1579 was substantially correct: daughters of kings without surviving sons inherited ahead of the former king's younger brothers or more distant male kin. One kingdom, Sweden, usually a French ally, reversed its position on female inheritance, permitting it twice and forbidding it twice between 1593 and 1720 before permitting it again in 1980.

A few European kingdoms, including its most prestigious unit, the Holy Roman Empire, were elective rather than hereditary. This amounted to a de facto bar against female rule because no woman would be freely elected to head any European government until Margaret Thatcher in 1979. However, in old Europe no elective monarchical state, including the empire, ever prospered politically. Poland became consistently elective after 1572 but soon declined in power and significance before being erased as a state in 1795. Only one woman ever campaigned in any Polish royal election: in 1668 the papacy proposed the former queen Christina of Sweden for its vacant throne, but she received almost no support, even among a devoutly Catholic nobility.[11] Bohemia occasionally behaved like an elective kingdom, exercising this privilege in 1618 and 1740, both times with highly unfavorable consequences for its political elite. By

1743, under military occupation, Bohemia was compelled to crown a Habsburg heiress.

Demographically, because monarchies made considerable efforts to produce sons as dynastic heirs, daughters inherited only about once in every seven or eight royal successions. On the other hand, only one European kingdom, Denmark, was inherited by twelve consecutive generations of sons after 1440. Like their three beleaguered twelfth-century predecessors, female monarchs in Latin Europe between 1300 and 1800 were overwhelmingly (twenty of twenty-four, or 83 percent) daughters of kings without surviving sons. They include several who followed childless siblings, most often a brother (Naples 1414, England 1553, Sweden 1718) but sometimes a sister (England 1558, 1702). The exceptions included a permanent regent of two kingdoms (Denmark and Norway 1386) and a royal usurper crowned jointly with her husband (England 1689), while Castile needed a lengthy civil war after 1474 to decide between an aunt and her niece. All of these women were *also* daughters of kings, but each faced major impediments to her claims. The Scandinavian ruler had an older sister whose son promptly claimed his grandfather's Danish throne; both Castilian female claimants had been disinherited at different times by the previous king; and the English usurper had a very young half brother whom she slandered as a changeling. The only complete aberration was the widow of a royal usurper (Cyprus 1474), and she possessed almost no personal authority.

## Did Women Rule Differently from Men?

Despite an abundant prescriptive literature preaching female subjection, once a woman had established a valid claim to rule a particular kingdom of Latin Christendom she governed it by divine right and faced no fundamental objection from its all-male political elites on grounds of her gender. *King* may have no female form, but political power has no sex. As Simone de Beauvoir once noted, Europe's most successful women rulers "were neither male nor female—they were sovereigns. It is remarkable that their femininity, when socially abolished, should no longer mean inferiority."[12] Women monarchs could govern effectively in most places at most times because most men adapt quickly to obeying orders from a legitimate commander who happens to be female. Today, in what is probably the closest approximation to absolute rule among civilians in a democracy, male crew members will unquestioningly obey a female airline pilot. Her voice sounds different, but the messages it transmits are not.

Throughout the five centuries after 1300, for all the talk about female inferiority and frailty, having a woman as divine-right sovereign made very little practical difference in the way governments actually operated. Again, the voice was different but its messages were the same. It is true that women rulers demonstrated greater flexibility, both political and personal, than male rulers; women, but not men, occasionally served as regents after having been sovereigns (see chapter 4), and women, but not men, sometimes changed both their personal names and their religion before becoming rulers (see chapter 7). But this flexibility did not extend to personal appearance. It seems significant that Europe's female rulers rarely felt any need or desire to dress like men in order to rule like men. The unusually tall Mary Stuart of Scotland reportedly wore male clothing in occasional private escapades and even staged one escape dressed as a man;[13] but to the best of my knowledge, no European female monarch ever put on men's clothing in public until Peter the Great's equally tall daughter Elisabeth held cross-dressing masquerades in mid-eighteenth-century Russia, and no woman wore military clothing in public until her spectacularly brazen successor Catherine II staged her coup d'état.

Because women rulers had been so extraordinarily rare in most parts of the world, they had not interacted with each other. But the early twelfth-century armed conflicts between Urraca of León-Castile and Teresa of Portugal suggest that when they did, female rulers behaved exactly like male rulers. After 1300, whenever Europe had two or more women ruling nearby kingdoms simultaneously they interacted no differently from their male counterparts. In 1386 a sister ruling in Poland (now officially a saint) seized two disputed border provinces from her older sister, who had been temporarily deposed as Hungary's sovereign and was then imprisoned. In the fifteenth century two women disputed the same throne and waged war against each other. Although husbands were deeply involved in both early cases, the women themselves were the official protagonists. In the sixteenth century a female monarch ordered the execution of another female monarch, something male kings never did to each other in the early modern era. In mid-eighteenth-century Europe two women, both sole sovereigns of major states, made a military alliance and waged a long and often successful war against the greatest warrior-king of the time, Frederick II of Prussia.

Women and men conducted nearly all royal business, from making minor appointments to conducting international diplomacy, in essentially identical fashion. Female sovereigns declared wars and ended them; exactly like their male counterparts, they held daily consultations with their principal advisers and made occasional formal public appearances. Both female and male monarchs also managed what was invariably the largest household in their kingdom, the royal court, and directed its official entertainments. Here, women and men sponsored the same kinds of coeducational activities, although, overall, female rulers probably held relatively fewer hunts and more dances and card games.

Old Europe first adapted to the anomaly of female monarchs by investing them with male attributes. As Albertus Magnus remarked in the thirteenth century, "There is no woman who would not naturally want to shed the definition of femininity and put on masculinity," and the women who exercised kingship coded themselves as men whenever this tactic seemed convenient.[14] Male mimesis was most blatant in the late fourteenth century among Europe's earliest successful female sovereigns: Joanna I of Naples appeared on some of her gold coins with a coat of armor and a man's bare legs, and Margaret of Denmark became the husband of two kingdoms (she was essentially a permanent regent, and her peculiar-sounding title becomes more comprehensible if *husband* is regarded as a verb rather than a noun). Traces of the transformation of female monarchs into honorary men persisted for centuries; in seventeenth-century Sweden and eighteenth-century Hungary heiresses were still acclaimed as *rex* rather than *regina* at their coronations.[15]

Female rulers could bend standard gender roles. A useful example compares the indirect audacity of Isabel of Castile with the more direct role of Maria Theresa in manipulating chivalric orders that formally excluded women. In 1476, during her civil war against her niece, Isabel, surrounded by loyal prelates and jurists, personally entered a plenary election meeting of the Knights of Santiago, one of Spain's three great chivalric orders; speaking through male surrogates, she intimidated the assembled knights into electing her husband as grand master, thereby acquiring the order's considerable revenues for her treasury. Three centuries later, after Maria Theresa's husband refused to head an honorary Hungarian order which she had revived, she herself presided over its first meeting as grand master, "by virtue of the masculine status which she acquired at her coronation," as her master of ceremonies explained.[16] All four eighteenth-century Russian empresses had themselves painted wearing the blue sash of St. Andrew, Russia's most prestigious chivalric order, created by Peter the Great, although its statutes expressly forbade awarding it to women.

After 1500 a linguistic factor, the widespread use of conveniently gender-neutral forms for addressing them, facilitated the acceptance of numerous women as rulers. Such terms as *Your Majesty* and *Your Royal Highness* were increasingly adopted in all principal European languages simultaneously with the unprecedented multiplication of female rulers, both monarchs and regents, in the mid-sixteenth century. Even Elizabeth I, sometimes considered the creator of a specifically feminine ruling style, often called herself a prince; as she told the new Venetian ambassador a few weeks before her death, "My sex cannot diminish my prestige nor offend those who treat me as other Princes are treated to whom . . . Venice sends its ambassadors."[17] Because the basic meaning of *king* and *queen* (as king's wife) never changed, such ungendered forms of address either promoted or at least reflected the increasing acceptance of female rule in Europe during the second half of this period. The subject deserves further investigation now that our capacity to digest massive amounts of information permits a cross-national, multilingual, and diachronic comparison of the official forms of address employed by and for Europe's female kings.

Although my account emphasizes that, overall, Europe's female rulers had some long-term overall improvements in their ability to rule autonomously between 1300 and 1800, such advances were neither linear nor uniform, nor did all of these women rule successfully. Far from it. About one in three—a much higher rate than among male monarchs—suffered some form of political catastrophe. Before 1500 their collective record is littered with depositions. Three female monarchs were deposed during the 1380s (Naples 1381, Portugal and Hungary 1385); afterward, another woman was deposed (Cyprus 1463), and a fifth abdicated involuntarily (Cyprus 1489). In 1479 the woman who lost Castile's civil war was forced to enter a convent.

Various forms of female political failure also occurred after 1500. In 1506 Castile's widowed heiress refused to exercise any of her political responsibilities; although she never lost her official titles, she was effectively imprisoned for nearly fifty years. In mid-sixteenth-century England a teenage female puppet known as the Nine Days' Queen was deposed and beheaded. Another young female monarch abdicated involuntarily (Scotland 1567), while two did so voluntarily (Sweden 1654 and 1720); an older woman suffered an irreversible mental breakdown (Portugal 1792). All four of these women lived for at least twenty years after they had ceased to govern. Royal statistics should not be pushed too far, but it seems evident that the political "casualty rate" was much higher for female than for male monarchs. Between 1500 and 1800, while five of sixteen female sovereigns ceased governing prematurely, a sample of well over a hundred male European kings (a ratio of about eight men to every woman) produced a larger number but a much smaller ratio of sudden endings. Only men experienced violent deaths in battle (Portugal 1578, Sweden 1632 and 1718), by assassination (France 1589 and 1610), or were beheaded by rebellious subjects (England 1649, France 1793). However, only five male monarchs were deposed (Sweden 1568 and 1599, Holy Roman Empire 1609, Bohemia 1619, England 1688), and only three men abdicated voluntarily (Spain 1555 and 1724, Poland 1668).

Even in the enlightened late eighteenth century, no matter how bizarre their behavior, Europe's divine-right sovereigns, male or female, were almost never officially removed because of insanity. In 1772 King Christian VII of Denmark (r. 1766–1808) had to be replaced for twelve years of de facto regency by his stepmother and his physically disabled half brother until his son could become the legal regent. When Frederick's brother-in-law, George III of England, appeared to require a regent because of insanity in 1788, he was pronounced cured shortly afterward.[18] In 1792 the same physician who cured George III tried but failed to help Maria I, the mentally disturbed female monarch of England's close political ally, Portugal. However, Maria's adult son did not become official regent of Portugal until seven years after his mother had ceased to govern.

The life expectancy of Europe's female monarchs was no greater than that of their male counterparts. Most died from natural causes but few lasted into extreme old age. Three late medieval heiresses died in their midtwenties, but only one succumbed to the aftereffects of childbirth; the other two died from riding accidents. However, only two heiresses outlived Elizabeth I, who died at seventy, and neither was ruling: Juana of Castile, who died at seventy-five, had exercised no political responsibilities for almost half a century, while Maria I of Portugal, who died at eighty-one, had been insane for twenty-four years. Only two adult female monarchs died violent deaths: one was murdered by her male successor in 1382 and the other was beheaded in 1587. On the other hand, three (Naples 1345, Scotland 1567, and Russia 1762) were widely suspected of arranging the murder of their politically inconvenient husbands.

As political leaders the most noteworthy trait of Europe's female monarchs is that they appear even more deeply enmeshed in Christendom's religious politics than most of their male counterparts. The subject is vast enough to deserve a separate volume, and only a few highlights can be sketched here. In Orthodox Christianity religious preoccupations emerged as early as the Empress Irene of Byzantium, who promoted the restoration of icon worship, and, much later, the future saint Tamar of Georgia, who patronized distant Near Eastern shrines. Religious politics similarly dominated the architectural legacy of Latin Christendom's first female monarch, Urraca of León-Castile, who, like Tamar, patronized famous distant shrines. Religious politics became even more vital among fourteenth-century female monarchs. Only consistent support from her papal suzerains enabled Joanna I to govern an important Mediterranean kingdom for almost twenty years, and her role in the Great Schism of 1378 fatally compromised her rule.

While no male monarch has ever been seriously proposed for sainthood since 1297, when Louis IX of France was canonized less than thirty years after his death, two female monarchs have been nominated in the twentieth century, one of them successfully. Jadwiga of Poland, who enthusiastically promoted the eastern expansion of the Latin church, was first proposed for this honor during her husband's lifetime, but it took almost six centuries after her death in 1399 before a Polish-born pope finally made her a saint. In 1496 Isabel of Castile owed her new papal title of Catholic king not just to a successful crusade against Muslims in Granada and her persecution of converted Jews through Spain's new state-run Inquisition, but also to the major religious reforms she carried out in her kingdom. After 1970 a serious effort by Spanish reactionaries to beatify her was quietly buried by the papacy.

After the Protestant Reformation religious politics became a primary concern of all the numerous mid-sixteenth-century women rulers. Two famous examples were half sisters: Mary and Elizabeth Tudor each overturned England's established church in opposite directions within a single decade (1554–63). Conversion to Reformed Protestantism led Jeanne III of Navarre to overturn her husband's authority in her hereditary kingdom in 1562. Two female Catholic regents adopted quasi-monastic behavior. Juana of Castile wore a veil while governing Spain as a secret Jesuit in 1554–59 and retired young to build a convent; her niece Isabel Clara Eugenia later dressed as a Franciscan nun while governing the Low Countries in 1621–33. In 1654 conversion to Catholicism became the decisive factor in the early abdication of Christina of Sweden, heiress to a solidly Lutheran kingdom.

Even in the century of Enlightenment female sovereigns continued to be (or at least to act) more pious than their male contemporaries. Maria Theresa's only critics were either Protestants

or Jews settled in Habsburg territories who suffered religious
discrimination during her reign. Although Catherine II justified her
usurpation of the Russian Empire largely as a defense of the imper-
iled Orthodox church and required her daughters-in-law to convert
to it, she subsequently extended state-supervised toleration not just
to schismatic Old Believers but also to vast numbers of her newly
acquired Muslim, Jewish, and Catholic subjects. The mental breakdown in 1792 of Europe's last female monarch of the old regime,
Maria I of Portugal, was attributed partly to the severity of her
confessor.

## Male Accessories to Female Rule

Despite widespread ambivalence about having women as divine-
right monarchs, European men never developed a coherent theoretical opposition to female rule; John Knox's notorious trumpet blast
of 1558 had no imitators. Instead, male critics preferred a more insid-
ious denigration of female sovereignty: the slogan 'when women
rule, men govern' became almost proverbial before 1800. This adage
used conventional beliefs about female frailty to assume that the
man with greatest access to a female ruler was necessarily the most
prominent person in her state. Such reasoning explains the frequent
late medieval coronations of husbands of female sovereigns and the
debate in book 3 of Baldassare Castiglione's *The Book of the Courtier*
about the role of Isabel's husband in her success. It also explains both
the frequent rumors of sexual liaisons between women rulers and
their favorites and the persistent tradition of historians to see the
principal ministers of women rulers as the primary agents shaping
state policy, from fourteenth-century Naples to the Austria of Maria
Theresa.

There is corroborative evidence to support this approach.
Husbands were considered indispensable to every young royal
heiress as late as the nineteenth century, Queen Victoria being the
most prominent but not the only example. At the same time, some
far older women monarchs, as early as Joanna II in early fifteenth-
century Naples, clearly governed through male favorites.
All-powerful male favorites reappear with Russia's first two

eighteenth-century empresses, Prince Alexander Menshikov with Catherine I and Count (later Duke) Ernest Biron with Anna Ivanovna. However, female rulers as early as Queen Anne of England also had politically prominent female favorites. Rule by royal favorites was never peculiar to female monarchs; both before and after Joanna I, many adult male kings did exactly the same thing. Because men comprised 90 percent of all European monarchs it is appropriate that the outstanding collaborative study of rule by royal favorites should include only one female ruler.[19]

If rule through favorites was endemic and independent of gender, were there any important differences between Europe's female and male kings? Although most of the time men and women governed in identical fashion, two special areas remained segregated by gender. The political peculiarities of female royal rule might be represented by a large central circle overlapped at both ends by smaller circles. The large circle represents ordinary government business (appointments, diplomacy, edicts, and so on) that was exercised in essentially the same way by both men and women. The small circle at one end represents an exclusively male sphere of warfare; throughout the five centuries considered here sovereigns were also military commanders, a role that remained taboo for female rulers. The small circle at the other end is the female zone of queenship centered around legitimate dynastic reproduction, so essential to hereditary monarchies. Male rulers needed female accessories in order to have legitimate heirs; female rulers needed male accessories for the same purpose, but for a long time they also needed them to command their armies. In Sweden a tradition of personal military leadership by the monarch remained sufficiently strong to influence the abdication of its two women sovereigns, both of whom succeeded kings who had been killed in battle.

Nevertheless, Europe's female sovereigns, who often found themselves entangled in wars, compiled a remarkably successful overall military record. Between the capture of the king of Sweden on the battlefield by the army of Margaret of Denmark in 1389 and the defeat of the previously invincible Frederick II of Prussia by the armies of two female monarchs in 1760, one finds the ten-year

conquest of Granada, the last Muslim state in Europe, by the armies
of Isabel the Catholic; the defeat of Philip II's Invincible Armada by
the navy of Elizabeth I; several great Swedish victories in the Thirty
Years' War during Christina's reign; and the humbling of Louis
XIV's armies by those of Queen Anne. Such military successes far
outweighed their reverses. Meanwhile, eighteenth-century female
monarchs found novel ways to cope with the problem of military
leadership by such tactics as portraying themselves on horseback
carrying a weapon, founding military academies to train their officer
corps, and creating honorary orders for outstanding military service;
Maria Theresa did all three, even naming the new order for herself.
In western Europe royal military leadership ceased being a political
concern; after 1745, no male monarch led an army in person. In
more recent times, Margaret Thatcher, the first democratically
elected female head of a major European state, continued this tradition of military success (see fig. 17).

The most obvious difference between male and female
monarchs is that women, in addition to their ordinary governmental
tasks, were also expected to undertake the burden of dynastic reproduction. Being kings made it harder for these women to be queens;
fulfilling their reproductive responsibilities proved extremely difficult.
High child mortality rates compounded the difficulties of locating
politically suitable spouses during their childbearing years, so that
only about 40 percent of Europe's female monarchs (far below the
70 percent rate for their male counterparts) were succeeded by their
direct descendants. All but one of these heirs came from marriages
made before the mother began her personal reign.

Royal heiresses inevitably confronted an extremely narrow
choice of possible husbands. Their dilemma had three horns.
Marrying one of her own subjects almost guaranteed disaster by
raising a single clan far above every other noble lineage in her
kingdom.[20] Marrying any foreigner of nonroyal status reduced her
own prestige, but marrying another king or crown prince would
automatically merge her kingdom with his and compromise its
autonomy. Somehow all these pitfalls had to be avoided in order to
preserve their heritage intact.

From a man's perspective, marrying a royal heiress entailed risks as well as advantages. A military leader was assassinated when he tried to marry the last female ruler of Sassanid Persia, and we do not know what happened to the first husband of Queen Tamar of Georgia; he simply disappears from the record. In Latin Europe, although their military potential sometimes played a role in their selection, no royal husband ever died in battle; however, a few of them were murdered, beginning in 1345 with the first husband of the first major European heiress. Among the few from nonprincely backgrounds, one was driven from his wife's kingdom in 1419 and eventually retired to a foreign monastery, while the last husband of Mary Queen of Scots ended in a Danish prison, where he died insane.

Whatever scriptural and customary wisdom said about the subordination of wives, such conventional notions were rarely applied to or internalized by women rulers. Folk wisdom knew that a married woman who was older than her husband had a better chance of exercising authority autonomously, so it is not surprising that some of Europe's greatest heiresses married men younger than themselves. At Naples, Robert the Wise did this with his grand-daughter, Europe's first major heiress. In 1469 and 1477 two women whose inheritance rights were sharply contested and who were able to choose their own husbands, Isabel of Castile and Mary of Burgundy, also did this, with highly satisfactory results. In the following century Mary Tudor was better positioned to retain England's autonomy after her marriage by being almost twelve years older than her husband. Even Mary Stuart of Scotland, seldom praised for her political astuteness, chose a man four years younger than herself when she decided to remarry during her personal reign. No subsequent female monarch ever remarried, although a few extremely successful female rulers flaunted affairs with much younger men in their old age. The earl of Essex was thirty-three years younger than Elizabeth I. The interchangeable gigolos of Catherine II's final years averaged thirty years younger than their employer, although her only politically important bedmate, Grigory Potemkin, whom she may have secretly married, as Louis XIV did his last mistress, was just ten years younger.

When they were fortunate enough to have surviving children, reigning mothers were able to avoid the often severe and occasionally murderous antagonism between fathers and crown princes. No mother who was a divine-right monarch ever abdicated in favor of an adult son, although Maria Theresa officially shared power with hers after her husband's death; Catherine II went to the opposite extreme by excluding hers from any political responsibilities. Daughters may have been even more difficult to manage than sons. Old Europe produced only one mother–daughter royal inheritance, and relations between Isabel the Catholic and her second daughter, Juana, turned remarkably bitter after Juana unexpectedly became heiress-apparent in 1502. After Isabel died two years later, the only daughter to acquire a major European kingdom from an extremely politically active mother became the only female sovereign in European history who refused to exercise any political authority whatsoever.

There was no standard formula for how female kings approached the tasks of government. Europe's most successful examples, the women who exhibited the greatest staying power in major states—Isabel the Catholic, Elizabeth I, Maria Theresa, and Catherine II—each developed strategies tailored to maximize the possibilities of her particular situation, and each manipulated very different images of how a woman wielded supreme political power. Isabel maximized the possibilities of a married woman in a dual monarchy in which her kingdom held most of the joint resources, including those acquired during the marriage; yet she always remained part of a partnership called the kings (*los Reyes*), and her husband held far more authority in her kingdom than she did in his. A half century after Isabel's death, Elizabeth I dodged the burdens of marriage and dynastic reproduction while presenting herself as either (virgin) mother of her subjects or wife of her kingdom, in either role providing safety and prosperity through prudent stewardship. A century and a half later Maria Theresa, flanked by a husband with an imperial title and a large flock of children, maximized the strategy of becoming truly the "mother of her country" (*die erste und allgemeine Landesmutter*). All three were native princesses, but the foreign-born Catherine II had usurped her throne from an incompetent and overtly foreign husband. She compensated by becoming a patriot in her adopted country and working tirelessly to acquire both glory for herself and improved conditions for her subjects, ultimately becoming the only female ruler generally known as the Great both at home and abroad.

Regardless of their individual styles after achieving power, all of Europe's most successful female rulers from the fourteenth through the eighteenth century shared one vital life experience with their most famous predecessors in such places as Egypt and China. Starting with Joanna I of Naples and Margaret of Denmark, these women had invariably surmounted major political obstacles before attaining sovereign authority in their own name. Isabel had to fight a civil war with her niece; Elizabeth spent much time imprisoned in the Tower of London. Even Maria Theresa, despite all her father's efforts to permit female succession throughout his possessions, had to overcome great difficulties before officially acquiring either of her two royal thrones. Women who managed to survive such testing experiences invariably relished the exercise of supreme power afterward; none of them ever retired gracefully like Japan's female tennos, relinquishing effective control to an adult male relative. Instead, European history offers a counterexample. Sweden's meticulously mentored and highly gifted seventeenth-century crown princess Christina, the woman with the least contested path to the throne and the only one who had been carefully groomed for the tasks of royal government, abandoned her monarchical responsibilities at the age of twenty-eight after only ten years of highly successful personal rule.

# 3

# Difficult Beginnings
## Heiresses with Crowned Husbands,
## 1300–1550

The Magnifico asked, "What prince has there been in our days, or
for many years past in Christendom, who deserves to be compared
with Queen Isabel of Spain?"
    Gasparo replied, "King Ferdinand, her husband."
        —Baldassare Castiglione, *The Book of the Courtier* (1528)

After 1300 the history of female sovereigns shifted to Latin
Christendom. A pioneering article by Armin Wolf identified twelve
female claimants among one hundred royal successions in eighteen
different kingdoms during the century between 1350 and 1450.[1] But
two other women, including Europe's most famous fourteenth-
century female ruler, had already inherited their thrones before 1350;
and some significant developments occurred shortly after 1450,
including some bizarre events in Cyprus, a small kingdom that Wolf
omitted. Both the number of women occupying thrones—at least
fifteen between 1328 and 1504—and the variety of situations involved
permit an aggregate picture of the governmental record of Europe's
female monarchs during the first half of these five centuries.

Most of these women were between the ages of ten and twenty
when they inherited a kingdom, but nearly all were already married.
Few remained without husbands; even the oldest woman in this
group, a widow past childbearing age, remarried shortly after inheriting. Although the primary purpose of their marriages was to ensure

legitimate dynastic succession, a goal which fewer than half of them managed to fulfill, the political status of the men they married appears to have been the single most important factor in their governments. If their husbands had received the equivalent of formal coronations—a situation that had occurred at least ten times by 1506—they shared formal political authority with the heiress and normally handled most government business. The only exception, Blanca of Navarre (r. 1425–41), was twelve years older than her husband and had previously served five years as regent of a different kingdom. Three childless royal heiresses were succeeded by their husbands. Three others, also childless, who were deposed or overthrown would eventually bequeath their claims to their husband's heirs, and all three donations are still preserved in the archives of their former in-laws.[2]

At the opposite extreme, between 1362 and 1430 three women, all over the age of thirty, successfully governed important European kingdoms for at least fifteen years without any male associate—a novelty in Latin Christendom. After 1450 joint rule reemerged as the dominant form of female sovereignty in Europe, with husbands of heiresses again playing prominent rules—a model incarnated in Spain by the best-known and most successful late medieval "power couple," Isabel and Ferdinand.

## The Divorce of France and Navarre

Both female inheritance and female exclusion acquired special importance after Europe's largest hereditary monarchy annexed its smallest monarchy, and the same princess was involved in both developments. Her experiences offer dramatic evidence that the rights of heiresses were more easily accepted in smaller and weaker monarchies because in 1328 a woman who had just been excluded for the third time from her father's inheritance in France was invited to rule her father's (and grandmother's) small kingdom of Navarre, which thus became separated from the French crown to which it had been joined for fifty-four years.

In 1300 the "Very Christian King" Philip IV of France was Latin Christendom's most powerful monarch. His wife, Jeanne of

Navarre, was the only child of the king of a small state near the southwestern corner of modern France, and also heir to some French provinces; she was one of several heiresses that Capetian kings of France married in order to increase their territory, wealth, and status. Navarre may well have been Europe's smallest kingdom, but even the meanest monarchy outranked any duchy or principality in prestige, and Philip IV's seals identify him as the first king of both France and Navarre.[3] After Jeanne's death in 1305 Navarrese authorities insisted that her oldest son, nineteen-year-old Louis, not his father, was now their legitimate ruler. After brief hesitation Philip IV sent his son, escorted by senior royal officials, to Navarre's capital at Pamplona, seat of its only bishopric, for a coronation. When the dauphin returned to Paris an official seal (now in the French national archives) described him as the "oldest son of the king of France and king of Navarre." Louis had the seal for four years until his father's death in 1310, but no documents attest to its use in Navarre. Afterward, he became Louis X of France and Navarre and ruled both kingdoms for six years.

Jeanne I had become heiress to Navarre when she was three years old. Her first grandchild, a girl, was barely four when her father died in 1316. When a posthumous brother, whom French genealogies call Jean I, died after a few days, Capetian France "fell to the distaff" for the first time. However, royal succession followed different trajectories in very large and very small kingdoms. After 1274 Navarre had been governed by regents until its heiress married. In France the obvious regents in 1316 were her father's two younger brothers. The older one bypassed his young niece and claimed the throne himself, staging a hastily organized coronation ceremony at Rheims.

Navarrese notables accepted this fait accompli and sent a delegation to the French court to offer homage. The new king promised in Paris to uphold Navarre's traditional privileges, or *fueros*, rights about which Navarrese remain extremely prickly seven centuries later. When Philip V died after a six-year reign, he left daughters but no sons. Following recent precedent, his younger brother Charles succeeded him and informed his Navarrese subjects that they could perform homage when he visited Toulouse, the seat of royal administration in southern France.[4] Navarrese sources insist that this king never swore to uphold their fueros, and they gave him a strikingly different nickname: in France he is Charles the Handsome (Charles le Bel), while in Navarre he is Charles the Bald (Carlos el Calvo).

History proceeded to repeat itself: this king also died after a six-year reign also leaving a daughter but no sons. At this point (1328) the succession issue acquired special urgency in both kingdoms. Its resolution in France, where the Capetian male line had finally ended, proved extremely significant in European history. France's political nation rejected a claim from England's crown prince (who, like France's two previous kings, was a descendant of Philip IV, but on his mother's side) and provoked what became the Hundred Years' War with England. Although the term would not appear until 1358, the fully developed Salic law had become operative in Europe's largest and most prestigious hereditary kingdom: henceforth only the strictest possible direct descent through an unbroken male line provided a legitimate claim to its throne.[5]

However, when describing the momentous choice of a new French king in 1328, both French and English historians tend to overlook its consequences for the long-standing union of the French and Navarrese crowns. While French political notables reinforced their taboo against female succession, those in Navarre vigorously asserted a woman's hereditary right to their throne. They had an heiress, one directly descended from another heiress two generations earlier, who was now sixteen years old. She was also legally an adult because, like most other princesses in the later Middle Ages, she was already married—to a French prince, Philippe of Evreux, with only a remote claim to the French throne.

When they notice it at all, French historians usually see the divorce between France and Navarre in 1328 as essentially amicable. Navarrese historians, on the other hand, emphasize its violence, which included some anti-Jewish riots. The rupture came even before France had resolved its disputed succession. An assembly composed of eight aristocrats (*ricoshombres*), forty-three lesser nobles (*caballeros*), plus deputies (*infanzones*) from Navarre's six administrative districts (*comarcas*) and forty-four communities met where the two main pilgrimage roads to Santiago de Compostela converge at Puente la Reyna and overthrew their unpopular French governor, replacing him with two local ricoshombres. Acting as regents, they promptly summoned a broader assembly (*Curia general*) at Pamplona, the traditional capital of the kingdom, in May 1328. With the notable exception of Navarre's lone prelate, the French-born bishop of Pamplona, it declared that the crown belonged "by right of succession and inheritance" to the princess who had been passed over in 1316 and 1322 and invited her to claim their throne in person as soon as possible.[6]

When news of the uprising and the offer reached them in northern France, the heiress and her husband rapidly reached an agreement with the new French king in July 1328. After she dropped her claims, through her grandmother, to another French province, he permitted them to accept the Navarrese throne. Each spouse quickly accredited three representatives; her husband (who had received no official invitation) already entitled himself king of Navarre. A month later, from Avignon, the pope, possibly unaware of the actual terms of the proposals, offered his congratulations to her husband, but not to his wife, as Navarre's new monarch.[7]

As these representatives hurried south to arrange the official coronation they encountered Navarre's emissaries just north of the major pass across the Pyrenees headed in the opposite direction. Preliminary discussions were followed by hard bargaining with Navarre's interim regents south of the summit at Roncesvalles. His chief agent reported to the heiress's husband that the Navarrese laid down four preconditions:

> First, you and Madame must come here together.
> Next, the two of you must take the oath jointly.
> Next, the oaths made to you must be made jointly.
>
> Afterward, our Lady (Madame) is raised [on a shield] and throws money [to spectators], because she is the heiress [*dame naturele*] and no one can be raised except an authentic heir [*seigneur naturel*].

These terms, so radically different from what was happening in France, were confirmed in separate meetings over the next few weeks with representatives of Navarre's towns, its secular Estates, and its clergy. Surviving summaries of these negotiations offer a precious glimpse into fourteenth-century gender politics because the crucial issue was the exact status of the new monarch's husband. Navarrese officials insisted that the crown was hers alone, while the representatives from both husband and wife insisted on a fully joint coronation in which both were raised on shields and threw money.[8] Local authorities ultimately yielded and, as a gesture of good will, abandoned their siege of their former French governor in southern Navarre.

Within six weeks, in midwinter, the new royal couple crossed the Pyrenees to Pamplona. Their coronation oaths, in local dialect, remain in Pamplona's archive. Navarre's new sovereign then officially handed her kingdom to her husband during his lifetime, together with a magnificent gift of one hundred thousand *livres tournois*. Two months later they concluded an agreement about the succession, stipulating that if her husband survived her and remarried he ceased to become the guardian of their children.[9]

In important respects Navarre's situation changed very little after 1328. Its newly restored heiress was a French princess who never mastered Navarre's language. For the next fifty years French officials continued to represent its usually absent monarchs. Until 1375 all eight chancellors were French; none of them even visited Navarre until 1364. The first Navarrese-born treasurer was appointed in 1363. Even when residing there for two years after their coronation the royal couple never became accustomed to their distant little kingdom; their presence always seemed provisional, and they spent nothing on their Navarrese residences. Apart from a second visit in 1336–37 to conduct official business, they lived at her husband's seat in Normandy or at the French court.[10]

The most significant political feature of their reign is the minor official role played by Navarre's female sovereign. Her husband visited Navarre more often and conducted most actual governmental business. Pamplona's archives preserve eighty-five official decrees from the fourteen years of their joint reign (1329–43). Just under half of them (forty-one) were issued in the names of both king and queen: seventeen are in Latin, nineteen in the local Romance, and five in the Languedoil of northern France. Philip of Evreux issued an almost equal number of decrees (thirty-eight) exclusively in his name: seventeen in Romance, eleven in Latin, and ten in northern French. Only six decrees, less than 10 percent, were issued exclusively in his wife's name. After Philip died at the end of 1343 Jeanne II ruled alone until her death in autumn 1349. She remained in northern France and issued another sixteen documents, only three of which were in Latin and none in Romance.[11]

Thus functioned what I propose to call the Navarrese solution to female inheritance. It became the dominant form among European monarchies confronting this issue in the fourteenth and fifteenth centuries and was followed in Navarre itself on every subsequent occasion (1425, 1483, and 1555) when a woman inherited its crown. A young heiress to a small kingdom, usually one struggling to maintain (or, as in the case of Navarre in 1328, to recover) its autonomy, was married as quickly as possible to a suitable prince in hopes of producing a male heir. Upon her predecessor's death, she and her husband were jointly invested with sovereign powers. Afterward, he took primary responsibility for governing his wife's kingdom, particularly its military affairs. Such political arrangements seemed obvious to contemporaries. As her Hungarian mother-in-law argued in the mid-1340s to a much more important royal heiress, Joanna I of Naples, "Didn't she agree that for the good of the kingdom as well as for her own peace of mind, it would be preferable that her husband assist her in sharing the burden of power? . . . There exist issues that their subjects would rather see a man tackle than a woman, and if enemies had to be repulsed, this would be a matter for the husband more than the wife. . . . All that would be needed would be to set limits that he should not infringe upon."[12]

If the couple had a son to succeed her (which actually happened on all five occasions between 1274 and 1555 when women inherited the throne in Navarre), the new king had a different dynastic name but royal government functioned essentially unchanged. If the heiress outlived her husband, she governed essentially as a regent for their son. But problems arose if her husband outlived the heiress; after this happened in Navarre in 1441 the consequences permanently compromised the little kingdom's long-term political stability. Moreover, heiresses of other kingdoms adopting a similar policy often left no surviving children, while their husbands frequently outlived them and inherited their kingdom.

## The Heiress with Four Husbands

The next female succession in fourteenth-century Europe occurred very soon after the heiress excluded in Capetian France had been crowned as Navarre's monarch. Close family ties also united this larger kingdom, located in southern Italy (known as the *regno*, or kingdom) and southeastern France (the county of Provence), to the now rigidly female-exclusionist French crown. Its rulers, technically kings of Sicily and Jerusalem, were a cadet branch of French royalty; the mother of its child heiresses designated in 1330 was a sister of the prince who acquired the French throne in 1328 (she died in 1331, leaving both daughters orphans). Like France in 1316, an heiress was also dynastically unprecedented here, and the previous king had two younger adult brothers.

Nevertheless, after his only son died in 1328 Robert the Wise of Naples chose female succession. In the light of recent French history—and King Robert had followed the events of 1328 closely—his decision seems remarkable. In 1330 he not only bypassed his younger brothers, thereby ignoring the order of succession followed by France in 1316, but also excluded them from a regency council headed by his widow. Instead, he bestowed his extensive domains on a four-year-old granddaughter and made his principal vassals acknowledge her as his heir. Twelve years later Robert reaffirmed this choice in a final testament that left virtually everything to his now-adolescent granddaughter—or, if she died childless, to her younger sister.

Like her grandfather, the woman who inherited Robert's title to the kingdoms of Sicily and Jerusalem in 1343 never ruled either of them. Because her actual possessions were governed from Naples modern English usage usually identifies Europe's first major royal heiress as Joanna I of Naples. Because Joanna was unmarried and thus technically a minor, Robert's widow became regent, heading a large council. The dying king ordered his heir to marry her fiancé— the younger son of a Hungarian king and her second cousin, who had lived at Robert's court for over a decade—as soon as possible but gave him no specific privileges.[13]

From the standpoint of female sovereignty this remarkable royal testament had equally remarkable consequences. Before this heiress died almost forty years later, she had had four marriages (a record among these thirty female monarchs) but left no surviving children. Her earlier marriages show similarities to Navarrese-style joint rule. Her first husband's representatives negotiated a joint coronation which never took place. Her second husband enjoyed an official coronation and used it to exclude her from exercising significant political authority until his death, making Joanna a Navarrese-pattern female monarch for ten years. Afterward, contemporaries agree that during her final two marriages she governed her large inheritance by herself for almost twenty years. Her posthumous fame is as uneven as her personal authority. Joanna acquired a negative reputation in her Neapolitan capital, while Provence, where she lived for some years, remembers her as *bello reino Jano*, "good Queen Jeanne." Contemporaries provide much evidence about her, including generally favorable but occasionally very negative opinions from such well-known people as Giovanni Boccaccio, Petrarch, and St. Bridget of Sweden.

Joanna needed official recognition of her position from the popes. Then residing at Avignon (a city she inherited and eventually sold to them in 1348), they claimed suzerainty over her Italian possessions under a charter dating from 1262. Although her grandfather had carefully excluded papal representatives from the regency council, a French legate arrived shortly after his death and promptly nullified his testament. Meanwhile, uncertainty about the future political role of Joanna's husband provoked intervention with the papacy from his anxious relatives. Joanna's formidable mother-in-law, who later made her older son king of her native Poland, traveled from Hungary to promote her younger son's coronation at Naples. Before she returned in spring 1344 the Avignon papacy had awarded her son a royal title but without specific political rights.

A political stalemate ensued at court between Joanna's faction, strongly opposed to sharing authority, and those favoring her even younger husband, Andrew of Hungary. Describing the power imbalance between them, Matteo Villani argued that these problems stemmed from the fact that the wife was "both master and lady of her Baron, who, as her husband, should have been her lord."[14] After spring 1344 Clement VI, the Avignon pope, addressed his official letters to both as king and queen, but his instructions to his legate about the kingdom's major business (for example, Joanna's oath of fealty to her papal suzerain or negotiating a truce in Sicily) never mention her husband. Yet the political situation of King Andrew gradually improved. By December 1344 Clement ordered her not to exclude him from her kingdom's administration. Six months later he told Joanna not to make "contrary suggestions" against having her husband crowned, anointed, and allowed into her administration.

By mid-1345 the papacy had decided that Joanna's seventeen-year-old husband should play a real role in Neapolitan government. A legate was sent to Naples with a bull empowering him to perform a double coronation in which, as at Pamplona in 1329, husband and wife would be anointed together as corulers. But even at this juncture, with their child soon to be born, Andrew still possessed no specific powers. Instead, he had to sign a document stating that he could not inherit if his wife died without surviving children, and the Neapolitan clergy and nobility swore a public oath that if Joanna died they would not declare him king.

The greatest scandal of a reign that eventually produced far more than its share of them occurred two days before the pope sent separate warnings to both husband and wife not to delay their joint coronation further. It never happened. Instead, during the night of September 18, 1345, King Andrew was brutally murdered at a royal hunting retreat just north of Naples, strangled like a common criminal and thrown from a window. All our evidence agrees that his pregnant wife remained in her room ("like a dead cat," said one chronicler) after her husband was enticed outside and immediately assaulted by numerous thugs. Joanna's subsequent behavior scarcely inspired confidence. A few weeks later she requested papal permission to remarry her first cousin, Robert of Taranto. By early 1346, however, she preferred his younger brother Louis. Since both men were widely considered major suspects in her first husband's murder, her reputation suffered permanent damage, even though an official inquiry by the papacy eventually absolved her of any responsibility.

The papacy's attitude toward Joanna's second marriage is highly instructive. By summer 1347 she was cohabiting with Louis in her palace. Next January, abandoning her young son by Andrew, they fled together to her French possessions in order to escape from the king of Hungary, who had invaded Naples to avenge his brother's murder (Louis's brother Robert was captured and imprisoned in Hungary for several years). Joanna and Louis of Taranto had two daughters, including one born in June 1348 while she was arranging the sale of Avignon in order to finance their return to Naples. After considerable delay Clement finally granted a dispensation in May 1352 to legalize their marriage and approved her second husband's coronation at Naples. As with Andrew of Hungary, the papacy insisted on upholding an essential clause of King Robert's testament by excluding the new king in favor of Joanna's younger sister if his wife predeceased him without leaving heirs. Joanna regained a minor share in government, an official seal, and a sizable staff of attendants; but her husband undeniably ruled, and his name preceded hers on their decrees and coins.

Ten years later Queen Joanna buried her second husband. At the age of thirty-six she was finally in full possession of her inheritance. "The Queen enjoys governing," noted the archbishop of Naples. "She wishes to do everything, because she has waited a long time for this moment." When the French king proposed his son as a suitor, she composed a polite refusal, arguing from personal experience that marriages to cousins were sterile, and she had sworn to have no more. But Joanna had no surviving children. Her best surviving contemporary portrait (only two are known) adorns a chapel in Capri and depicts her praying to the Virgin, presumably for a male heir. Joanna's lack of offspring dictated a third marriage. She soon asked permission from the papal nuncio at Naples to marry a prince much younger than herself from the minor kingdom of Mallorca, a man who had recently escaped after a long imprisonment. When Avignon again recommended the French candidate, she replied, "After all, marriages are free, and I don't see why this doesn't apply, especially to the detriment of my own freedom."[15]

About this time, Boccaccio returned to Naples, a city he loved, carrying an almost completed manuscript with a novel twist on Plutarch: a collection of lives of illustrious women. Boccaccio dedicated it to another noblewoman, while telling her that he originally intended it for Joanna, and added a final essay, the only one about a living woman, extolling the queen of Sicily and Jerusalem. It begins by describing her, correctly, as "more renowned than any other woman of our time for lineage, power and character" and as governing "a mighty realm of the sort not usually ruled by women." Boccaccio avoided naming any of her husbands and ended by calling her "a singular glory of Italy . . . never seen previously in any nation." Although composed very early in her long personal reign, it remains her most durable monument, surviving in numerous manuscripts and being reprinted many times during the Renaissance.[16]

Joanna avoided any suggestion of a coronation for her third husband. He soon began quarrelling incessantly with both the Neapolitan baronage and his wife, who avoided giving him any important military responsibilities. After experiencing a miscarriage in 1365, Joanna encouraged him to go abroad to claim his own throne. Although the range of documentation for her personal reign does not equal that for Navarre, there is every reason to believe she now ruled as autonomously as her grandfather had; surviving records indicate that she governed her French possessions effectively. Much evidence shows that throughout her personal reign she also collaborated loyally with her pontifical suzerains until the schism erupted in 1378. Joanna even provided them military aid, sending ten ships in 1367 to escort the pope back to Italy (the other Italian naval powers combined sent only thirteen). The following year Joanna became the first woman ever awarded the Golden Rose, which the papacy usually reserved for crusading knights.

After her third husband died in 1375, why, one might ask, did Joanna feel the need to marry yet again? By now she was far beyond childbearing age and had experienced three unsatisfactory marriages. Nevertheless, both she and her papal suzerain agreed that she needed a reliable soldier without too much political baggage, and Gregory XI advised her to marry the younger son of a German duke, Otto of Brunswick. Even older than Joanna, he had been a mercenary commander in Italy for thirty years and had once married the widowed second wife of her third husband's father. Her negotiators denied him royal rank and excluded him from the succession; his bride's wedding gift was a principality confiscated from a rebellious vassal. Otto sailed to Naples on four galleys loaned by Neapolitan barons, and they were married about a year after her third husband's death. It was undeniably a scandalous *mésalliance*; Gregory sent a circular letter emphasizing that the queen had freely chosen him and advised her subjects to honor him as her "true husband." However, the marriage proved a useful political expedient. Joanna's final husband served her faithfully until her death, then continued to serve under her successors.

Joanna I, the first woman to put *Dei Gratia Regina* on a few of her coins, left an abundant numismatic legacy, more of it from her French territories than from southern Italy. Her most ornate coins, called golden queens (*Reines d'or*), directly imitated French royal *souveraines* and show her full length, holding both sword and scepter like a male king. The first version, from 1370, shows Joanna wearing a long dress, but another struck only two years later shows her wearing a coat of armor with bare legs like a man. No fewer than 316 of her gold coins of the latter type were found in a single Parisian hoard, and this design was reused by her male successor in Provence, who changed only the name.[17]

As Elizabeth Casteen has pointed out, Joanna's change of papal obedience at the beginning of the Great Schism in 1378 proved disastrous: it not only destroyed her carefully reconstructed reputation for piety, but also led directly to her deposition, imprisonment, and death. She shifted her allegiance to Avignon after the new Roman pope, who knew Naples well, reportedly told her ambassadors that her kingdom "had been poorly led and governed for a long time by a woman, and he wanted to give it a man to lead and govern . . . and wanted the queen to enter a religious order of her choice."[18] The succession to Joanna's large possessions soon became linked with the schism. After her three children all died young, she had adopted the orphaned son of a first cousin as her heir. After repudiating the Roman pope for his Avignon rival, she replaced him with a French prince. In June 1381 Joanna legally transformed her new heir into her biological son and named him coruler throughout her territories. But her original heir, already crowned at Rome exactly three days earlier by the rival pope, invaded Joanna's kingdom. Outmaneuvering her fourth husband, he soon captured both of them at Naples and forced her to abdicate before her new heir could intervene. By the time his French rival invaded Italy, the original heir had moved Joanna to a remote fortress; when his enemy approached the kingdom, he had the old queen killed. Joanna's body was taken back to Naples and exhibited at the foot of the splendid mausoleum she had built for her grandfather.

As the first autonomous female sovereign to rule a large European state for a long period, Joanna I set many precedents. She had more marriages than any other female monarch in European history. She was Europe's first heiress to break tradition by subordinating her last two husbands, whose names are omitted on her coins or official documents. Joanna also set some dubious precedents. She was the first modern heiress (but not the last) to be accused of murdering her husband. She became the first female monarch to be deposed and the only one to be murdered afterwards—both by her adopted heir. Her biography inspired a theatrical performance at Marie Antoinette's court in the 1780s, but it seems rich enough to furnish sufficient plots for several operas, films, or television series.[19]

## Two Older Women Rule Independently

After Joanna I's death, two other childless women also managed to rule European kingdoms autonomously. First, after her son died in

1386, Margaret of Denmark made the transition from regent to de facto monarch of two Scandinavian kingdoms, and she folded her husband's kingdom into her father's so tightly that Denmark would continue to govern Norway for many centuries; then, shortly after Margaret died, Joanna II of Naples inherited the Italian (but not the French) parts of Joanna I's possessions from her childless brother Ladislas in 1414. Each woman would govern alone for many years. Margaret, only twenty-seven when her husband died, apparently never considered remarriage; Joanna II remarried, but after a few years she drove her new husband from her kingdom. When they first acquired monarchical status Margaret was thirty-three and Joanna II forty-five. Their maturity probably helped both women to govern successfully during an age replete with adolescent royal heiresses; after all, Joanna I did not govern autonomously until the age of thirty-six, and Blanche of Navarre, the only married late medieval heiress to become a monarch beyond the age of thirty-five, was also the only one who managed most of her kingdom's routine business.

"As a female historian," notes Vivian Etting, the recent biographer of Margaret of Denmark, "I must admit that women who climb to the summit of power usually are just as ambitious and ruthless as their male colleagues," and her subject seems an illustrious predecessor of Margaret Thatcher, another Iron Lady who shares her name. Little is known about how Margaret persuaded Danish magnates in 1376 to overturn her father's treaty giving his kingdom to an older grandson by his older daughter, except that Margaret showered some of them with gifts. One of the stranger aspects of her Danish coup was the complete lack of involvement by her husband, the king of Norway. When Hanseatic merchants requested her to confirm their Norwegian privileges after her husband's death in 1380, she informed them that these privileges "had died with the king." In Denmark she consolidated power during the 1380s by refusing to name successors to its virtual viceroy (*drost*) or its field commander (*marsk*) after they died. Both had served her loyally. She also dismissed the governor of Scania (now part of southern Sweden) for disloyalty, and again appointed no successor. Margaret put talented foreigners in key positions: her military commander at a decisive battle came from Pomerania, and she employed a German as Norway's chancellor.[20]

Margaret's determination to hold power became evident in 1386 after the sudden death of her seventeen-year-old son deprived her of any legal claim to govern either Denmark or Norway. Her father's original heir, her Mecklenburg nephew, immediately claimed the Danish crown. However, Denmark's old drost needed exactly one week to arrange Margaret's election by various notables as "Almighty lady and husband and guardian for the whole kingdom of Denmark." This unprecedented document constituted sovereignty in everything but name; it made her a de jure regent for an indefinite period, "until the day when *she* and we agree to elect and appoint a king, with *her* and our advice." Four provincial assemblies soon confirmed this remarkable arrangement. This tactic was then imitated in Norway, which, unlike Denmark, was a hereditary kingdom. The archbishop of Norway, whose name headed the list of notables at the Danish meeting, soon summoned his kingdom's royal council. Overlooking the rules of succession which favored the king of Sweden, they named Margaret "Mighty Lady and Righteous Husband of Norway . . . in all the days of her life."[21]

Now ruler of two kingdoms, she intrigued to dethrone another Mecklenburg enemy from the Swedish throne, but she also needed to name a successor. For that purpose she chose a six-year-old grandson of her older sister, a Pomeranian princeling named Bugislav. His father brought him to Denmark, where Margaret adopted him and renamed him Erik. Six months later her troops defeated the Swedish king, capturing him and his son. Margaret kept the king imprisoned for almost six years. After this success, by 1391 she was using a privy seal with all three Scandinavian crowns. Nevertheless she still needed prolonged negotiations with the Hanseatic League before gaining control of Stockholm. The road finally lay open to the Union of Kalmar, which in 1397 unified the three Scandinavian crowns for a second and last time.

Margaret of Denmark micromanaged her adopted successor, arranging his marriage to an English princess and sending her twenty-three-year-old heir an eight-page set of personally written

instructions for his first independent state journey to Norway. She
also had a man who claimed to be her dead son extradited from
Prussia and executed after smashing his official state seal in his presence (almost four centuries later, Catherine II did this to
Pugachev).[22] The only privilege of sovereignty this remarkable female
ruler did *not* exercise was to issue coins bearing her name in any of
her three kingdoms. No matter how powerless she was in practical
terms, every fourteenth-century royal heiress had her name and title
on coins; but they had legitimate claims, which Margaret, despite all
her power and her royal father, lacked.

Joanna II, a childless widow, was the oldest woman who ever
acquired a European kingdom when she inherited Naples from her
brother. Although she remained on her throne for twenty years, her
reign ranks among the most obscure of any late medieval woman
sovereign. Unlike that of Joanna I, her government left no documentary evidence outside Italy to compensate for the destruction of the
Neapolitan archives in 1943. Joanna II, like her better-known predecessor, collaborated successfully with the papacy and also built a
mausoleum for the man who had made her his heir. But she also
repeated some of her predecessor's political mistakes in selecting
husbands and adopted heirs.[23]

Joanna II's worst political error was her remarriage to a French
nobleman, Jacques de Bourbon, in 1415. Although their prenuptial
contract, like Joanna I's final marriage, refused him royal authority,
he arrived with a military entourage, claimed royal rank, and soon
made her a virtual prisoner. By 1416 she had reversed the situation
through a mixture of cunning and bribery, fomenting a rising by
local barons that liberated her and imprisoned him instead. By
winter 1418 the Roman pope officially acknowledged Joanna II's
sovereignty, and his legate performed her coronation in January 1419.
A few months later her husband escaped from captivity and soon
returned to France, where he eventually retired to a monastery.

For fifteen years Joanna II governed her kingdom alone. Like
Joanna I and Margaret of Scandinavia, she employed ministers from
nonaristocratic backgrounds, but the succession question also bedev-

iled her reign. Joanna II revoked her first adopted heir in 1423 but subsequently revoked her new heir in 1433 for her original choice before changing her mind again two months later. Joanna II's death in 1435 provoked sixty years of sporadic aggression from her adopted French successor and his heirs, while her original Aragonese heir and his descendants governed her kingdom (ironically, one of them left his wife in charge of his own kingdom for over twenty years). Joanna II also left the largest surviving statue of any early European female monarch. It sits alongside one of her brother in the Neapolitan chapel which she endowed, near a smaller monument (with an epitaph by Lorenzo Valla) to the only notable murder victim of her reign: her long-serving principal minister, Ser Gianni Carraciolo.

## Four Young Royal Heiresses

Between 1377 and 1384 four young heiresses, all between the ages of ten and sixteen, claimed thrones in widely dispersed kingdoms: Sicily, Hungary, Portugal, and Poland.[24] Relatively little is known about them; for example, it is unclear when Portugal's heiress died, although her place of burial is known.[25] None of their final testaments survives, if indeed they bothered to make any, and no published documentary base as rich as that from Navarre survives in any of their kingdoms. Nevertheless, all four satisfy both fundamental criteria for identifying authentic female sovereigns: each woman left behind a handful of coins with her name followed by "D.G. Reg." and a few original signed documents.

These four contemporaneous heiresses have some interesting distinctions. Two full sisters acquired separate royal thrones in Hungary and Poland, a unique occurrence in European history, and each promptly made suitably impressive royal seals. Three girls inherited before the age of twelve; in Portugal and Hungary, their widowed mothers closely supervised their actions and arranged their marriages. All four heiresses were married to men of princely rank, one in Poland exactly at the canonical minimum age of twelve and another in Portugal even earlier. All four husbands carried out the ordinary business of government in their kingdoms; in other words, by the end of the fourteenth century the Navarrese solution of 1328 had already been repeated elsewhere four times (or five, counting Joanna I's second marriage).

However, this solution failed everywhere except in Navarre. Despite their early marriages, none of these four heiresses produced a surviving heir to her kingdom. One, whose husband already had a son by a previous marriage, remained childless; the others had only one child each, and all three (like Joanna I's three children) died in infancy. The childless heiress had already been deposed five years before her husband's death; the husbands of the other three outlived them. All three men had enjoyed official coronations in their wife's capital and therefore continued to rule her kingdom after her death as legitimate sovereigns. Unsurprisingly, all three widowers promptly remarried, but only one eventually founded a new dynasty, an accomplishment which took him twenty-five years and required three more wives.

These were indeed difficult times for royal heiresses. If they died young and childless after their husbands had received joint power, they risked being virtually erased from their kingdom's history—except, perhaps, for numismatists.[26] Two were deposed in the same year (1385) in widely separated kingdoms, Hungary and Portugal; one later recovered her throne. The papacy's Great Schism, which had undermined Joanna I's rule at Naples, further compli-cated their situation. One heiress, whose small kingdom backed the Roman pope, was held hostage for fourteen years by a larger kingdom, whose rulers backed his Avignon rival. On the other hand, the one heiress who lined up early and consistently behind the Roman pope achieved a unique distinction among Europe's female monarchs: six centuries after her death, Jadwiga of Poland has finally become a saint.

In 1377 Maria of Sicily inherited a monarchy which recognized papal suzerainty and maintained a fragile autonomy between two larger kingdoms, Naples to the north and Aragon to the west; her father gave Malta to his illegitimate son and made him heir to Sicily if his unmarried daughter died childless. Her uncle, the Aragonese king, vainly protested to the pope that women should not inherit; then he kidnapped Maria. After fourteen years of closely supervised captivity outside Sicily, the next Aragonese king used a dispensation from the antipope at Avignon to marry her to his nephew, who was barely half her age. When Maria returned for a joint coronation with her husband, she was "exhibited as a powerful fetish, an object or symbol of sovereignty, lost some time ago and recently recovered." Only four surviving documents bear her signature.[27]

Like her Sicilian counterpart, Beatriz of Portugal was an unfortunate political pawn. Her father, after losing several wars against Castile, was compelled on his deathbed to betroth her to the son of his hated enemy. However, the Castilian king suddenly became a widower and decided to marry Portugal's underage heiress himself. The decision soon proved to be a serious political mistake. He lost control of his child-wife's kingdom when rebels supported an illegitimate prince who won a dramatic victory in 1385. Because the victor founded a new dynasty, Portugal's unlucky heiress has been expunged from its official record, which still describes the two years separating her father's death from her bastard uncle's coronation as an interregnum.[28]

Europe's next heiress, Maria, was the older daughter of Louis the Great, king of Hungary and Poland. Her luck was little better: she became the second female monarch to be deposed by the same Angevin prince who had removed Joanna I of Naples in 1381. Within a week of Louis's death in 1382, his ambitious widow staged a solemn coronation making the twelve-year-old Maria king (rex) of Hungary. This act not only overturned her husband's intentions (Maria supposedly inherited Poland), but it also bypassed a German fiancé whom her mother disliked. For a few years the dowager governed Hungary; but disaster struck when her autonomous Croatian cousin invited Joanna I's assassin to add the Angevin heritage in central Europe to his Mediterranean possessions.

Advancing rapidly, the invader met little resistance. In late 1385 he was crowned as Hungary's new king, while its young heiress made a humiliating renunciation and her mother stood by helplessly. But within two months the dowager had organized a conspiracy that resulted in the assassination of the usurper. Maria and her mother then moved south to Croatia, where both were soon imprisoned. In early 1387 her captors murdered the dowager regent. Maria's original fiancé finally reached Hungary and became the third person crowned as its king within five years. A few months later she was finally liberated with help from Venice. Their subsequent marriage and joint reign until her death in 1395 seem anticlimactic.

The destiny of her younger sister Hedwig (Jadwiga in Polish), separated from her mother and pushed into her father's other kingdom, took a totally unpredictable turn. One must penetrate very thick clouds of incense concealing a thin layer of surviving documents in order to grasp events in Poland before and after Jadwiga's coronation as its king in October 1384. She was obviously manipulated by Polish magnates, who prevented her from marrying the Habsburg prince with whom she had been raised. Instead, they promised her to their powerful non-Christian neighbor, the grand duke of Lithuania. In exchange for accepting Catholic baptism and marrying Poland's official monarch, he would be crowned king of Poland. And so it happened. The thirty-six-year-old Jagiello was already unanimously accepted as king and lord of Poland even before being baptized at Cracow, the kingdom's capital, taking a new Christian name, and marrying Poland's other "king" three days later, on her twelfth birthday. His coronation, which required additional negotiations, followed five weeks later.

Understandably, objections were raised: the Habsburgs opposed the wedding, and the Teutonic Knights opposed the conversion. In 1386 and 1388 two papal legates investigated, but both found the marriage to be canonically legitimate and the conversion authentic. In order to reduce their dependency on Poland's magnates, this oddly assorted royal couple, though unable to speak a common language, quickly established a working political relationship. With Jadwiga's mother and sister imprisoned in Croatia, Poland's new king sent his young wife off to claim a disputed province from Hungary; she accomplished this successfully while he began implementing the conversion of Lithuania. A few months later she reminded Polish officials that Jagiello was the kingdom's "natural lord." Poland's queen remained active in Hungarian affairs; after the death of her sister Maria, Jadwiga added "heiress of Hungary" to her official titles.[29]

Jadwiga took great interest in promoting Latin Catholicism in her husband's territories, which were populated mainly by Orthodox Christians. In 1398 she endowed a college for Lithuanian theology students at the University of Prague. When she died a year later (between 1126 and 1853 she was Europe's only female monarch to die from complications following childbirth), her jewelry was sold to help reestablish a university in Cracow that still bears her husband's name. Twenty years later, churchmen who owed their careers to her began campaigning for her beatification.[30] Her sainthood is unquestionable; but the extent of her political agency in Poland seems much less than that of her paternal grandmother, who governed this kingdom for many years with minimal intervention from her son. From a political perspective, St. Jadwiga was simply the least ineffective of these late fourteenth-century Navarrese-style heiresses.

## Navarre Unravels

Although the Navarrese solution to female inheritance generally worked well in the small kingdom that had originally developed it, one of Europe's most energetic and capable fifteenth-century heiresses, Blanca of Navarre, became involuntarily responsible for undermining its long-term autonomy. Her first husband, Martin the Younger of Aragon (who had acquired the kingdom of Sicily by outliving his first wife), died childless in 1409 and bequeathed Sicily to his father, who then appointed his son's widow to govern this nominally autonomous kingdom. Despite having no hereditary ties, Blanca did so successfully for five years before her Aragonese in-laws repatriated her. (Aragon's fifteenth-century kings were unusually comfortable with female surrogates; as Theresa Earenfight has recently demonstrated, a Castilian wife administered Aragon for her husband for twenty-one consecutive years after he had inherited the kingdom of Naples from Joanna II.) Blanca unexpectedly became the heiress to Navarre in 1420 and, now a thirty-four-year-old childless widow, married the twenty-two-year-old Aragonese prince who had followed her as Sicily's viceroy. Their marriage produced a son and two daughters before Blanca's father died five years later. Navarre's heiress and her husband (not a crown prince) later held an elaborate joint coronation at Pamplona in 1429.[31]

Blanca had previously governed Sicily, and her young husband was preoccupied with the far larger kingdom of Castile, so she ordinarily managed most governmental business in Navarre. Until Blanca became chronically ill after 1437, almost three-fourths of Navarre's state documents were issued in her name and usually bore her signature. Afterward, her son, Carlos (born in 1421), became increasingly involved in governing Navarre (see table 3.1).

During Blanca's lifetime all three of her children had been sworn as potential heirs by Navarre's representative assembly with their order of succession confirmed, and all three had been married off, the crown prince to a German bride. Despite such precautions, one unforeseeable circumstance caused the Navarrese solution to unravel after Blanca's death. All three of her children would eventually claim her throne, but none ever enjoyed official recognition because of their father's exceptionally long survival. Juan I of Navarre lived until the age of eighty-two; after making a second

## Table 3.1. Government under Blanca of Navarre, 1426–40

| Year | Joint names | Queen only | King only | Crown Prince |
|------|-------------|------------|-----------|--------------|
| 1426 | 29 | 177 | 7 | |
| 1427 | 48 | 134 | 0 | |
| 1428 | 17 | 131 | 1 | |
| 1429 | 37 | 235 | 19 | |
| 1430 | 42 | 355 | 29 | |
| 1431 | 33 | 274 | 0 | |
| 1432 | 123 | 121 | 4 | |
| 1433 | 60 | 211 | 11 | |
| 1434 | 21 | 177 | 7 | |
| 1435 | 6 | 227 | 9 | |
| 1436 | 27 | 177 | 5 | 1 |
| 1437 | 13 | 128 | 16 | 3 |
| 1438 | 12 | 57 | 73 | 22* |
| 1439 | 18 | 19 | 35 | 78 |
| 1440 | 15 | 44 | 7 | 168 |

*also 5 signed jointly by king and crown prince

Source: Florencio Idoate, ed., Archivo General de Navarra: Catálogo de Comptos

marriage that produced his famous son Fernando the Catholic, he later inherited his father's kingdom, becoming Juan II of Aragon. Every key document in the gradual erosion of Navarrese autonomy, from the prenuptial agreement of 1420 to the testaments of all three children, is still extant. They outline what could and did go wrong when a formally crowned "dowager king" outlived a royal heiress by thirty-eight years but refused to let any of their adult children rule her kingdom. In this political tragedy, the most important document was Blanca's testament, long and "barely legible in places," as its leading expert acknowledges.[32] It confronted an unprecedented situation: she was Europe's only royal heiress who was survived both by a crowned husband and an adult son already accustomed to exercising authority, and she bequeathed her jeweled crown to a son who never wore it. The political abilities of all parties involved make Blanca's testament and its subsequent manipulations exceptionally important in the history of late medieval joint monarchy.

After King Juan remarried the daughter of a Castilian grandee in 1443, relations between father and son deteriorated rapidly. Within a decade, a very small kingdom had two parallel administrations. The father imprisoned his son for two years; the prince then fought an unsuccessful civil war, infuriating his father by minting his own coins as they traded mutual accusations of falsifying Blanca's testament. Juan summoned Navarre's Estates and formally disinherited both his son and his older daughter "as if dead of natural causes," considering them "erased [*suprimidos*] from the royal House of Navarre." The prince fled abroad, spent much time imprisoned, and died in exile. His older sister died shortly afterward while imprisoned by her younger sister and her husband, whom king Juan named as governors of Navarre. The younger daughter, now widowed, outlasted her octogenarian father by only a few weeks in 1479. This fifty-two-year-old heiress, the oldest in European history, lived just long enough to make a will bequeathing Navarre, still split between two warring clans, to her grandson, advising him to avoid Aragon and rely on French support to maintain its independence.[33]

Four years later, what remained of a very small kingdom acquired a very young heiress, Catherine of Foix. Alvaro Adot has

demonstrated how Navarre—now joined to the independent principality of Béarn across the Pyrenees, which she also inherited
from her father—experienced a brief renaissance as a viable trans-
Pyrenean state under Catherine and her French husband, Jean II
d'Albret. Their marriage proved both biologically and politically
fruitful. To an even greater degree than their better-known Castilian
contemporaries Ferdinand and Isabel, theirs was truly a joint government: almost 80 percent of the 434 documents issued for Navarre
between their joint coronation in 1494 and their expulsion in 1512
bore both their names. Catherine's official testament, drawn up at
Pamplona in 1506, resembles that of her fourteenth-century predecessor Jeanne II in its generous provisions for her "husband and
good companion." Its primary clauses awarded him fifty thousand
gold florins "for good marital love" plus one-fourth of Navarre's
revenues even after their heirs occupied the throne—unless he
remarried, in which case his paternal rights and revenues would
"cease immediately."[34]

Catherine's and Jean's downfall came suddenly and unexpectedly. In 1512 their overmighty neighbor Fernando the Catholic, son
of Juan II of Aragon (Juan I of Navarre) by his second wife, invaded
their kingdom, conquered it, and annexed it to Castile. Navarre's
ruling dynasty lamented his "completely unreasonable" actions (*gran
sinrazón cometida por el rey Fernando*) and retreated north of the
Pyrenees. Their defeat was not quite total or permanent. Within
twenty years their son had reclaimed the northernmost bit of their
Navarrese kingdom from Spain and governed it from Béarn.[35]
Within eighty years, their great-grandson unexpectedly inherited
France and thereby reunited two crowns which had been separated
by the Salic law in 1328.

## Cyprus: The Last Crusader Monarchs

The kingdom of Cyprus, Europe's last surviving state founded by
crusaders, lost its independence through the misfortunes of its two
fifteenth-century female rulers. Their fates were truly extraordinary:
the first was overthrown by Muslim intervention, and the second
was deposed by a republic which had legally adopted her. In the first

case an Egyptian sultan (who ignored the sacramental status of Christian monogamy and the associated notion of legitimate birth) sent a *jihad* to replace a young woman ruler with her bastard half brother; the second woman ruled as a puppet of Venice, which ultimately forced her abdication when she threatened its interests.[36]

When John II, the last legitimate male king of Cyprus, died in 1458, his island had become a protectorate of Egypt's Mameluke sultans, to whom it paid an annual tribute. By his second wife, a Byzantine princess, John II left a daughter, Charlotte; by another Greek noblewoman he also had an illegitimate son, whom he intended to make the island's Latin archbishop. Since a legitimate female, although younger, outranked an illegitimate male, the Cypriot barons duly arranged Charlotte's coronation in October 1458, absent the archbishop-elect of Nicosia. The major political issue was to arrange her marriage to a younger son of the duke of Savoy, which duly took place a year later.

Meanwhile, her half brother escaped from virtual house arrest and fled the island. The political fate of this crusader kingdom would now be determined by its Egyptian suzerain, and the extraordinary tale is best recounted primarily through Egyptian chroniclers, who provide its basic narrative: "On Sunday 28 Ramadan 863 [May 29, 1459] Jakum the Frank, son of Jawan, ruler of the island of Cyprus, arrived in the Egyptian realm with a request of the sultan that he be granted possession of Cyprus in his father's place. The people of Cyprus had installed his sister, supplanting him, since he was the product of adultery, or some such condition that did not legitimate his succession in their community." Help was soon promised. Three months later "the sultan convened a ceremony in the royal courtyard of the Citadel of the Mountain. He presented Jakum ibn Jawan and draped him with a Kamiliyya robe of honor, enrobing two other Franks who were presented with him. The sultan gave him a horse with a golden saddle and mantle with gold and silver brocade, which he rode for the duration of his stay in Egypt. The sultan designated him governor of Cyprus and pledged to establish him there, delivering Cyprus to him." A few weeks later, "the sultan commenced construction of the vessels designated for the jihad, with Jakum accompanying them to Cyprus." Four days later, he sent an emissary to Cyprus "to inform its populace that the sultan desired the sovereignty of this Jakum over Cyprus in place of his father, and the deposition of his sister, censuring them for the lack of sovereignty of this Jakum and the preferment of his sister in his place."

Greater honors followed: "On Sunday 25 Rabi [864/January 19, 1460], the sultan celebrated the Prophet's birthday in the royal courtyard as per tradition every year. The sultan presented Jakum al-Firanji, son of the ruler of Cyprus, and seated him among the notable officials of state." As the chronicler observed, "This distressed the populace grievously. So I have said: Possibly the sultan did not present him at this court session, except to see him glorify Islam and diminish unbelief." Jakum al-Firanji was surely the only Latin archbishop-elect who ever attended such a ceremony, and rumors about it "distressed the populace grievously" on the Christian side as well: his enemies insisted he had renounced his faith, and no pope ever trusted him again.

On Cyprus, many Frankish barons protested the sultan's repudiation of their queen. When his emissary returned to Cairo on March 24, 1460, he was accompanied by "a large group of Frankish princes and people from Cyprus in two factions: one unit requesting that the designated queen be confirmed; the other demanding her deposition and installation of her brother." When the sultan finally decided the matter a few months later, events took two unexpected twists. On May 27, 1460, reports the Cairene chronicler, "a heinous event occurred in the realm: the sultan convened the notable Cypriot Franks, filling the royal courtyard. He intended to confirm the queen as ruler of Cyprus as she was established." The sultan had changed his mind because the queen's emissaries had offered to raise the island's tribute and brought the money with them: "He enrobed her emissaries, the notable Franks," and "appointed [his falconer] as her escort, bearing her diploma and her robe of honor." Meanwhile, "her brother was in attendance, seated below the commanders of 1000. The designation of his sister . . . pained him. He rose to his feet and called for support. He spoke words to the effect that he had come to Egypt, taken refuge with the sultan, sought his protection, and submitted to him this lengthy period. [He asserted] that he had more right to the kingship than his sister. The sultan did not heed him, being resolved upon confirmation of his sister, and ordered him to depart to his residence. Thus, Jakum had no recourse but to depart from the middle door of the royal courtyard. His adversaries, his sister's entourage, followed after him."

At this point, chaos ensued because James's chief adviser and a Mameluke interpreter had outbribed his sister's representatives among the emirs.[37] "Then some veteran Mamelukes extended their hands against the adversaries of Jakum among the Franks. They inflicted blows and lacerations upon them, tearing up the robe [of honor]. They called in one voice that they wanted nothing but the confirmation of this Jakum in his father's place. The tumult heightened, leaving the sultan no recourse but to yield immediately, deposing the queen and acclaiming Jakum. Thus was Jakum confirmed in spite of the sultan. The sultan immediately enrobed Jakum. He ordered the departure of an expedition of officers to invade Cyprus and to proceed with Jakum to Cyprus." Twelve days later "the sultan summoned the sultani Mamluks to the royal courtyard. He designated a group of them for the jihad, that is: to depart in the company of Jakum al-Firanji for Cyprus."

This jihad was successful. By November 1460 Mameluke military muscle had enabled Jakum to gain the upper hand on Cyprus, pinning his sister's loyalists into an impregnable coastal fort. He spent three years rallying support among the Cypriot barons and finally forced his sister and her Savoyard husband off the island. Once firmly in control, James massacred his remaining Egyptian elite troops in cold blood and sent an emissary to Cairo accusing their commander of "abducting comely youths from their parents." Relating this tale, the Cairo chronicler expresses skepticism before concluding laconically, "Jakum took possession . . . on the grounds that he was the sultan's viceroy. In any case, [he] remained as ruler of Cyprus." On the Christian side, his sister found shelter with the Knights Hospitallers on Rhodes, and the papacy refused to acknowledge the island's new monarch.

James had no fleet, and his island kingdom required protection from Venice; he therefore decided to marry the daughter of a

prominent Venetian aristocratic family with many investments on
the island and few scruples about his right to rule Cyprus. In July
1472, two months before she sailed to Cyprus, the Republic of St.
Mark officially adopted his bride, Caterina Cornaro. This ceremony,
unique in the Republic's long history, sufficed to give legal footing to
another unprecedented event after James died in 1473. When Queen
Charlotte tried to persuade a Venetian fleet that "James, now dead,
was a bastard and held the kingdom wrongfully, for it is wrong that
while the heir is alive others should take the kingdom . . . in justice,
you are bound to help her win [the kingdom]," the commander
refused because James was "the king appointed by the sultan."[38]
Instead of restoring the heiress, the Most Serene Republic
proclaimed the pregnant widow of the sultan's king the new ruler of
Cyprus. Charlotte sent another embassy to Egypt, but her claim was
refused and her emissary sent in chains to her female rival.

After the infant son of King James died in 1474, his teenaged
widow became the island's official sovereign. Money was coined and
decrees were issued in the name of Catherine of Venice, *Caterina
Veneta*. The pope and the sultan were duly informed of her eleva-
tion; the sultan sent an official robe and asked for his unpaid tribute.
She herself enjoyed scant respect. Her father received permission to
visit her soon after her proclamation (she was Europe's first titular
female monarch with a living father) and complained that she was
treated worse than her married sisters. Theoretically, she ruled
Cyprus for fifteen years, until the Most Serene Republic, upon
hearing rumors of her projected remarriage, sent her brother to force
her resignation. This constitutional charade ended when, for the
only time in European history, a large, powerful republic swallowed
a small, weak monarchy: on February 13, 1489, the Lusignan standard was lowered on Cyprus and replaced by the Lion of St. Mark.
Unlike accounts of her official adoption, elaborate descriptions of
her abdication ceremony have been preserved. In return for her
cooperation, Venice permitted her a dignified retirement at full
salary governing the minuscule lordship of Asolo, while the republic
ruled Cyprus for more than seventy years.

## Successful Joint Rule in Castile

The thirty-year reign of Isabel I of Castile (1474–1504) is deservedly far better known than those of her late medieval female predecessors. It marked the first time a woman had exercised supreme authority for such a long time in one of Europe's largest kingdoms; not only was Castile vastly larger and more powerful in 1474 than when Urraca had inherited it in 1109, but Isabel's kingdom increased greatly in size and influence during her reign. It has also been noticed that a sudden development in the game of chess, involving the greatly increased powers of the only female piece on the board, the queen, originated in Castile shortly after Isabel's greatest military success, the conquest of Granada; the new rules were first described in a treatise dedicated to her son.[39] In the history of female kings, both the beginning and the end of this well-studied reign hold special significance. It began with a succession disputed between partisans of two women that was resolved only after a lengthy civil war, and it ended with one woman leaving her kingdom to another woman, the only such occurrence in European history until the twentieth century. On both occasions Isabel's husband proved indispensable both in ensuring victory over her niece and in preserving Isabel's Castilian heritage from their politically incompetent daughter thirty years later. To a degree not always recognized by current scholarship, he proved no less indispensable throughout the long period between these events. The Catholic kings enjoyed the most successful truly joint reign in European history.

Isabel's marriage in 1469 to Ferdinand, her slightly younger second cousin and crown prince of Aragon, required elaborate prenuptial arrangements—particularly since her brother, the king of Castile, opposed it and soon used her disobedience as reason for disinheriting her. Seen in the context of similar arrangements between her fiancé's father and his first wife and those involving another Navarrese heiress in 1485, its provisions do not seem unusual. Its most important clauses required the husband to spend most of his time in his wife's kingdom; he could not remove her or their children from it without express permission. Royal authority was to be held jointly: they must share all titles and sign all documents together. The agreement employed the plural form throughout.[40] Ferdinand's father donated the Sicilian crown to enhance his son's rank and forged a papal dispensation. They married and soon had a daughter.

Five years after this marriage, Isabel's brother died after having repudiated her as his heir. She immediately claimed the Castilian throne, arranging an official proclamation in Segovia while her husband was in Aragon. Isabel acted so hastily because she knew that her brother's only child, her unmarried thirteen-year-old niece, would also claim his throne once she became a legal adult. Surprised by Isabel's gesture, Ferdinand returned to Castile and soon assured Aragonese authorities that he had been quickly confirmed as its king: "In the field, I was sworn, received, and raised as king of these realms." Under emergency conditions, their prenuptial contract obviously required some retouching, although its essential provisions required only minor modifications: for example, his name preceded hers on joint declarations, but her coat of arms preceded his on the attached seals. A few months later, as war was breaking out, this revised arrangement was updated a second time, giving her husband power to make appointments "without my intervention, consultation, or authorization." For his part, Ferdinand made a testament leaving his titles to his daughter with Isabel, who must also raise her husband's two previous illegitimate children.[41]

The ensuing civil war became Europe's last lengthy struggle between rival female claimants to a major throne (in 1553 England had one that ended within a few days). Each side exercised the prerogatives of sovereignty by issuing decrees and coining money. In important ways this conflict mirrored that between Portugal and Castile ninety years before, but with the protagonists reversed. Both times, a very young heiress lost her kingdom after being forced to marry a neighboring older king who already had a male heir; both times, the women who lost ended up in convents in their husband's kingdom; and both times, prominent noblemen and church prelates who backed the losing side became permanent exiles.

One major difference is that in the 1470s, as Carrasco Manchado has emphasized, the older woman manipulated various strategies of legitimation throughout the struggle, even turning military setbacks into propaganda victories after her husband's first campaign ended in failure. It took four years to conclude the fighting (the Castilians eventually did better), but Isabel won the peace quickly. In 1479, with her husband away reorganizing his dead father's kingdom (this was also the moment when Ferdinand's widowed half sister successfully claimed the kingdom of Navarre), Isabel personally handled negotiations with Portugal. Preoccupied with permanently neutralizing a dangerous niece whom she never referred to by name (Juana was always *aquella*, "that woman"), Isabel insisted on forcing her into a convent. Subsequently known in Portugal as the "excellent lady," "aquella" apparently never stayed in a convent and long outlived her aunt; she eventually donated her Castilian rights to the Portuguese crown in 1522. But Isabel won the representational war so thoroughly that her unlucky rival's story has not been pieced together until quite recently.[42]

After Ferdinand and Isabel emerged victorious, this power couple drove the last Muslim government out of western Europe, sent Columbus on multiple voyages to explore a new continent, and opened a new chapter in religious persecution via the Spanish Inquisition. Their reputation as joint rulers is substantially correct because they worked tirelessly to implement their famous slogan to "command, govern, rule, and exercise lordship as one" (*mandar, gobernar, regir, y señorear a una*). In several ways they were the ulti-mate and certainly the most successful embodiments of a general late medieval phenomenon: the heiress with a husband possessing royal authority in her kingdom.

They differed from the Navarrese model because of the excep-tional political activity and talent of the heiress. Their political rela-tionship is represented with didactic clarity on their various gold coins, from early *castellanos* issued during the civil war to their dazzling new *excelentes* of 1497: all of them depict both as crowned monarchs, either seated or facing each other, with him in the posi-tion of honor on the left and his name preceding hers. But their most remarkable coin was not struck in Spain. Their silver *carlino*, made in 1503 for the recently conquered kingdom of Naples, was the first two-headed male and female coin seen in the Mediterranean world since the time of Antony and Cleopatra, and its single contin-uous inscription covering both sides represented Europe's closest numismatic approximation to gender parity during the high Renaissance (see fig. 4).

Castilian chronicles, composed by Isabel's well-paid officials and often published in the vernacular, tend to emphasize her role over her husband's. Juan de Flores, her first official chronicler, said that Isabel ruled "like a powerful man" (*como esforçado varón*). "It may be," he reports her as saying, "that women lack the discretion to know things and the strength to stand up to others, perhaps even the language to express themselves properly; but I have discovered that we have the eyes to see." And to read a great deal: Isabel read so many letters and documents that she became the first female monarch to own several pairs of spectacles. She also read printed books, relatively new cultural products that reached her kingdom during her reign. It is no accident that one of the earliest preserved portraits of a European female monarch, made about 1490, shows Isabel holding one of these.[43]

Contemporaries disagreed about which half of the Catholic kings was the dominant force in their partnership. In 1526 a Venetian diplomat praised Isabel as "a rare and most talented [*virtuosísima*] woman, who is universally spoken of throughout Spain much more often than the king [Ferdinand], although he also was very prudent and rare in his time." Two years later, another Italian diplomat, Baldassare Castiglione, raised the issue of her husband's influence in his famous *Book of the Courtier* but gave the longest speech to Isabel's champion rather than to her husband's. However, Ferdinand of Aragon also had Italian admirers; the most famous, Machiavelli, praised him as "almost a new Prince."

Ferdinand's grandson, Emperor Charles V, certainly believed the king was the dominant force in the partnership. When arranging the marriage of his son Philip to his cousin Mary Tudor, Charles advised him to imitate his Aragonese great-grandfather by acting "so that while he in reality does everything, the initiative should always seem to proceed from the Queen and her Council."[44] Some seventeenth-century Aragonese authors, led by Baltasar Gracián, reduced Isabel to her husband's collaborator and subordinate; but after the French Bourbons, who had cause to dislike Ferdinand, claimed the Spanish throne, Isabel's moral preeminence has dominated the couple's posthumous reputation.

How did their much-praised joint rule actually work? The subject has not yet been adequately studied, despite (or perhaps because of) a superabundance of documentation.[45] Joint rule should not be confused with equality or even symmetry. When she first visited his lands in 1481, Ferdinand gave his wife a few unusual privileges, but there was no symmetry between his authority in her kingdom and her authority in his. Every Castilian coin after 1474 bears his name, but no Aragonese coin uses hers. In Castile, this famous couple apparently behaved similarly to their younger counterparts in the small neighboring kingdom of Navarre, which was also being ruled at the end of the fifteenth century by an heiress and her husband. In both places, jointly proclaimed decrees outnumbered those issued by either sovereign alone, and the husband issued more individual decrees than his wife. In the 1480s Ferdinand usually handled certain types of routine royal business that generated lucrative fees, such as legitimations of bastards or appointments of public scribes. Much Castilian international business was signed by Ferdinand alone, even when Isabel was present, although the reverse was occasionally true.[46]

In some other areas of state policy, Isabel's participation consistently outstripped that of her husband. Although they remain jointly famous as the Catholic kings, a title officially given them in 1496 by the Spanish-born pope Alexander VI, she took a far more sustained interest than her husband in improving the educational and moral level of senior appointments in the Castilian church. In Aragon, on the other hand, Ferdinand made his nine-year-old bastard son archbishop of Saragossa and later approved the nomination of the pope's bastard son, the notorious Cesare Borgia, as bishop of Valencia. At another point where religion intersected with politics, Isabel manipulated the incorporation of Castile's three great chivalric knightly orders into the royal domain by employing some remarkable displays of female authority over these supposedly entirely masculine organizations. The process began during the civil war, in 1476, when she personally attended the meeting to elect a new Master of the Order of Santiago (her husband, of course, was chosen). It concluded seventeen years later, when she persuaded the papacy to grant her the administration of all three orders—something "against all law," grumbled papal officials, "and a monstrous thing that a woman could administer such Orders."[47]

The most famous, or notorious, intersection of religion and politics in Isabel's kingdom was undoubtedly its new royally controlled Inquisition, founded in 1478. She personally conducted some of the necessary high-level diplomacy: after a papal suspension of its proceedings in Aragon in 1482, Isabel, not Ferdinand, signed a long letter to Rome defending inquisitorial procedures in both of their realms and eventually received a satisfactory answer. Nevertheless, as Henry Charles Lea demonstrated over a century ago, Ferdinand intervened far more often than his wife in the Inquisition's early affairs in Castile, frequently writing in the first person singular, while some of Isabel's interventions attempted to protect her *converso* officials.[48]

## Burgundian and Castilian Heiresses, 1477–1506

When her father was killed in battle early in 1477, nineteen-year-old Mary of Burgundy became the richest heiress in Christendom, inheriting a total of thirteen provinces with more than sixty-three hundred parishes. An embryonic great power, created essentially after 1430 by two ambitious Burgundian dukes in the Low Countries along the border between France and the empire, its constituent parts were vassals of these great overlords; Flanders, the largest and wealthiest province, was legally divided between them. This unmarried heiress, aided primarily by her shrewd stepmother, Margaret of York (sister to Edward IV of England), struggled to retain control of her sprawling inheritance. Despite an eloquent plea to the authorities of the Duchy of Burgundy, from which her house took its name, she was unable to prevent its reabsorption into France. Other parts of her father's possessions located in what is today France were also lost in 1477, some in the south permanently, others temporarily. Farther north, things went better. In exchange for extending local privileges which her father had infringed, Mary collected political and financial support from the core provinces of the Low Countries, but sometimes their loyalty was negotiated only after serious bargaining: for example, Holland, her third most important province, insisted on replacing court French with the local Low German dialect as its official language.[49]

Threatened by the French king Louis XI, who proposed to marry her to his son and heir, Mary needed a husband to provide military leadership to defend what remained of her patrimony. She and her stepmother quickly concluded an arrangement with her father's preferred choice, Maximilian of Austria, the eighteen-year-old heir of the Holy Roman emperor. In a region already famous for its elaborately opulent public ceremonies, they were married with minimal pomp at a moment when making war was more urgent than making love. It was a union of political equals; in 1479 a highly unusual two-headed medal depicted them with similar inscriptions on each side. Afterward, Maximilian did what was asked of him both by fathering heirs (three children in four years) and by winning a major victory against the French in 1479. Advised by his wife's stepmother, he also reorganized Burgundy's famous chivalric order, the Golden Fleece, after a five-year hiatus. However, Burgundian coinage testifies that Maximilian never enjoyed the official rank of other contemporary royal husbands like Ferdinand of Aragon in his wife's possessions. Burgundy's heiress managed many internal affairs in her remaining lands and attended any political assembly where she and her husband needed to raise revenue.

Mary of Burgundy was genuinely mourned when she died after a hunting accident at the age of twenty-five. Despite her short life, she left a noteworthy cultural legacy. She loved hunting with falcons and was the first woman ruler in Europe whose official seal showed her on horseback holding a falcon. Her most distinctive legacy to posterity is as Europe's only female ruler with a beer (*Duchesse de Bourgogne*) named for one of the last native rulers of a land unusually rich in breweries. Its current label adapts a portrait of her (with a falcon) that was commissioned by her widower three years after her death, itself an unusual distinction, Much later, the chivalric Maximilian reshaped his youthful adventures in the Low Countries into an illustrated fairy tale about a hero entitled the White King (*Weisskunig*).[50] Mary of Burgundy also left her two surviving children a sizable political legacy as the Burgundians became the Habsburgs. In 1494, faced with increasing responsibilities in the empire, Maximilian handed a stable state to their sixteen-year-old son Philip. Two years later Maximilian approved his children's marriages to the son and second daughter of Spain's Catholic kings, Ferdinand and Isabel. The long-term consequences after the Spanish legacy passed to their Burgundian-Habsburg heirs proved far more important than anyone imagined at the time.

Spain's transition to Habsburg rule demonstrated in acute form the risks of female inheritance in an age of joint rulership. Isabel the Catholic had to change her official heir several times because her only son died childless in 1497 and both her oldest daughter and her first grandson also died by 1501. In 1504 Castile's succession therefore fell to Juana, another married daughter whose Habsburg husband already governed Europe's largest nonmonarchical state and was desperately eager to claim royal rank through his wife. Upon learning of Isabel's death, the so-called Burgundian theater-state staged a remarkably elaborate funeral service for her at Brussels. Jean Molinet, the official Burgundian chronicler, praised the Castilian ruler as a female crusader, a "very Catholic queen who besieged the strongholds and fortresses of the Moors in the absence of her husband: she received magnificently all embassies sent to her and gave elegant replies without using a spokesman such that everyone admired her prudence and noble countenance." He also explained that the archduke spent fifty thousand florins on this ceremony "because Lady Jeanne was the one who will succeed to these kingdoms." At its conclusion, the herald of the Order of the Golden Fleece named husband and wife as joint successors to the dead monarch, then formally invested Philip with a sword of state. In a complete reversal of her mother's central role at her own official proclamation thirty years before, Castile's new heiress remained a passive spectator as royal authority was ceremonially transferred to her husband.[51]

Like his father, Ferdinand of Aragon outlived a royal heiress; but unlike him, his authority in his wife's kingdom ended with her death. Isabel did what she could to protect her husband's position through a lengthy final testament which envisaged the possibility that her oldest surviving child would be either unwilling or unable to rule. But in the end there was no legal alternative to repeating the same formal proclamation that Isabel's followers had devised thirty years before, jointly acclaiming Castile's new proprietary heiress "and her legitimate husband." The royal couple took over a year to reach Castile, whereupon Ferdinand relinquished his regency, remarried, and retired to his hereditary possessions.

Castile's new regime would not be a joint monarchy. Instead, its proprietary monarch became the exact antithesis of her mother by refusing to exercise any political responsibilities. Juana's self-erasure as sovereign became evident during her brief appearance in July 1506 before Castile's first parliament or *Cortes* held under its new rulers. The *diputados*, all of whom had experienced thirty years of Isabel's government, asked her daughter four specific questions. First, did she intend to govern her kingdoms? Second, would her husband reign jointly with her? Third, would she please dress like a Spanish lady? Fourth, would she please appoint Spanish women in her household? Only their third request received an encouraging answer; she promised to dress differently. However, she refused their fourth request "because of her husband's temperament [*naturaleza*]." Juana's responses to their two main questions reflect her experience when her husband had publicly claimed Castile's crown without associating her. She now refused to exercise any authority because "the Flemings do not have the custom of permitting women to govern." Her remark was patently false, although she may not have been aware that her husband had inherited his lands from a mother who had governed them alone before her marriage.[52]

Seen in the context of female sovereignty, Juana the Mad deserves her sad nickname. Spaniards were probably fortunate that her overbearing husband died within a few months of his arrival, but they were unfortunate that his politically catatonic widow survived him by

almost half a century. By failing to participate in any rituals of government, she became the only reigning monarch in European history
considered a political cipher by her husband, her father, and her son,
all of whom governed successively in her name. Significantly, her
magnificent tombstone in the new royal chapel in Granada was made
without her knowledge at least two decades before her actual death,
and she was never told when her husband's corpse was moved there.

Spain's resulting constitutional quagmire had various official
consequences. The British Museum possesses a seal of Philip and
Juana with the husband in primary position on the left; it was used
on a document four years after his death, with his name erased.
Although Juana's was a phantom reign, her name generally precedes
her son's name on thousands of official Spanish documents—none of
which she signed during the last forty-eight years of her life. Almost a
year after her death, the official cession of the kingdom of Sicily to
Philip II was still drawn jointly in the names of Charles and Juana.[53]

Spanish coinage reveals even greater confusion. Juana's husband
died too soon to issue coins, but her de facto abdication in combination with her de jure title created major problems. During her father's
regency, a *real* minted in Granada proclaimed "Ferdinand and Juana,
by God's Grace King and Queen of Castile, León, and Aragon." After
news of Ferdinand's death reached Brussels in 1516, his grandson
immediately had Spanish coins struck there, imitating the earliest
coins of Ferdinand and Isabel, but with the important difference that
his mother's name preceded his. Next year, in a document which
never mentioned Juana, the papacy officially acknowledged Charles I
as the Catholic king of Castile and Aragon. Afterward, the names of
both mother and son appear on all Spanish coins; most inscriptions
name her first. In Aragon, a gigantic one-hundred-ducat piece, more
a medal than a coin, shows her in the primary position on the left,
facing her son, with both wearing crowns (see fig. 5). In their Italian
possessions, Juana's name usually comes first, but in their American
possessions, her son's name precedes hers.[54]

In assessing the overall political record of late medieval female
sovereigns, one must remember the failures as well as the successes,

Juana the Mad as well as her mother, Isabel the Catholic, while realizing that their contemporary Catherine of Navarre offers a more typical example than either of them. A royal heiress meant a change of dynasty, especially when her husband outlived her, which happened about half the time, partly because their husbands were often younger. The advent of female monarchs eroded political autonomy in some of Europe's smallest and weakest kingdoms, such as Sicily, Norway, Cyprus, and Navarre. Nevertheless, probably because opening royal successions to legitimate children of both sexes increased the possibilities of direct inheritance from one generation to another, only France unambiguously prohibited women from inheriting a royal throne.

The most common feature among these fifteen late medieval female monarchs was that, apart from two childless widows with no hereditary claim to their former husband's kingdom—Margaret of Denmark in Norway and Catherine of Venice in Cyprus—they were heiresses who were married during most, if not all, of their reigns. Like queens, husbands of royal heiresses were expected to play a political role in a spouse's kingdom. But whereas queens might be a temporary regent for an absent husband or an underage son, husbands were expected to perform most—but never all—of the work of governing their wife's kingdom. This general practice was best described in 1683 by Diego Dormer, an Aragonese with little knowledge of northern Europe. He argued that throughout Spain, including Urraca's reign in twelfth-century Castile and León and Isabel's reign three centuries later, husbands of heiresses had invariably governed their wife's kingdoms. But Dormer had to admit that this situation was not universal, and he lamented the "much greater unreasonableness and more unjust and dishonest pretensions of both Queen Juanas of Naples, who excluded some of their husbands from the title and rule of their kingdom."[55] Although the practice would have a final revival a few years later during England's so-called Glorious Revolution, expecting husbands of royal heiresses to govern their wife's kingdom had already become the exception rather than the rule when Dormer printed these remarks.

How did this come to pass?

# 4

## Female Regents Promote Female Rule, 1500–1630

*A woman is never as respected and feared as a man, no matter what rank she holds.*

—Mary of Hungary, resigning as regent, 1555

A considerable gulf separated the political authority of female regents from that of female monarchs. A regent, whether male or female, always governed on behalf of an authentic sovereign who was unable to exercise authority personally because of physical absence, youthfulness (the age of legal majority was fourteen or higher), or generally recognized incompetence. For this reason, the authority of regents was by definition delegated and temporary: young monarchs would mature, absent monarchs would return, and even monarchs declared mentally incompetent might, like George III of England, be restored to sufficient health to resume their duties. Like their male counterparts, some female sovereigns were therefore replaced by regents when under the age of majority, absent, or proclaimed incompetent. All three situations happened more than once; but overall, women were far more likely to become regents than to require regents. It was usually a monarch's closest female kin, most often mothers of underaged kings or wives of absent kings, who commonly filled such temporary voids in sovereign authority; but the most important long-serving female regents in early modern Europe also include sisters, aunts, nieces, daughters, and even a grandmother of male sovereigns.

No regent had the propaganda possibilities that coinage offered to monarchs, nor did regents claim to govern by divine right. Nevertheless, regents who served for lengthy periods often found other methods to buttress their political stature. It is a central contention of this book that the gradual acceptance of women rulers in Europe during its long transition from politically subordinated female monarchs with crowned husbands to female monarchs who governed alone even when married was greatly assisted by various printed, painted, sculpted, and engraved endorsements of women's capacities for ruling, and that the most audacious of these were sponsored or commissioned not by female monarchs (whose sovereignty was permanent and divinely ordained) but by eight female regents, each of whom governed a major state for at least five years between 1507 and 1633. Among them, the two who patronized the most extreme written and painted promotions of female rule were those with the most experience in governing France—the most important kingdom in Europe to prohibit any trace of female inheritance rights.

Female regents had been common throughout the Middle Ages, and a few of them had served for lengthy periods. The wife of one chronically absent fifteenth-century Aragonese monarch governed his kingdom for over twenty consecutive years. However, the political visibility of women regents increased after 1500. Several high-profile women now became regents for indefinite periods because of their political skills, especially in the Low Countries—a densely populated, wealthy region which lacked monarchical status, although it presently includes two hereditary monarchies and a hereditary grand duchy. After mistakenly assuring Castilian deputies in 1506 that "the Flemings do not permit women to govern," Isabel's heir would live long enough to see her husband's hereditary lands governed for over forty years by his sister and one of his nieces. Four women governed the Habsburg Netherlands without a male associate for more than half the time between 1507 and 1633, and each of them sponsored some novel cultural promotion of female rule. In 1529 the first treatise arguing women's general superiority to men was dedicated to Margaret of Austria, who governed her native lands for over twenty years. Afterwards, her niece and former ward, Mary of Hungary, governed this region for twenty-four years. She became Europe's first living female ruler since Cleopatra to commission a life-size statue of herself, and her exceptional capacities as ruler became the central feature of her state funeral. A few years later, Mary's niece Margaret of Parma, who governed the region while her husband remained in Italy, commissioned the first medal honoring a woman's rule. Much later, a fourth Habsburg princess, Philip II's oldest daughter, governed this region for twelve years while dressed as a Franciscan nun.

In the mid-sixteenth century two other Habsburg princesses, the younger sister and a niece of the veteran regent Mary of Hungary, each served five years as regents of Spain and Portugal, and both women left significant cultural legacies. Soon afterward, during the final phase of her long de facto regency in France, Catherine de Medici sponsored the most impressive sixteenth-century treatise defending the principle of female rule. Exactly a half century later, Marie de Medici, another ambitious Tuscan princess who served many years as de jure regent of France, commissioned Europe's most famous artist to create the most elaborate cycle of pictorial propaganda glorifying a woman's political career. In terms of political propaganda, the cultural innovations associated with Europe's early modern female regents far surpassed those of its female sovereigns.

## A Self-Fashioned Female Regent

After his only legitimate son, Philip, died in Spain in 1506, Emperor Maximilian I ignored suggestions from the Flemish Estates-General that Philip's widow become regent.[1] Instead, he named his twice-widowed daughter Margaret to govern her native lands. Maximilian was already aware of her diplomatic skills and her ability to select talented and dedicated officials when he named her guardian of his grandchildren and regent of Burgundy. His grandson, who became Charles I of Spain and Emperor Charles V, thus had extensive but contradictory experiences with women rulers during a lifetime (1500–1558) when he dominated European politics. Raised in the Low Countries by an extremely capable aunt, he stripped her of her authority upon reaching his majority at age fourteen. Two years later he acquired a distant Spanish crown that technically belonged to his mother, and for almost forty years they officially ruled jointly, although she remained completely inactive.

Because he needed to govern important states that were distant from each other, Charles required regents. He often selected women: his early experience of a clever aunt apparently outweighed having a politically inert mother. One of Margaret's protégés, Mercurino Gattinara, soon persuaded Charles to restore much of her authority. By 1519 she was once again "regent and governor" with "authority, faculty, and full power" over finance, justice, and military affairs in the Low Countries. After Margaret died in 1530, he chose his younger sister Mary, the widowed queen of Hungary, to replace her. Charles V remains enormously popular in his native region, where he spent barely four and a half years after 1517. Although theoretically supervised by absent male relatives, both female regents were in practice autonomous and gave as much advice as they received.

Margaret of Austria was both politically successful and culturally self-fashioning to an unusual extent. Her regency began with a notable diplomatic triumph for her father by negotiating the League of Cambrai in 1508: Maximilian used it to invade Italy and almost destroyed the Venetian Republic. It ended with another diplomatic success on behalf of her nephew when Margaret negotiated the so-called Ladies Peace of 1529 with her former sister-in-law, the dowager French regent; it produced several years of peace during the interminable Habsburg–Valois wars. A true Renaissance princess, Margaret was the first woman ruler in Europe to compose poems; she also created a personal motto about the benefits of adversity, *Fortune infortune fort une.* She supervised two major building projects: a new official residence in her capital city of Mechelen and a magnificent mausoleum for herself and her second husband in her Savoyard dowry lands. Her commissions continue to interest historians of art. Musicologists have published facsimile editions of her private collections, while her numerous manuscripts and books have been reconstructed from her private inventory. With good reason, a study of her personal possessions is entitled "Life with art and influence through art."[2]

Margaret sat for portraits as an adolescent and later commissioned them as a regent. No fewer than five depictions of her at the age of fourteen survive, all by unknown artists. Afterward, Margaret considered a court painter a political necessity for anyone governing this talent-rich area, and Bernard van Orley created what became her official portrait, at least ten copies of which went to relatives and courtiers in the 1520s. Recognizable versions also survive in many other forms, including a tapestry, an illuminated manuscript, a stained-glass window in a cathedral, and even a small-scale carving used as a game piece. Margaret kept no copy of this official portrait in her exquisitely furnished palace at Mechelen alongside her numerous portraits of relatives and prominent contemporary figures, but she did keep one of her prenuptial teenage portraits.[3]

Margaret's literary patronage has some protofeminist accents. She preferred manuscripts to printed books, possessing not only the oldest illustrated manuscript of Boccaccio's *Famous Women* but also an extensive acquaintance with the works of Christine de Pizan. Margaret eventually acquired five works by her and purchased a second copy of the *City of Ladies* in 1511. During a meeting with Henry VIII of England in 1513, she also received a six-panel tapestry illustrating scenes from the *City of Ladies*. Her first court historiographer, Lemaire des Belges, composed a poetic "crown" for her that included a comparison to her politically illustrious namesake, Margaret of Denmark. Lemaire's poetic license twisted the Scandinavian Margaret into a legitimate heiress to both Denmark and Norway; he also claimed she had released a captured Swedish king with "singular moderation," whereas she had actually made him resign his throne through six years of close confinement.[4]

The most novel treatise dedicated to Margaret of Austria was undoubtedly Henry Cornelius Agrippa's paradoxical argument that reversed conventional wisdom by asserting that women were superior to men. It was composed in Franche-Comté (part of her lands) in 1509 and eventually published twenty years later in another part,

Antwerp. Like most Renaissance discussions of women's general capacities, the treatise pays minimal attention (two paragraphs) to the role of women in politics and uses only examples from antiquity, except for an unnamed Maid who was recently commemorated by a statue at Orléans. After praising the biblical Deborah, Agrippa simply noted that the infamous biblical queen Athaliah "was sovereign for seven years in Jerusalem," and his next sentence notes that Semiramis governed for forty years. Margaret rewarded him with an appointment as court historiographer, a position which required him to compose her funeral oration a year later.[5]

## A Female Warrior

After Margaret's death, Charles returned to the Low Countries to reorganize its government before entrusting it to his widowed sister Mary of Hungary. Her political talents had impressed observers in Hungary; before the fatal battle of Mohacs (1526) that cost her husband his kingdom and his life, a royal official had remarked, "I wish that . . . the queen would become the king; the fate of the homeland would then be better."[6] In 1527, one month after a rival candidate had been crowned as king of Hungary, Mary helped engineer her brother Ferdinand's election by arranging a rival election. Four years later, her other brother, Charles, named her to succeed her aunt and foster mother as regent of the Low Countries.

Europe's two earliest long-serving female regents, Margaret of Austria and Mary of Hungary, offer an interesting set of comparisons and contrasts. Both of them governed as childless widows, and each supervised a young niece who eventually occupied her position. On the other hand, it was already something of a commonplace in the sixteenth century that the first "governed the Low Countries with sweetness and the other with rigor." Charles V employed both women but seemed far more comfortable with his younger sister than with his aunt. Over time, the emperor increasingly asked Mary for advice about matters outside the Low Countries and let her govern there even when he was physically present. Erasmus, who knew both regents well, considered Mary of Hungary the greatest woman of her time, and his assessment is generally confirmed by high esteem from Venetian

diplomats. Anyone wishing to understand the achievements of women
rulers in Renaissance Europe must study the record of this early Low
Countries Iron Lady, as the Dutch feminist Monika Triest calls her.

Although the second major female regent of the Netherlands
served uninterruptedly across a longer period than her predecessor,
enjoyed even greater legal authority, and managed an even larger
block of territories after 1543, only recently has Mary of Hungary
begun to come into sharper focus, primarily through various international conferences about her, the proceedings of which have
appeared in the Netherlands (1993), Hungary (2006), Germany
(2007), and Belgium (2008). For various reasons, Mary has been
neglected both politically and architecturally. Margaret's state correspondence was published in the nineteenth century, while Mary's,
which is far more voluminous, began to appear in print only in
2009. Both of Margaret's principal buildings, her new palace at
Mechelen and her magnificent tomb in her Savoyard dowry lands
(now in France), have survived with minor changes. Mary, however,
had wretched luck. Both her new palace at Binche, the scene of
internationally famous festivities in 1549, and her elegant new
hunting lodge, Mariemont, were destroyed by the French within a
decade after she built them. Even her new village named
Mariembourg was overrun by the French in 1554 and renamed for
their king (after Mary's death the Habsburgs recovered it and
restored her name, which it still bears).[7]

Mary of Hungary kept herself well informed about contemporary
religious and intellectual issues, while getting much outdoor exercise.
During the period between her widowhood and her regency she
studied scripture intensively, including works by Martin Luther. Like
her grandmother Mary of Burgundy, she greatly enjoyed hunting with
falcons imported from Prussia; during her regency, Mary of Hungary
acquired no fewer than 191 of these. In order to hunt more effectively,
Mary not only rode like a man (*mannelijke jageres*) but even named
herself chief huntsman (*grand veneur*) of the Duchy of Brabant in 1544,
personally supervising 23 people and 76 dogs. Brantôme considered her
"a little mannish" (*un peu homasse*) and assures readers that "she made
war well, sometimes through her lieutenants, sometimes in person,

always on horseback, like an Amazon." Mary also took a close interest in military architecture: in 1546 she became Europe's first female ruler to create a fortified town designed by Italian military engineers.[8]

Less dazzling than her predecessor at cultural self-promotion, Mary of Hungary nonetheless compiled an impressive record as a patron of art, music, and literature. In the 1520s her court composer arranged a polyphonic setting for one of Luther's German Psalms. In 1529 Erasmus dedicated a treatise on Christian widowhood (*De Vidua Christiana*) to her; Mary's library held eight titles by him, including his complete works. Between 1532 and 1535 she paid for at least seven portraits of herself in a style resembling Margaret's official portrait, but not until 1548 did she sit for what became her favorite portrait, painted by Titian at Augsburg. However, the second major female regent of the Netherlands also commissioned a life-size bronze statue of herself from a famous Italian artist, Leone Leoni. Not completed until 1555, it is the only known contemporary sculpture of any female ruler of Renaissance Europe; this antique art form was normally reserved for heroes and warriors. To any viewer aware of Mary's extensive involvement in military affairs, her hood—a prerequisite for depicting sixteenth-century widows—suggests a warrior's helmet.[9]

Weighed down by the burdens of government, especially wrangles over financing her brother's interminable wars, Mary of Hungary finally resigned in 1555. She timed her departure to coincide with her brother's abdication and justified it with an eloquent memorandum. Charles was reluctant to see her go, and forty-five years later the Estates-General of the Habsburg Netherlands would nostalgically recall the "good old days" of her regency. In her farewell address Mary insisted that "the more experience I have, the more I realize that I am unable to accomplish my task properly. Whoever acts as regent for a ruler," she explained, "must have more understanding of affairs than the person who governs on his own account" because "a regent has to account not only to God but also to his sovereign and his sovereign's subjects." Mary boasted, "I have often done more than was fitting for my position and vocation as a woman, from eagerness to serve you . . . as well as possible." But no

woman, regardless of rank, ever received as much respect as a man.
Mary continued, "Even if I possessed all the aptitudes necessary to
govern well (and I am far from doing so), experience has taught me
that a woman is not suited to this purpose, neither in peacetime nor
even less in time of war." War was especially frustrating because she
lacked the authority to make decisions: "as a woman, I was
compelled to leave the conduct of the war to others." Thus she could
never claim credit when Habsburg armies performed well but
became a convenient scapegoat whenever things went badly.
Everyone in Renaissance Europe knew that war posed the ultimate
limitation on a woman's ability to command men, but only this
exceptionally tough, hard-working female regent ever bothered to
make the point so explicitly for posterity.[10]

Seeing a younger generation acquiring power in the Low
Countries, Mary protested, "I would not wish to rule over such
people, even if I were a man and sufficiently capable" and begged to
accompany Charles to Spain so that "I would be able to withdraw
from all affairs of government." He granted her wish. But even after
her retirement, Charles constantly leaned on his sister's advice,
including her opinions about governing Spain. This habit provoked
howls of protest from Spain's regent, Mary's young niece Juana.
"The character of the Queen of Hungary is such," she warned her
brother Philip II, "that she will not be content with offering advice
but will wish to command, and the authority given to me to govern
cannot suffer such a change. . . . I would rather retire and renounce
the Spanish regency."[11]

Three years after leaving office, Mary of Hungary received a
glowing funeral eulogy that reverses her necessarily pessimistic letter
of resignation. Delivered at Brussels in the presence of Philip II by
François Richardot (Cardinal Granvelle's vicar for his bishopric of
Arras), it was soon printed by Plantin.[12] "Divine favor," it began,
"was not given to men alone, but also to women. God has so
honored this sex that they have sometimes . . . surpassed the virtues
of men of their time . . . in the government of states [*estats publics*]."
Citing Deborah "and several others celebrated in both sacred and
profane scripture," Richardot admitted that such women were rare,

but some could be found in every age; and "the pearl and Phoenix of Ladies of this age" was undoubtedly the dowager queen of Hungary.

The middle part of the eulogy profiled a remarkable female ruler at work. "As for public affairs and government," Richardot began, "Mary gave very clear proof of a rare felicity of mind, facility of apprehension, and dexterity of advice, showing energy and vivacity in all things: in her speech, her opinions, and her judgment." As a newly appointed regent, she devoted incredible energy and diligence to understanding public affairs in the Low Countries: "In a short time, she learned and understood all the special features even better than those who had been managing such business. This was one of the most admirable things about her: that among so many different public matters, whether finance, appointments, wages, tributes, customs, legal or judicial privileges, offices, treaties, and infinite other matters, there were no points or articles which she did not know and recall, as if she understood the complete anatomy of the state [*République*]." Consequently, "no matter what the business at hand, there was no man in her Council who could better debate the pros and cons, nor come to a better-informed decision, through which she gained a reputation throughout Europe of having the most alert mind and the greatest understanding of statecraft of any person alive in her time. Thus," he continued, "this virtuous princess had often been the adviser of her advisers, and like an oracle for state business, seeing far in advance what was going to happen next." Moreover, "beyond the particular government of her country, she advised the Emperor by correspondence about numberless matters involving the friends and servants of the House of Austria, and even about any notable and important matters affecting all of Christendom." Richardot praised Mary's meticulous administration of justice, "giving the most and best remedies to all inconveniences and with the least possible burden to the poor people," despite "often very difficult times and very urgent perplexities." Like the biblical Deborah, "she fulfilled the role of Judge, Governor, and Captain." He praised even her conduct in military affairs, in which "she did everything possible which her sex permitted."[13]

This eloquent requiem for a female ruler was printed by the famous house of Plantin just as John Knox's scurrilous diatribe on the "Monstrous Regiment of Women" appeared in anonymous obscurity. Neither treatise was reprinted or translated.

## Young and Old Female Regents in Iberia

Between 1554 and 1562 two other Habsburg princesses governed Spain and Portugal, at this time the only European kingdoms with overseas empires, for five years apiece. They were closely related by marriage as well as by blood, being mother-in-law and daughter-in-law as well as aunt and niece. One was remarkably young, ruling on behalf of an absent father and then of an absent brother nine years older than herself; the other was remarkably old, ruling on behalf of a young grandson (the son of the other regent). When the younger woman retired in 1559, she was less than half as old as her aunt had been when she started her regency in 1557.

When the English marriage was forced on him in 1554, Philip II persuaded his father to appoint his newly widowed youngest sister, Juana, as his replacement in Spain, and he confirmed her next year after Charles's abdication. Juana was only eighteen in January 1554, when the Spanish ambassador to Portugal, who attended her three weeks later in childbirth, proposed returning her to Spain "in order to dedicate her to tasks of government." Her widowed aunt and great-aunt had begun their regencies in their midtwenties, but Juana's father had ruled the Low Countries at fourteen, and her brother had become regent of Spain at sixteen. Juana's character—"so energetic in her decisions that she even expressed regret at not being born male," noted a Venetian ambassador—seems remarkable even among Habsburg princesses. "Much testimony," says her biographer Antonio Villacorta Baños-Garcia, "confirms that she filled her responsibilities with rigor, resolution, and authority, including bursts of arrogance."[14] Spaniards know her as the founder of a famous Madrid convent, but Juana probably deserves to be remembered primarily as Europe's first and only female Jesuit.

Juana's powers resembled those of previous Spanish regencies; Philip ordered his sister to hear Mass in public, to maintain a regular schedule for hearing petitions, and to pay close attention to guarding Spain's borders. Unsolicited praise for her rule came early. In August 1554 a Jesuit told Loyola that she "proceeded with more care and wisdom in fulfilling governmental obligations than seems possible for a woman her age"; a month later the president of her council assured the emperor that "the Most Serene Princess undertakes business with such prudence and consideration that Your Majesty will never repent of having entrusted her with governing these kingdoms." Considerable legislation was passed, including a new censorship code. Juana's regency also experienced serious problems. After the loss of a fortress in North Africa in 1556, its commander was returned to Spain and beheaded in her capital on her orders. A state bankruptcy in 1557 created endless wrangling with her brother. In 1558 Protestant heretics were discovered in both the capital and the largest city, leading to a spectacular *auto de fe* over which she presided in 1559.[15]

Juana's spiritual adviser was Francis Borgia, a high-ranking nobleman and future saint who had secretly joined the Jesuits in 1546. Before she became regent, he mediated her request to be associated with a recently established order whose founder had asked the papacy in 1547 to "liberate the Company forever from having women under its obedience." The candidate Borgia proposed to Loyola under the code name Mateo Sanchez posed huge risks but offered equally huge advantages. On January 1, 1555, after consulting five senior colleagues, Loyola told Borgia that the rules had been bent in order to accommodate her request through a secret papal bull that enabled her to take three of the four Jesuit vows. Some of the exceptions and secrecy employed when Borgia himself had joined were repeated; "in no way," Loyola insisted, "is it suitable that she make a formal profession" because "it cannot go on record that such a person has been admitted." Two days later Loyola wrote to Juana, announcing that the request of an unnamed person (herself) had been approved, "although there was no small difficulty in this business." She repaid him by establishing the Jesuits in Aragon over stiff local opposition; but in 1556 she also ordered Loyola not to send Borgia to England and another Spanish Jesuit to Rome "because these two fathers cannot travel abroad without my express permission."[16]

Juana retired in 1559 when her brother returned from the Netherlands. Although Brantôme, who met Juana in retirement, believed she had left government so young "more from spite than from any great piety," she now refused to discuss either remarriage or political assignments. Juana's portraits—most notably, those depicting her relationship to dogs—changed remarkably between her regency and her retirement. In 1557 she sat for the first authoritarian portrait of a female ruler; Alonso Sánchez Coello copied a setting from one of Titian's most famous portraits of her father to depict this young secret Jesuit standing alongside a hunting dog. Five years later, after her retirement, Coello's studio again painted her, but this time Juana is seated and holding a lap-dog.[17] After 1559 Juana concentrated on one great project: constructing a Franciscan convent on the site of her birthplace. Her most important cultural legacy remains the convent she founded, the Descalzas Reales, which is still a tourist attraction in Madrid. Like her brother, who built his own apartments within his great palace at the Escorial, Juana lived in a part of the convent building. Like male Jesuits, she neither wore conventional monastic garments nor practiced reclusion. She died at the age of thirty-eight.

"Although for kings there are better realms than Portugal," her older sister remarked before Juana's marriage to Portugal's crown prince in 1553, "I believe that for Queens it is the best of all, because nowhere else do they enjoy so much authority in government or are so respected and obeyed." She was describing the situation of their aunt Catalina, the youngest daughter of Juana the Mad. Born after her father's death, Catalina had been raised at Tordesillas during her mother's forced confinement and had been married in 1525 to the king of Portugal.

Catalina's intelligence, energy, and attention to detail compensated for her husband's taciturn, procrastinating style, making her a perfect example of a royal woman exercising indirect rule. She became Portugal's only queen ever to be formally acknowledged as a member of its privy council. In 1539 a Spanish ambassador noted that she was "held in great esteem in the kingdom, and the king, knowing this, informs her about everything; there is nothing great or small that does not pass through her hands." In 1544 his successor noted that the privy council always met in the queen's apartment and that "nothing was done without Her Highness." A year later the papal nuncio claimed that she, not her husband, governed Portugal. In 1552 Antonis Mor eloquently depicted her political authority: the magnificently dressed queen is standing, and a folded piece of paper lies on a nearby table, a Renaissance code implying access to privileged information that was almost never applied to women. Mor's parallel portrait of her husband, João III, reveals lassitude in his horizontally held scepter.[18]

They had nine children. But the last of them, Juana's fifteen-year-old husband, died in early 1554, leaving as Portugal's heir a grandson born three weeks after his father's death and known as *el deseado* ("the desired one"). Eager to assume the Spanish regency, the widow abandoned her infant son. When João died in 1557 without leaving a will, Catalina simply continued her preeminence in Portugal's government, encountering little opposition in becoming regent for its three-year-old monarch. At fifty, she was Europe's oldest woman regent and the first grandmother to hold such responsibility since the tenth century.

As regent, Catalina operated much as she had before her husband's death, collaborating closely with a veteran royal secretary who did for her what William Cecil was then doing for Elizabeth in England. Portugal's great nobles were kept at arm's length; major positions which they normally filled remained vacant, while she granted privileges to Portugal's wealthy Jewish "New Christians." Catalina also patronized the Jesuits, who tutored the young king and opened Portugal's second university in 1558. Her five and a half years of regency saw both domestic and international problems. In 1559 five witches were executed at Lisbon, the only such occurrence in Portuguese history. The Casa de India declared bankruptcy in 1560, and Portugal's vital overseas empire faced military threats in 1562, when the sultan attacked their remaining stronghold in Morocco while the French attacked Brazil. Both were repulsed.[19]

Discontent with her rule coalesced around her husband's younger brother Henry, a cardinal and inquisitor-general. In December 1560 Catalina announced she wished to retire and organized a national referendum on the issue. About a hundred responses have been preserved, most of which praised her government. However, continuing pressure from the kingdom's highest-ranking nobles caused her to summon Portugal's Cortes in December 1562. After the opening ceremonies, she sent a letter of resignation, ordering the deputies to replace her with Cardinal Henry in ten days; she had signed it more than two months before without informing him. Afterward, she continued as guardian of Portugal's child-king, but the task became so frustrating that she threatened to move to Spain. Catalina also built a lavish tomb for her husband and joined him in 1578, shortly before their grandson's fatal crusade in north Africa plunged Portugal into political chaos.

Early in her regency Catalina patronized a remarkable book. Ruy Gonçalves, a law professor recently appointed to Portugal's appellate court, dedicated to her a 110-page treatise entitled *Privileges and Prerogatives possessed by the female sex through common law and royal ordinances, above the male sex.* "Most high and most powerful Queen, our lady," it begins, "Emilius Papinius (one of the best jurists of civil law) writes that women are in worse condition than men in many sentences and conclusions, and from this the doctors have accumulated many cases and doctrines to prove that men have more legal privileges and prerogatives than women; others choose . . . to write against the lives and customs of women, almost accusing Nature for producing females instead of males, as many texts of common law repeat." Admitting that "the consensus is that Papinius's view is truthful," he asserts that "nevertheless one can affirm, Most Powerful Lady, that for the most part men and women are treated equally in legal cases and decisions and that the male gender normally includes the female." Justifying his enterprise "because so many have written to the contrary," Gonçalves insisted that in some situations, especially those involving the guardianship of minor children, women have privileges equal or even superior to those enjoyed by men. Under a female regent, the Portuguese Inquisition approved publication of this upside-down version of Renaissance jurisprudence, a treatise as paradoxical as Agrippa's far better known *Declamatio*. More than two centuries later, during the reign of Portugal's first official female monarch, it was republished unchanged.[20]

## Catherine de Medici and Salic Law

France had known lengthy female regencies before 1560 and would experience two more in the next century, but none had a greater impact than Catherine de Medici. Among Europe's numerous mid-sixteenth-century female regents, she most closely resembles her Portuguese namesake, who was twelve years older and died eleven years sooner. Both had been foreign queens-consort and consequently always remained vulnerable to xenophobic attacks. Both produced large broods of children (ten and nine, respectively), yet neither could prevent her kingdom from falling into dynastic chaos immediately after her death. Both acquired supreme political authority in middle age by outmaneuvering their dead husband's nearest male relative. Finally, both held de facto control of royal government for a much longer period than their official regencies, although their influence declined sharply during their final years.

The French Catherine played her political role on a much larger stage, surrounding herself at the peak of her influence with anywhere between eighty and three hundred ladies-in-waiting in her famous Flying Squadron, all of whom were dressed like goddesses in silk and gold cloth. A flood of printed invectives, mainly from her later years and often linked to her role in the infamous massacre of St. Bartholomew in 1572, has ensured Catherine's posthumous reputation as a sinister Italian black widow (after 1559, she always wore black). Her numerous biographers have rarely explained how this particular French queen managed to acquire and maintain so much authority for so long over a kingdom where, as a Habsburg princess remarked in 1553, queens had less authority in government and enjoyed less respect than anywhere else in Europe. Many biographers explore her rich cultural legacy, but few have noted her patronage of works undermining the origins of France's Salic law, which opposed female inheritance of sovereignty.

After her husband's death in 1559, Catherine was never officially regent of France except for three months in 1574, but she soon took an increasingly decisive political role alongside her fifteen-year-old son, François II. By mid-1560 his acts began, "This being the good pleasure of the Queen, my lady mother, and I also approving of every opinion that she holds." At his death in December 1560, she staged a coup d'état, outmaneuvering the king-consort of Navarre, Antoine de Bourbon, who was also France's military commander, to gain de facto control of French government. The Estates-General proclaimed her "governess [*gouvernante*] of France" and president of the king's council, with authority to receive foreign ambassadors and official correspondence and to appoint officials on behalf of the new king, her ten-year-old son, Charles IX. An ornate official seal showed her full-length, crowned and holding a scepter, with the legend "by the grace of God queen of France and mother of the king." She continued to use this title, with its implication of divine-right status, long after the king had been declared legally adult.[21]

By 1561 Venetian diplomats noted that "she governed as if she were king." Catherine developed a cumbersome system of opening every official letter addressed to the king and composing two answers, one from her (the real response) and one from the king (the official response). She worked diligently: between 1561 and 1575, omitting the king's official replies, more than 3,250 letters of her state correspondence survive. Catherine, who hunted until she was sixty, despite suffering numerous falls and serious injuries, adopted Mary of Hungary's method of riding horses and complemented it with an early form of female underpants. Thus the queen-mother looked more imposing when accompanying her army in person, as she did at the siege of Rouen during the first religious war.

Evaluating Catherine's political record as France's de facto head of state remains difficult. In this era, religious conflicts coexisted with female rule throughout northern Europe, from Scotland to the Low Countries. In France, which had perhaps the most dynamic Protestant movement anywhere in western Europe, an insecure woman ruler sought various religious compromises in order to hold it together peacefully. Although she ultimately failed, Catherine's record also includes some considerable achievements. She opposed religious persecution and devoted the first half of her political ascendancy to creating workable compromises between rival religious factions at court. In 1561, Michel de l'Hôpital, who became chancellor even before her coup d'état, arranged a national summit conference on religion and crafted some remarkably evenhanded legislation. Although enforcement proved impossible, they persisted in this goal even after civil war interrupted their attempts in 1562.

Catherine's most original political tactic followed the official proclamation of her son's majority (*not* made at Paris, another innovation). She sought to increase loyalty and obedience through a gigantic visitation covering much of Europe's largest kingdom, taking along the court, including foreign ambassadors, and royal administration, including the chancellor. No contemporary European monarch ever attempted anything remotely similar: upwards of ten thousand people spent twenty-seven months journeying across France. Royal camping equipment included portable triumphal arches for entries into major cities and miniature carriages for the nine dwarves accompanying the queen-mother; most of the time on this interminable journey, it also had a traveling zoo of about three dozen animals, including bears and camels. Government became portable. L'Hôpital presided over the first royal *lit de justice* ever held outside Paris; in 1565, the only full year of the trip, his office produced the largest number of acts in its history while the Parlement of Paris reached its nadir. A new legal code that reinforced royal control over the judiciary was promulgated at a minor but centrally located town.[22]

Then things fell apart. Protestants attempted to capture the king in 1567, rebellion broke out again, and Catherine dismissed l'Hôpital. A longer and more bitter cycle of religious wars ended in 1570 with a more restricted version of the peace of 1563. Catherine last attempted a religious settlement for France by marrying her youngest daughter to the son of the Huguenot matriarch Jeanne III of Navarre. Although completely overshadowed by the bloodbath that followed, in which the groom was lucky to escape alive, the ceremony itself constituted Europe's first politically important mixed confessional marriage. By 1572 her influence over her second son, now married and the father of a daughter, had begun to diminish. After 1574, during her third son's reign, she rarely shaped royal policy. However, as late as 1582 she was still capable of claiming Portugal's throne against Philip II and used her personal funds to equip an ill-fated naval expedition under her Florentine cousin Filippo Strozzi.

If her political record in her adopted country was problematic, the cultural legacy of Catherine de Medici was more positive. She introduced France to such Italian refinements as ballet, forks, and handkerchiefs. In the 1560s her propagandists created Europe's most elaborate set of political tapestries, celebrating her as a modern Artemisia, the greatest widowed queen of antiquity.[23] Her architectural projects reveal the same flair, but here Catherine was unfortunate because her principal undertakings were either abandoned or demolished. A vast mausoleum for the Valois dynasty at the royal cemetery of St. Denis, begun in 1563, was interrupted in the 1570s and torn down in 1719. Nothing remains of Catherine's town house, built in 1572, except a pillar with 147 steps which stood in the center of her courtyard, Now called the Colonne de l'Horoscope, the first astral observatory in Paris held three people at a time. Her major architectural legacy was the Tuileries palace and garden complex, an extension of the Louvre begun in 1564. But after 1572 budgetary restrictions left it to be completed by her successors.

Catherine's de facto regency coaxed even Frenchmen into voicing occasional praise for female rule. In 1564 the famous court poet Pierre de Ronsard, rarely considered a protofeminist, exclaimed, "The female sex, hitherto removed from royal sceptres, is naturally very generous and worthy to command. . . . [T]he greater and better parts of Christendom would be very wrong to complain, seeing themselves presently governed by princesses whose natural intelligence, seasoned by long experience of good and bad fortune both in wars and domestic matters, have put a great many kings to shame." When Catherine de Medici negotiated a military alliance with Elizabeth I despite their religious differences, Ronsard again praised the "prudent gynocracy" of both kingdoms, remarking that "it is sometimes more profitable to a commonwealth [*République*] to be governed and commanded by a princess of benign and accommodating mind than by a lazy and idle king."[24]

Critical discussions of France's Salic law, undermining its historical authenticity without daring to suggest that it be abandoned, also peaked during her de facto regency among officials close to the queen-mother. The most influential assessment, printed in 1570 and reissued often in the next forty years, called it an invention but nevertheless found it "handsome, admirable, and profitable"; its manuscript predecessor had called it "a special law . . . founded on the greatness of the French, who cannot tolerate being dominated by women." Brantôme reported that Catherine went further in private, once remarking that if the Salic law were abolished and her daughter Marguerite allowed to inherit the kingdom "by her just rights, as other kingdoms also fall to the distaff," she would make an excellent monarch. "My daughter," she boasted, "is just as capable of governing, or more so, than many men and kings whom I know."[25]

In the 1570s Catherine de Medici inspired the most radical sixteenth-century discussions of female rule, both positive and negative. In one direction, French Huguenots, infuriated by her role in the St. Bartholomew's massacre, even tried to extend the Salic law by arguing that women were unfit to act as regents for underage kings. But at almost the same time (1573), another Protestant named David Chambers composed *Discourse on the legitimate succession of women to the possessions of their parents and on the government of princesses in empires and kingdoms.* This brief but extremely broad defense of female rule was written in French by a close associate of Mary of Scotland's ill-fated third husband, the Earl of Bothwell. Chambers, who had fled to France when Mary surrendered in 1567, dedicated it to Catherine de Medici, "a woman who has accomplished more than any previous governing princess for a long time past in Europe." It was not published at Paris until 1579.[26]

The preface claims that "this subject has never been treated before" because most writers on the subject had either overpraised women rulers or else utterly condemned them and they always relied on "the least probable testimony." Chambers tried to be both more comprehensive and more concise than previous defenders of female rule. In only sixty-eight pages, he examined female succession by the law of nature, the law of nations, "positive divine law" and "human positive law," offered a historical survey of women's hereditary succession to public governments, and connected the dots by considering female succession in public governments according to all four types of law—all before examining two current issues, the status of Mary Queen of Scots and France's Salic law.

Because in hereditary monarchies "the eldest daughter inherits from her father in the absence of sons" and because "no difference of sex is needed to follow [laws], but only prudence and reason," Chambers insists that "careful upbringing [*bonne nourriture*] of the daughter of a prince with no sons is of considerable value for advancing her to her father's government." While admitting that "in ordinary elections, one rarely finds women elected as commanders in chief in the Empire," Chambers claims that "histories testify that some have governed, and their rule was very well accepted by their subjects." In kingdoms and lesser hereditary governments, "it is a general rule that women succeed in the absence of males" and "their government in such cases is universally received at all times and approved by all nations," unless "some great consideration by a special positive law orders the contrary." To support the near-universality of female inheritance, he resurrects some relatively obscure European female monarchs. The German Protestant chronicler Johann Sleidan told him how "Charlotte, daughter and heir of King John of Cyprus, was prevented from succeeding her father by the trickery [*finesse*] of the Venetians." Chambers also sketched how France had acquired and lost the kingdom of Navarre through heiresses, unraveling the tangled history of a small kingdom with numerous female sovereigns. As a foreigner in France, Chambers prudently avoided mentioning Isabel of Castile and offered cautious praise for France's English ally, where "Elizabeth, presently reigning, is considered to have a good and quick mind with many good qualities and capable of good advice."[27]

After summarizing the refutation of Knox by John Leslie (cited here by his alias, Morgan Philips), Chambers concludes by discussing "how the government of Queens and Princesses is profitable to France." He began by noting French exceptionalism: "In all hereditary kingdoms presently known (at least in Europe), daughters succeed, except in France, because of a positive law, called 'Salic,' or some old custom." However, "one can easily conjecture that the aforementioned Salic law, or old custom of frustrating women of their possessions, was introduced by constraint." Summarizing his sources, who include *Christina de Pise, femme Italienne*, Chambers asserted that "no state has been governed by princesses more often than France, nor with greater profit to the public; and it seems a counterweight to foreclosing them from reigning officially over that kingdom."[28]

It is not difficult to understand why a foreign Protestant like Chambers sought Catherine de Medici's patronage, even after 1572. In her capacity as de facto regent and guardian of a kingdom allied to German Lutherans against their Catholic Habsburg rivals, she remained a conventional Catholic; but even after sharpened Protestant–Catholic differences had degenerated into religious warfare in the 1560s, she sometimes cooperated with two female Protestant monarchs, Elizabeth I of England and Jeanne III of Navarre, despite their confessional differences. In 1564, during her son's "great tour" across France, the queen-mother learned that her prominent and thoroughly heretical vassal Jeanne d'Albret had been summoned to Rome to appear before the papal Inquisition. Catherine exploded with indignation because popes had no authority over any sovereign. Grateful for her support, Jeanne III wrote that she would kiss Catherine's feet "more willingly than the Pope's"; she joined the royal tour for several months and did homage for her many French fiefs before returning to her sovereign state. In 1570 Catherine de Medici similarly refused to publish the papal bull excommunicating Elizabeth; twelve years later England's Protestant queen quietly repaid her by unofficially loaning several ships for Catherine's futile attempt to invade Portugal and claim its throne from Philip II.[29]

## Female Regents in the Low Countries, 1559–1633

Soon after hearing Richardot's funeral sermon for Mary of Hungary, Philip II of Spain left the Netherlands permanently. Having promised his sister Juana that he would never employ her again, he turned to his illegitimate half sister Margaret of Parma to govern this region;

like her two predecessors, she had been born there. Margaret was also Europe's only married female regent, but during her term of service her husband remained in Italy governing his duchy. Three portraits of her by the same painter, Antonis Mor, made before (1557), at (1559), and during her appointment (1562), offer a sequential progression in official gravitas appropriate to a ruler. Though not without some successes, her tenure in office proved to be much briefer and more conflictual than those of her female predecessors. Margaret was the only regent of the Low Countries to resign her office, and her government is generally seen in hindsight as the prelude to the long war for Dutch independence from Spain.

The regent herself believed that she had overcome a serious threat to her authority in late 1566 by raising an army in Germany that defeated local noble malcontents a few months later, and she celebrated by creating Europe's first heroic medal specifically honoring a female ruler. In the inscription accompanying her image on the front, her personal title as Duchess (by marriage) of Parma and Piacenza is abbreviated *D.P. et P.*, while her official rank as governor of Lower Germany (*Germaniae Inferioris Gub.*) takes far more space. The reverse features a beleaguered Amazon holding both a sword and an olive branch, protecting both church and state amidst storms and waves. The Italian adviser who designed it proudly sent copies to both Cardinal Farnese and the pope in Rome.[30] Even after Margaret had pacified the region, Philip II viewed her earlier compromises with local nobles as disastrous and sent the Duke of Alba with a large army and full authority to crush all opposition; the regent, humiliated and furious, resigned. The consequences after Alba replaced her were eighty years of military struggle and eventual Spanish failure; in retrospect, Margaret's triumphant medal of 1567 seems ironic and even modest alongside the large public monument to Alba made by the same artist a few years later (it was soon demolished).

After more than thirty years of rebellions in the Low Countries and after three years of study, Philip II decided on his deathbed to separate this war-torn region from his Iberian possessions, which now included Portugal. He would be succeeded in the Netherlands not by his son but by his oldest daughter, Isabel Clara Eugenia, who must marry her Austrian cousin, Archduke Albert, already the region's governor general. But these lands would not be separated permanently from Spain. If Isabel, already thirty-two years old, died without children, her younger brother (soon Philip III of Spain) or his heirs would succeed her; if she produced an heir of either sex, he or she must marry back into the Spanish ruling house; and if her brother died without an heir, Isabel must return to Spain to govern all of her father's possessions. Before marrying the new heiress, Albert assumed power in the southern Netherlands in Isabel's name. Because the former monarch had died, the governor general also had a new state seal made in 1598. It depicted Philip II's daughter enthroned, but with a half-empty coat of arms under its crown, because the man who designed it was not yet her co-sovereign. It was replaced after they married and reached their joint state.[31]

The political status of the archdukes lay in an intermediate zone between genuine sovereigns and viceroys or regents. Like sovereigns, they could coin money, manage civil government, and establish permanent embassies in a few major foreign courts (England, France, and Rome). But like regents, they could not operate independently: a large army of occupation remained on hand, paid and commanded from Spain, with its own treasury and legal system. Until 1609 only one Belgian appreciably influenced high policy on the Council of State, and even he was excluded from military issues; domestic policy eventually became more autonomous. In 1616, when it became obvious they would have no children, Isabel's younger brother made local notables take an oath to recognize him as the successor to either spouse. Under these restrictions, their high-value coins reflected a dubious sovereignty through the most varied numismatic depictions of joint rulers anywhere in Europe. Some poses were traditional; some gold coins showed husband and wife seated on parallel thrones, while others showed their heads facing each other, with a crown on the reverse; after 1618 a novel arrangement depicted them in profile, facing in the same direction with the husband foremost and over-shadowing his wife. When Albert died in 1621, a new Spanish king, Philip IV, canceled Isabel's sovereign status, but he also named her as the region's governor general (her husband's original position), and she remained in office until her death in 1633.[32]

The militant piety of these quasi-sovereign regents was exemplary even by Spanish standards. Isabel was very much Philip II's daughter and had spent much time at Madrid's new convent founded by her aunt Juana; her husband had once been a cardinal. They were the last joint rulers of Europe to donate a stained-glass window to a cathedral that showed them kneeling in prayer. Both Isabel and Albert were popular, but Isabel overshadowed her diffident husband. She hunted frequently with falcons and bows, and in 1615 she won a traditional crossbow-shooting contest in Brussels with her first shot. A four-hour parade celebrated Isabel's triumph, and the sponsors suspended the annual competitions so she could remain king of the popinjay (*roi du papegay*) until her death.[33]

Isabel governed this region either jointly or alone for thirty-four years, even longer than her great-aunt Mary of Hungary, with whom she was frequently compared. The last two meetings of the Estates-General of the Netherlands, neither with prior approval from Spain, were held at the beginning of their joint reign (1600) and near the end of her governorship (1632). The horse she rode at her formal entry into Brussels in 1599 is preserved in a local museum, alongside one that Albert used in battle. Militarily, Isabel did as well as her husband; the last great victory of Spain's Army of Flanders, the capture of Breda in 1625, occurred on her watch. A Flemish artist, Pieter Snayers, depicted the victorious general Ambrosio Spinola greeting his civilian superior outside the conquered city; Isabel is dressed as a nun, having taken vows as a Franciscan Tertiary after Albert's death. She thus became not only Europe's only female sovereign to win an archery contest but also its only female regent to govern in nun's clothing (the only male ruler in Europe ever depicted in clerical garb was the pope).[34]

## Baroque Pretensions

The other seventeenth-century female regents of Europe all fit the traditional pattern of royal widows serving as guardians for their young sons. They seldom exercised as much personal authority as their sixteenth-century predecessors, and they have seldom enjoyed as high a reputation. Bearing out David Chambers's assertion, it was female-exclusionist France that experienced the two most important seventeenth-century female regencies. The first, Marie de Medici, lacked the exceptional political skill and energy of her sixteenth-century Florentine relative, but she enjoyed higher official status and shared some of Catherine de Medici's durability in power. Marie de Medici's most recent biographer, Jean-François Dubost, has restored her political credibility, especially during the years 1610–17, when she exercised effective sovereignty.

Her political ambitions preceded her coronation one day before her husband's assassination in 1610. In 1609 an engraving depicted her seated under a regal canopy and equipped with a crown, a sword, and the scales of justice; it bore the inscription, "I am the one who makes kings reign, who knows how to use weapons and laws, maintaining peace and good government by correcting the malice of men." Marie de Medici threw tokens to the crowd attending her coronation, something no other French regent, male or female, ever did. During her regency she commissioned several self-congratulatory medals. One from 1612 shrinks her obligatory widow's veil to a small ornament while her son, the king, disappears completely. The front calls her *Regina Regens*, "Queen Regent"—she was the only woman to flaunt this title in France. The reverse used even more boastful language, claiming, "A female leader has done so much" (*Tanti Dux Femina Facti*).[35]

In 1617 Marie de Medici was abruptly thrust out of power after alienating her son by monopolizing too much authority for too long. But unlike previous or subsequent female regents, she managed a political comeback during her son's reign. Her ambition continued to draw criticism: in 1623 a French pamphleteer claimed she resembled Semiramis, "that proud queen . . . who massacred her husband and her son in order to govern over men." This criticism contained the proverbial grain of truth. The almost two dozen large canvases celebrating her alleged triumphs undoubtedly constitute the most spectacularly overblown pomp associated with a female European ruler. In 1622 she commissioned, from the most famous artist of the time, Peter Paul Rubens, a cycle depicting her "highly illustrious life and heroic deeds" for the main room of her new Parisian palace. Completed three years later, the series continues to draw visitors to the special room at the Louvre which holds nearly all of it.[36]

Rubens's work demonstrates the limitations of gender stereotypes when heroic baroque portraiture had to glorify a woman ruler. His celebration of a military triumph of the regent's armies in 1610 foregrounds a mounted woman in a warrior's helmet but with one breast bared and riding demurely sidesaddle. A far more militaristic theme dominates his later portrait of her that accompanies her "triumph" cycle (see fig. 8). When shown the entire cycle, her son Louis XIII apparently remained unaware of his relative unimportance in it. However, Cardinal Richelieu was appalled, and not long afterward he abandoned her patronage. In 1630 Marie de Medici lost all political influence for the second time after failing to remove Richelieu, a disgrace that precipitated her permanent exile. Rubens was never paid in full for Marie's triumphs, and a planned second cycle was canceled. In 1639, a year after Richelieu wrote that "nothing can ruin a state like an evil mind hiding behind the weakness of their sex," one of his Catholic followers again proposed, as the Huguenots had in 1573, to exclude mothers from French regencies.[37]

Baroque portrayals of female regents can carry extremely misleading messages. The contrast between nearly simultaneous portrayals of two widowed female rulers by the same famous artist is instructive. At Paris, Rubens's final painting for the original "Apotheosis" cycle (not in the Louvre) portrayed the former French regent Marie de Medici as a triumphant female figure replete with military symbols: she not only wears Minerva's helmet but also holds a royal sceptre, while two cherubs overhead hold a laurel wreath and, at her feet, a pile of military equipment is visible. But at Brussels during the same year, Rubens also did a well-known realistic portrait of his main patroness, the Spanish infanta and governor general of the Netherlands, Isabel Clara Eugenia. It shows Marie's militarily more successful female counterpart as a smiling Franciscan Tertiary.[38]

Marie de Medici's commissioning of Rubens to portray her triumphs culminated a century of high-profile female regents.

Subsequently, Europe's female regents avoided ostentation. In the 1670s that incurable royal misogynist Christina of Sweden remarked that her mother, explicitly excluded by her father from having any role in a regency, "was no less capable of governing than anyone we have seen of the other maternal queens and princesses in this century; in truth, they were all as incapable as she of governing."[39] As in her other sweeping condemnations of female rulers, Christina remained blind to such inconvenient recent counterexamples as Louis XIV's mother, Anne of Austria, who served well for a long time under difficult circumstances while maintaining a modest political and cultural profile.

In Europe, female regents had a complex relationship to female sovereigns, who occupy the center of this account. For all their early associations with innovative political enhancements (beginning with the invention of chess queens around 1000), no female regent in Latin Europe was ever accused of trying to usurp sovereign status, although one tried to do so in Russia in 1686, and another probably planned to do so in 1741. Instead, in Latin Europe, it was possible for a female sovereign to move in the reverse direction and end as a regent. Isabel Clara Eugenia was the first, but not the only, example; after abdicating as Sweden's monarch in 1720, Ulrika Eleonora would briefly serve twice as its regent. By contrast, several male sovereigns (for example, Philip II of Spain), had been regents before becoming kings, but none ever served as a regent *after* being a sovereign.

The most important achievement of the long-serving female regents of early modern Europe was to serve as cultural pioneers for its female sovereigns during their gradual transition away from Navarrese-style royal heiresses to women ruling by themselves. These eight women, all of whom governed without husbands, sponsored various cultural promotions of female rule at a time when female monarchs began emancipating themselves from the political authority of their husbands (see chapter 5). However, there is no evidence that such novel affirmations of female political authority spread easily or quickly from regents to sovereigns. For example, Elizabeth I, who reigned over an important kingdom with great success for forty-five years, would have been the major beneficiary in the late sixteenth century. Although her courtiers took the art of painting a female ruler in triumphant poses far beyond her regent predecessors (one made in 1593 showed her kingdom under her feet), Elizabeth's literary defenders seem relatively timid: British treatises defending her sovereign rights against Knox were less vigorous than one printed abroad under the patronage of a female regent. There is no contemporary life-sized statue of Elizabeth, as there is for Mary of Hungary; and the English monarch did not commission a heroic medal of herself, despite having much better reasons than Margaret of Parma to do so.

The manner of riding horses—Europe's most prestigious form of transportation for a thousand years—illustrates that even incomplete mimesis of regent predecessors could take a long time, though never so long as the five centuries that separate the invention of the chess queen modeled on female regents from the more powerful versions modeled on a female sovereign, Isabel of Castile. In the mid-seventeenth century Christina of Sweden still rode sidesaddle, even in Sébastien Bourdon's portrayal of her on a rearing horse. Not until far into the eighteenth century did any female sovereign ride in public in the manly fashion practiced by the sixteenth-century regent Mary of Hungary. In the 1740s both Maria Theresa of Austria and Tsarina Elisabeth of Russia were portrayed riding fully astride, but despite remarking that they wanted to take the field in person against their enemies, neither woman, unlike Mary of Hungary and Catherine de Medici, ever accompanied her armies on campaign.

*Figure 1.* The first documented major female ruler: Hatshepsut (c. 1435 B.C.). This reconstructed statue in the Metropolitan Museum, New York, depicts her enthroned, with a female body but garbed as a male king. Most of its lower fragments were excavated in 1929 near her funerary temple, while her torso (discovered in 1845) was acquired from Berlin. Digital photo at Wikimedia Commons by Postdlf, licensed under the Creative Commons Attribution–Share Alike 3.0 license.

*Figure 2.* Cleopatra and son (c. 30 B.C.). In this relief from an Egyptian temple at Dendera, Caesarion precedes his mother Cleopatra VII, although her name precedes his in the accompanying inscription; the tiny figure between them is Caesarion's *ka*, or guardian spirit. Wikimedia Commons.

*Figure 3.* Spouses on medieval Georgian coin, 1200. Tamar's monogram, a theta, is above a delta for her husband, Davit. Image licensed under the Creative Commons Attribution–Share Alike 2.5 license by the Classical Numismatic Group, Inc., www.cngcoins.com.

*Figure 4.* Neapolitan coin of Spain's Catholic kings, 1503. The inscription on their two-headed silver *carlino*, now hard to read because of clipping, begins on his side ("Ferdinand and Isabel, by the grace of God") and concludes on hers ("monarchs of Spain and of both Sicilies"). Since 1282 there had been two separate kings of Sicily, one based in Naples. Courtesy of American Numismatic Society.

*Figure 5.* A female figurehead, 1528. Aragon's proprietary sovereign, Juana la loca, faces her son, Emperor Charles V, who monopolized state power throughout Spain and kept his mother imprisoned. Nevertheless, she outranked him; its obverse legend proclaims "by God's grace King [*Rex*] Juana and Charles, her firstborn son." Image at Wikimedia Commons licensed under the Creative Commons Attribution–Share Alike 3.0 license.

*Figure 6.* Floating-crown coin of married heiress, 1557. After Mary Tudor married Spain's crown prince in 1554, English coinage developed this new motif to depict the elusive location of sovereignty under joint rulers. Image licensed under the Creative Commons Attribution–Share Alike 2.5 license by the Classical Numismatic Group, Inc., www.cngcoins.com.

*Figure 7.* Elizabethan pictorial icon, 1592. England's aging monarch remains eternally youthful in this often-reproduced portrait, named for the location where she appears to stand. Wikimedia Commons.

*Figure 8.* Female regent as goddess of war, 1622. To conclude her apotheosis cycle, Peter Paul Rubens portrayed Marie de Medici as Bellona and surrounded her with weapons. Wikimedia Commons.

*Figure 9.* Christina of Sweden triumphant. Starting in 1647, her high-value coins replaced her crown with a classical motif used previously by some male sovereigns. Courtesy of American Numismatic Society.

*Figure 10.* Cavalier riding sidesaddle, 1653. Sebastian Bourdon's quasi-heroic portrait of Queen Christina of Sweden, intended as a gift to the king of Spain, depicts her on a rearing horse, accompanied by her falcon-carrying groom. Wikimedia Commons.

*Figure 11.* Sarcastic German medal of 1710 celebrating recent French defeats. On the reverse, a slogan in French about adapting to feminine tastes captions a scene with a woman wearing a crown (Queen Anne of England) playing a harp while an old king (Louis XIV) tries to dance on crutches. Courtesy of American Numismatic Society.

*Figure 12.* Statue of Tsarina Anna, 1741. The first life-sized modern vertical representation of a female ruler made shortly after her death (now in the Russian Museum of St. Petersburg) portrays a bellicose monarch in an uncharacteristically feminine pose. Photo by Rosellen Monter.

*Figure 13.* Maria Theresa as matriarch, 1764. The Habsburg heiress, not her husband, is the focus of this family portrait displaying the numerous children of the "first and general mother of the nation." Wikimedia Commons.

*Figure 14.* Europe's greatest female usurper, 1765. Catherine II hung Virgilius Erikson's almost life-sized canvas of her dressed as a Guards officer at her coup d'état of 1762 in Peterhof Palace; it is still there. Photo by Rosellen Monter.

*Figure 15.* Europe's last divine-right joint monarchs, 1779. On this gold coin from Brazil, the profile of Maria I of Portugal overshadows those of her husband and uncle Pedro III (compare fig. 3). Courtesy of American Numismatic Society.

*Figure 16.* Catherine II in her park, 1792. The earliest known portrait of an informally dressed female sovereign: an old lady walks her greyhound in the gardens of her Summer Palace, casually indicating a monument to her past military triumphs (compare fig. 7). Wikimedia Commons.

*Figure 17.* Margaret Thatcher inspects troops in Bermuda, 1990. Wearing traditional feminine headgear, Europe's first democratically elected example in a long tradition of militarily successful female rulers performs her role as commander in chief. White House Photo Office.

# 5

# Husbands Finessed
## The Era of Elizabeth I, 1550–1700

The reigns of women are commonly obscured by marriage . . .
whereas those that continue unmarried have their glory entire and
proper to themselves.
—Sir Francis Bacon, *Works*

In the second half of the five centuries 1300–1800, when
kingdoms were fewer in number but larger, the husbands of Europe's
royal heiresses generally enjoyed much less political power than previously. Like their predecessors, the first three royal heiresses after
1550—Mary Tudor, who acquired England in 1553; Jeanne III d'Albret,
who acquired Navarre in 1555; and Mary Stuart of Scotland, who
became a monarch as a baby and a legal adult through her marriage in
1558—already had or soon acquired husbands. The first married
soon after her coronation, not from personal inclination, she said, but
from desire to produce an heir; the second was already married and
had a son; and the third, soon widowed without children, later remarried during her personal rule. But instead of reigning as conventionally deferential Navarrese-style wives, all three placed significant
curbs on their husband's authority between Mary Tudor's marriage in
1554 and the disintegration of Mary Stuart's second marriage twelve
years later. In 1562 the Navarrese pattern even broke down in Navarre
itself.

Europe's next two royal heiresses, Elizabeth I of England and Christina of Sweden, avoided this spousal problem by remaining unmarried, as would the next unmarried woman who acquired a throne, Empress Elisabeth of Russia in 1741. Between 1550 and 1700, a total of six women, two of whom inherited as children, occupied monarchical thrones in Europe. During an age often described as strongly patriarchal, four of them would govern jointly with their husbands for at least part of their reigns. However, during almost ninety years of rule as adults, these six female monarchs actually had husbands barely 20 percent of the time (nineteen of eighty-eight years). Even excluding the exceptionally long and pivotal reign of Elizabeth I, which accounts for half of the total between 1550 and 1700, other female monarchs ruled jointly with husbands less than half the time, and all these men were foreign princes who usually operated under important restrictions.

Numismatics once again provides exceptionally illuminating examples of the uncertain governmental relationship between female sovereigns and their husbands in early modern Europe. In 1553, two of them, in England and Scotland, appeared alone on their kingdom's coinage before their marriages. Between 1554 and 1558, married female monarchs in three kingdoms, England, Navarre, and Scotland, had their effigies on high-value coins facing their husbands (all of whom were in the primary position on the left), with his name preceding hers on the inscriptions (see fig. 6). All three kingdoms used the same design to express the uncertain location of sovereignty under such circumstances: a single crown floats above the heads of both spouses without touching either. Written evidence suggests that this visual message is not misleading; these were joint reigns in which royal husbands continued to participate in exercising sovereign authority, as they had done previously. But they were no longer clearly the dominant partners; by 1566 Scotland's coinage reflected the political eclipse of the monarch's spouse by naming the wife first. As has been noted, the next royal heiresses finessed any political and numismatic problems with husbands by remaining unmarried.

However, seventeenth-century numismatic evidence also suggests two reversions to medieval female figureheads. One woman, the Spanish archduchess Isabel Clara Eugenia in the Habsburg Netherlands (r. 1598–1621), was devoutly Catholic, while the other, Mary II of England (r. 1689–94), was devoutly Protestant; both had childless marriages to first cousins. Both women appear on high-value coins in a new design that underlined their subordinate political positions: their profiles are partly concealed behind those of their dominant husbands. However, neither woman was a legitimate heiress, so their status as sovereigns was extremely fragile. The first woman held only a provisional sovereignty, granted by her dying father, Philip II, on condition that she marry the man he designated, and when they had no children, these lands reverted to the Spanish crown. The second woman became England's junior co-monarch after her Dutch husband had successfully usurped its throne from her father. Despite its progressive features, the so-called Glorious Revolution of 1688 also marked Europe's final regression to the medieval pattern of joint rule when a husband could rule alone after outliving his wife. When her brother-in-law died in 1702, Mary II's younger sister (also married to a foreign Protestant prince) selected Elizabeth I as her political role model.

## An Unmarried Adult Heiress

Many historians have pointed out that in 1553 the greatest political problem in Tudor England was not whether a woman would inherit its throne, but which woman. Its outgoing male regent attempted to arrange the coronation of his young daughter-in-law, Lady Jane Grey. Although usually known as the Nine Days' Queen, a doomed Protestant heroine, Jane Grey also deserves to be remembered as Europe's last failed teenage female royal claimant, seventy-five years after Isabel the Catholic overthrew her unfortunate niece. A well-educated Renaissance princess, Lady Jane challenged traditional assumptions by announcing that she might make her young husband, for whom she had scant respect, a duke, but not a king. In the event, Henry VIII's older daughter, Mary Tudor, managed to push aside this young rival with remarkable swiftness; no one died fighting, and at first only three of Jane Grey's principal supporters were beheaded. As Anne Whitelock has pointed out, "It was the only successful revolt against central government in sixteenth-century England." Mary's Council promptly issued a beautiful gold sovereign depicting their new monarch enthroned.[1]

Once the English succession had been settled, Europe's third-largest kingdom faced an unprecedented problem. Its monarch was already older than a dozen previous royal heiresses in other parts of Christendom; but unlike all of them—or for that matter Jane Grey—she had never been married. Although Mary Tudor's famous father had six marriages himself, he was never able to arrange one for either of his daughters, even after restoring both of them as possible successors. As Charles Beem has pointed out, nobody, including the monarch herself, really knew how to behave when an unmarried adult heiress acquired England's throne, and the peculiar rituals of Mary Tudor's coronation reflected this confusion. Much ritual was completely traditional, including being girt with a sword and having spurs touched to her. But also appropriated were elements from the so-called auxiliary coronations of English queens: Mary was presented with two scepters, the traditional one for kings and one with doves for their wives. Other aspects were entirely feminized. Mary was carried in a litter (men rode horses), dressed in white cloth of gold (men wore purple velvet) and with her hair unbound, like a girl being married (Mary would insist afterward that she had married her kingdom). Like her father and brother, she acquired the title of Defender of the Faith (*Defendrix Fidei*) at her coronation. A recent peculiarity of the English Reformation also made her, like her father and brother, Supreme Head of the Church in England. Mary quickly dropped this title while using the accompanying authority to remove Protestant ceremonies.[2]

When she soon decided to marry a foreign prince, a remark-ably one-sided prenuptial agreement was rapidly cobbled together in England and the Low Countries. Like those of earlier heiresses to major kingdoms (Joanna I of Naples and Isabel of Castile), it placed strict limitations on her future husband's powers. The bride already governed a major kingdom in her own right; her groom, Philip of Spain, eleven years younger but already a widower with a son, possessed a minor kingdom (Sicily) and was poised to inherit

Europe's most powerful kingdom. Such circumstances help explain the unusual precautions for preserving England's autonomy written into the prenuptial arrangement. This document—which Parliament promptly incorporated into statutory English law, preceded by a special act specifying that Mary enjoyed exactly the same royal prerogatives as her male predecessors—constitutes a watershed in the history of marriages of royal heiresses.

The official English copy began with a sentence appropriate for first marriages of every previous royal heiress throughout Europe: "So long as the matrimony endures, Prince Philip shall enjoy jointly with the queen her style and kingly name and shall aid her in the administration." Its final clauses also seem traditional: "Whoever succeeds shall leave to every dominion their privileges and customs to be administered by their natives. The dominions of the Emperor, the prince and his successors, and the queen shall aid one another," according to a treaty signed at Utrecht in 1546. However, its central passages disadvantaged Philip in multiple ways: "The prince shall leave to the Queen the disposition of all officers, lands, and revenues of their dominions; they shall be disposed to those born there. All matters shall be treated in English," a language of which Mary's relatively well-educated husband knew not one word. At the same time, "the queen shall be admitted to the society of the dominions the prince has or shall come to him during their matrimony." Its financial clauses were even more disadvantageous to her husband. "For her dowry if she outlives the prince," she was to receive one hundred thousand pounds per year, 40 percent of it from the lands "which Margaret [of York], widow of Charles, Duke of Burgundy, received"; but if he outlived her, he received nothing.

Most disadvantageous of all to the groom were the burdens it placed on his six-year-old male heir. To prevent controversy over the succession, "in England males and females of the marriage shall succeed according to law and custom." Neither Philip nor his son could expect to inherit England; the boy was guaranteed his possessions in Spain and Italy but accompanied "with the burden of the said dowry." However, "if there is any male child by this marriage," Philip's son and his heirs "shall be excluded from the Lower Germanies and

Burgundy"; and even "if only females are born of the marriage, the eldest shall succeed in Lower Germany" as well as in England (one must remember that at this moment, Lower Germany had been governed by women for forty years, and that its current female regent, Mary of Hungary, was the brains behind the Habsburg negotiators in Brussels).³ Philip, who constantly signed himself "your obedient son" to his father, secretly repudiated this prenuptial contract, which offered him neither political nor economic advantages, before agreeing to marry a woman whom he generally described as his "dear old aunt" (she was really his first cousin once removed).

Both their wedding ceremony and Philip's official entry into London displayed a bewildering confusion of male and female prerogatives. At the wedding, both bride and groom wore white, and Philip entered the church on the side traditionally reserved for brides. Even their new great seal of state featured a peculiar design that eloquently depicted the elusive location of sovereignty after the marriage of a royal heiress. Both spouses are on horseback, looking at each other; Philip is foregrounded with a raised sword, but Mary, riding sidesaddle and holding a scepter, precedes him in the primary position on the left. Neither wears England's crown, which appears alone in the upper right atop their joint coat of arms. At the same time, new high-value English coins were made in the names of both spouses, using an equally novel and politically similar design: a single crown above two heads (this time with Philip on the left) but once again touching neither. Otherwise, standard protocol for European joint reigns was observed, with all official documents issued in the names of Philip and Mary. One should not forget that Philip's authority would have increased dramatically if the marriage had fulfilled its primary purpose, the birth of a child: Parliament granted Mary's husband guardianship of a daughter to the age of fifteen and of a son to the age of eighteen, and his wife's will of early 1558, when she again believed herself to be pregnant, named him regent.⁴

But Mary remained childless, never offered her husband a formal coronation, and left his political role in England undefined. Although no consensus yet exists about Philip's actual share in the major events of Mary I's short yet eventful reign, some outlines emerge. His greatest practical disadvantage was undoubtedly his complete unwillingness to learn the language of his wife and her kingdom; but England's Privy Council, more than half of whose members received Spanish pensions, prepared Latin summaries for his perusal and, sometimes, his annotations. Both he and his wife signed its official Latin proclamations, he first and in larger letters. Most correspondence between Philip and his *conjunx noster charissima*, who wrote to him in French, was burned at her death; only two letters survive. Their great joint business was the restoration of papal authority, and here they seem to have collaborated as seamlessly as her grandparents Ferdinand and Isabel, who were also his great-grandparents. Philip's diplomatic service compensated for the absence of English representation at Rome; a Spanish source gushed that it was "a miracle by the hand of God that a people and kingdom so ignorant and dissolute could be persuaded to obedience and union with the Church without the least shedding of blood."[5]

Actually, much blood was shed soon after the reunion with Rome—but by England's government, not by the rebels. The most notorious aspect of Bloody Mary's reign, its relentless persecution of English Protestants, followed the same rhythm whether her Spanish husband was in England or abroad. Almost three hundred heretics were burned in just over four years, ranking among the very worst persecutions anywhere in Reformation Europe. In foreign policy, Philip, on his final trip to England, managed to evade one provision of their prenuptial agreement by exploiting a French provocation in 1557 to drag England into the last phase of the Habsburg–Valois struggle. Judith Richards has pointed out that, unlike any other major document of her reign after her marriage, Mary officially acted alone in declaring war—and she did so against a French king who seemed as clueless as his Ottoman allies about diplomatic protocol involving female monarchs. Henri II explained to his assembled ambassadors, "As the herald [declaring war] came in the name of a woman, it was unnecessary for [me] to listen to anything further."[6] The resulting war proved beneficial to Philip, who commanded many English soldiers at the time of his great victory of St. Quentin, but it was disastrous for the English, who lost their last foothold in France,

Calais, to a surprise French attack. When peace came in 1559, Mary was dead, Philip remarried a charming young French princess with a proper royal dowry, and the French retained Calais.

Mary Tudor's official funeral sermon in England noted that she was "a queen, and by the same title a king also." At Brussels, the capital of her "reverse dowry," a local prelate delivered a more eloquent commemoration in the presence of Philip's regent. It celebrated exactly what English Catholics admired in her: "courage in difficult matters, . . . and in every phase of life, integrity, truthfulness, and charity." Mary Tudor exhibited "great and heroic virtues," her eulogist affirmed; "the victory that this Princess achieved in surmounting so many adversities without a single false step, gave her the prize among women famed for the masculine virtue of power." The culmination, unsurprisingly, was Mary's piety: "After carefully considering her deeds, she needed a truly victorious faith in order to put down the lions who raged against her at the outset of her reign and . . . wished to take over her kingdom." Only after "dominating so many tumults and pacifying so many seditions" could she "destroy the fortress of the infidels and restore the honor of God and the Church in her kingdom, and rebuild Christian doctrine and discipline." This achievement evoked favorable comparisons to five male heroes of the Old Testament. Her eulogist, still unaware of her successor Elizabeth's religious policy, concluded that a great place awaited this other Queen Mary in heaven.[7]

But not on earth. Instead of being remembered as the next woman to rule a major European kingdom after her grandmother Isabel of Castile, Mary Tudor's posthumous fame in the history of female rule lies primarily in having inspired John Knox's diatribe against all female rulers. Visitors to Westminster Abbey seldom notice her tomb because it lies directly beneath the magnificently ornate funeral monument to her half sister and successor, Elizabeth. In some ways, this arrangement is appropriate because Elizabeth, during a reign nine times as long as Mary's, destroyed her great work of papal restoration and replaced it with a version of national church which still exists. It is also appropriate because Elizabeth's royal authority rested on some solid foundations laid by her half sister.

## Husbands' Authority Overturned in Smaller Monarchies, 1562–67

During Mary Tudor's reign in England, two other women became legal sovereigns of two small kingdoms: Jeanne d'Albret (r. 1555–72) in Navarre and Mary Stuart (r. 1558–67) in Scotland. Mary had become the first Queen of Scots as a week-old baby. By far the youngest royal heiress in European history, she had several illegitimate half brothers, the oldest of whom would play a major role in her reign. In 1553 Scotland imitated England by putting an image of its young female sovereign on a gold coin, although she would not become a legal adult until her marriage five years later to the crown prince of France. In 1555 a married woman with a three-year-old son inherited the northernmost remnants of the kingdom of Navarre, united with the larger sovereign principality of Béarn. Jeanne III (the only female monarch of Europe as yet to reach that modest numeral) became Navarre's fourth woman sovereign since 1328.

At first, both small kingdoms followed the now-traditional Navarrese solution to female inheritance, that is, marrying their heiresses to powerful princes who were expected to govern in her name. Both husbands were French princes of royal blood. After becoming the fiancée of the four-year-old French dauphin in 1548, Mary spent a decade at the French court preparing to become queen of France. In the late 1550s the constitutional situation of both small kingdoms is neatly captured on their silver coins, which imitate those of Philip and Mary in England by using a single crown floating above two heads, and with the husband's name first on the inscriptions. However, during the following decade, against a background of acute confessional conflicts which then dominated politics throughout western Europe, both female sovereigns would sharply curtail the political authority of their husbands. In Navarre, religious divisions shattered cooperation between royal spouses; in Scotland, they opposed the sovereign to her political nation, with her husband caught in between.

The joint coronation of Jeanne III of Navarre and her husband, Antoine de Bourbon, in 1555 essentially repeated the ceremonies for her distant predecessor Jeanne II and her husband in 1329. Despite stubborn resistance from local authorities, both heiresses insisted on including their husband as a fully equal participant. In 1555 the Estates of Béarn met a few weeks after the former king's funeral. Jeanne's husband, first prince of the blood in France, met a flat refusal when he demanded to be recognized as king, being "the lord of his wife and of all her property." A local chronicler reported that the heiress, "in order to please her husband," repeated his demand, reiterating that he was "lord of [her] person and [her] properties." The Estates replied that she was "their true and natural Lady" (*naturelle Dame*) and that there was a great difference between marital and royal preeminence. Under local law, her husband was king only accidentally (*par accident*) and merely the steward of her goods. After five days of debate, the Estates, exactly like their predecessors at Pamplona 226 years earlier, accepted joint rule. He, not she, took the oath in local dialect to uphold their privileges, whereupon the Estates took an oath of homage to both rulers. Their coinage copied England's floating-crown motif for joint sovereigns, identifying them as "Kings of Navarre and Lords of Béarn."[8]

Over the next few years Jeanne III's husband schemed incessantly to recover Spanish Navarre, engaging in treasonous negotiations with the Spanish king while serving with French armies who were fighting him. The marriage, originally very solid, began crumbling largely because of Jeanne's growing attraction to Reformed Protestantism. At Christmas 1560, while her husband was being outmaneuvered by Catherine de Medici in his bid to become regent of France, his wife converted publicly to the Reformed church; Elizabeth I of England and John Calvin immediately congratulated her. When France stumbled into religious war in 1562, Jeanne III separated from her husband and fled to her hereditary lands. As she noted later, when he tried to repress Protestantism in Béarn without informing her, "I used the natural power which God had given me over my subjects, which I had ceded to my husband, for the obedience which God commands; but when I saw that it was a question of my God's glory and the purity of His worship," she proceeded to arrest her husband's secretary and cancel his orders. She also revoked her permission for her husband to negotiate with Philip II to exchange Navarre for the island kingdom of Sardinia, which she had "given through force and fear, not having dared refuse a husband."[9]

Fortunately for her, Jeanne III's husband was killed a month later fighting Protestant rebels in northern France. His thirty-four-year-old widow wrote a sad poem, held a solemn funeral for him at her capital, and systematically removed every Catholic official whom he had appointed. "Since the government is entirely in your hands," Calvin told her, "be aware that God wishes to test your zeal and solicitude." She tried her best over the next decade, earning a well-deserved reputation as France's Huguenot matriarch and defiantly striking a medal in 1571 with a Spanish slogan "Until Death."[10] Jeanne III died in 1572, after arranging her son's marriage to a sister of the French king but before the notorious massacre of St. Bartholomew that followed it. She was able to establish the Reformed church in Béarn but not in the little Basque-speaking corner of the old kingdom of Navarre.

Scotland was the only kingdom in Europe ever governed for a female sovereign by a female regent; and during the 1550s the dowager queen, Mary of Guise, probably exercised greater political authority as its regent than her daughter would a decade later as its monarch. In 1548 Scotland's Auld Alliance with France degenerated into a French protectorate under a male regent (who received a French duchy), and its child heiress moved to France. When her mother returned in 1554, the French ambassador placed Scotland's crown on her head and handed her the scepter and sword of state, "to the great satisfaction of all the Estates." Four years later Mary of Guise had successfully arranged her daughter's marriage and Scotland's eventual incorporation into France. But soon after her daughter unexpectedly became queen of France in mid-1559, Scotland's Protestant nobles rose in revolt. English military aid helped overthrow her regency before Mary of Guise died in June 1560. When her widowed daughter reluctantly returned to Scotland a year later, she confronted the daunting task of ruling the turbulent nobility of a now-heretical kingdom without French soldiers.[11]

The personal reign of Mary Stuart as Queen of Scots (1561–67) has inspired sharply discordant opinions. Was she primarily a besieged Catholic expatriate trying to rule a newly Protestant kingdom, as her leading biographer, Antonia Fraser, sees her or simply a striking example of female political ineptitude, as her most important critic, Jenny Wormald, sees her? These conflicting interpretations are not necessarily mutually exclusive, because her record mingles political achievements with avoidable failures. If Mary Stuart became Europe's only crowned female monarch with the dubious distinction of being beheaded, she also became its only female sovereign to produce a legitimate heir through a marriage made during her personal government. The most useful approach is probably to view her as an illustration of the problems that marriage posed for a young royal heiress. Mary Stuart would marry three times before the age of twenty-six, and her marital politics closely resemble the last three marriages of the great fourteenth-century heiress Joanna I of Naples. Mary's first wedding virtually erased her political authority in her own kingdom, but each subsequent husband became increasingly dependent: the last one even removed his hat in her presence.[12]

Mary's coins shed much light on her political history before, during, and after her personal reign. Numismatists divide her reign into early years (1542–58), French marriage (1558–60), widowhood (1560–65), second marriage (1565–67), and second widowhood (1567); her brief third marriage had no coins. The National Museum of Scotland possesses more than two thousand coins from her reign, which, significantly, include several hundred counterfeits; they constitute a better treasure trove than we possess for any of her female contemporaries.[13] Almost three hundred of these coins are gold or silver (crowns are gold and *ryals*, or royals, are silver). Broken down numismatically, coins with the ruler's portrait reveal the pattern that appears in table 5.1.

Her effigies, which begin when she is eleven, appear on 30 percent of her gold coins (17 of 56) and only 9 percent of her silver coins (22 of 238). But only two out of almost forty are joint portraits, one with each husband. The gold Francis-and-Mary coin

## Table 5.1. Coinage of Mary Queen of Scots, 1543–67

| Period (years) | Gold coins (portraits) | Silver coins (portraits) |
|---|---|---|
| Girlhood (1543–58) | 55 (16) | 110 (3) |
| First Marriage (1558–60) | 1 (1) | 59 (0) |
| Widowhood (1561–65) | none | 18 (18) |
| Second Marriage (1565–66) | none | 46 (1) |
| Widowhood (1567) | none | 13 (0) |

Source: N. M. McQ. Holmes, *Scottish Coins in the National Museums of Scotland*, Edinburgh: Part I, 1526–1603 (Sylloge of Coins of the British Isles, #58: Oxford University Press, 2006); reprinted from Monter, "Numismatics and Female Sovereignty," *Journal of interdisciplinary History* 41 (spring 2011), 550.

may have been made (or at least designed) in France rather than Scotland; a single gold crown made during her first widowhood exists in London but not in Scotland. The silver ryals ('royals') from her second marriage are especially instructive. The only one with a portrait shows face-to-face busts of Mary and her younger husband, Henry Lord Darnley, in customary order, but with no crown visible; its inscription follows custom by putting his name first. But these coins were rapidly replaced in 1566 by new varieties without effigies and on which, for the first time in European history, the wife's name precedes her husband's, a detail that perfectly captures Darnley's diminished status.[14]

Marriage negotiations between Scotland and France in 1558 reversed the Anglo–Habsburg negotiations of five years earlier. Europe's largest kingdom, which inherited from women but forbade them from ruling, attempted to swallow a smaller one through marriage to its heiress. The dowager regent persuaded the Scottish Parliament to award Mary's husband the so-called crown matrimonial, giving him precedence in signing joint documents and full authority to sign acts by himself. Designs on the couple's coins privileged the French fleur-de-lys of a "dauphin-king" over the Scottish heraldry of a "queen-dauphine." The Scots negotiators, led by the bride's oldest half brother, insisted that French privileges disappeared if the heiress predeceased her husband, and they refused to send Scotland's crown to France for his coronation. Three weeks before her marriage, their heiress signed secret agreements with her father-in-law, nullifying any agreements she might subsequently make with her subjects.

During the eighteen months after May 1559 when Mary Stuart was queen of France, the dowager regent died, and the young royal couple lost all control over Scotland. Protestant nobles seized the state apparatus, and by the time Mary returned as an eighteen-year-old widow they had established the Reformed church in her kingdom. While a religiously divided Europe accepted the slogan *cuius regio, eius religio* everywhere else, from Tudor England to tiny Béarn, Scotland's sovereign was barely able to maintain her right to practice her religion privately. When she finally had to summon a parliament in 1563, her political skills proved better than expected.[15] In 1565 she decided to marry Henry Lord Darnley, a man four years younger then herself with uncertain religious preferences and genealogical links to both Scottish and English royalty; she hoped thereby to reinforce her claim to the English succession, relieve herself of some of the burdens of government, and produce a legitimate heir. She achieved only the last.

Darnley's constitutional position in Scotland was peculiar. Although he never possessed the crown matrimonial that her first husband had enjoyed, Mary proclaimed him king of Scotland immediately before their marriage and declared shortly afterward that all royal acts would carry both signatures (his signature was sometimes larger, but every surviving state document signed by both has her name in the place of honor on the left). The immediate aftermath of Mary's second marriage marked the peak of her political authority. Her oldest half brother and chief mentor rebelled, hoping to overthrow her with English help. In an Amazonian display, the queen, with a helmet on her head, a pistol in her belt, and her new husband at her side in gilded armor, chased him from her kingdom. Even her nemesis Knox, expressing admiration for her manlike courage, prudently retreated from her capital. During this personal and political honeymoon, she became pregnant even before the papal dispensation arrived. But Mary's relations with her young husband soon soured, primarily because she refused him the crown matrimonial. When he retaliated by refusing to sign joint documents, Mary used a dry seal of his signature. By December the English ambassador noted that Darnley was now called simply her majesty's husband, and his name now followed hers on proclamations and coin inscriptions.

During her pregnancy, her husband participated in the murder of David Rizzio, her trusted private secretary, in her presence. Mary recovered quickly from the shock, regaining her husband's loyalty and persuading him to betray his associates. She took the initiative in pursuing them, outlawing sixty traitors but condemning very few to death. After giving birth to a son, however, Mary could not divorce Darnley, who did not attend his son's baptism, without impugning the legitimacy of her heir. A solution was found: Darnley was murdered in February 1567 while presumably in his wife's care. It was the first such occurrence in over two centuries, and the last for almost two more. Each time, the female ruler was convicted of complicity in the court of public opinion, although never with formal proof.

The combined effects of her husband's murder, following that of Rizzio, her first childbirth, and the disintegration of a marriage that she had made herself provoked what even Mary Stuart's admirers admit amounted to temporary paralysis. She stopped writing and dictating letters; even worse, she suffered a complete breakdown in judgment. Not only did she ignore vehement advice from both Elizabeth I and Catherine de Medici to pursue the culprits remorselessly but she compounded this unforgivable negligence with the politically fatal act of marrying the head of her privy council, a man widely considered the mastermind behind Darnley's murder. The explanation is simple: he had raped her (a unique instance in European history), and she feared, correctly, that she was pregnant. By the time she miscarried, it was too late: she had been taken captive by rebellious Scottish nobles and forced to abdicate in favor of her infant son. Mary Stuart would escape from this captivity and live another twenty years, but her reign in Scotland had ended when she was only twenty-five.

## Europe's First Never-Married Heiress

In 1567 militant Calvinism undermined female rule throughout northern Europe, as Catholic women lost control of both Scotland

and the Low Countries and Catherine de Medici suffered serious political damage from religious warfare in France. At the same time, Elizabeth of England, who was the first Protestant female sovereign in Europe as well as the first to remain unmarried, adroitly navigated her ship of state past some major political problems that would include a Catholic rebellion in 1569 and papal excommunication a year later. Surviving numerous assassination attempts, she would remain on her kingdom's throne for forty-five years, the longest reign of any female monarch anywhere in Europe before the nineteenth century.

A superabundance of valuable English-language studies on England's Protestant Virgin Queen, together with the sheer length of her reign, renders any attempt at detailed reconstruction of her achievements superfluous. At the same time, her reign has rarely been set in the general context of European history. Insularity domi-nates much that has been written about her, both before and since Katharine Anthony commented more than eighty years ago that Elizabeth I "was in a sense too provincial and ignorant of the rest of the world, in spite of her linguistic attainments and the depth of her learning." Her first foreign biography had twenty editions in five languages before 1800, but it has yet to appear in English because its original subtitle called her a political comedienne. In the present-day European Union, where English has become a lingua franca, Elizabeth I rarely attracts non-Anglophone biographers.[16]

With the obvious exception of Mary Queen of Scots, her unwanted guest for nineteen years, Elizabeth I is almost never studied in the context of Europe's other female rulers. But her reign began amidst an unparalleled regiment of women, to which Knox objected so violently. When Elizabeth claimed England's throne in 1558, western Europe had two other female monarchs and three female regents, and two additional female regents appeared before 1561. These women were all older than she (except, once again, Mary Queen of Scots) and gradually faded away. Seen in the context of her female peers, therefore, the reign of Elizabeth divides into two phases. During her first fifteen years, Europe usually had three or occasionally four other female rulers. After Mary Stuart's abdication in 1567 and Jeanne III's death in 1572, Elizabeth became the lone reigning female monarch; after Catherine de Medici's eclipse in the mid-1570s, she was Europe's only female ruler until 1598, when Philip II of Spain made his oldest daughter co-sovereign of the Netherlands.

Elizabeth's distinctive personal style was already evident at her coronation, which both imitated and improved upon her half sister's recent version. "According to the ancient precedents," which in fact dated back only five years, Elizabeth made her triumphal procession in a litter rather than on horseback and married her kingdom during the ceremony. However, this time the ceremony and accompanying festivities enjoyed vastly improved publicity: an official account was printed within ten days. The extent to which Elizabeth appropriated her sister's Act of Supremacy of 1554 became apparent even before her coronation, when she told her assembled lords, "I am but one body naturally considered, though by [God's] permission a body politic to govern." It was her first formulation of the peculiar common-law doctrine of the king's two bodies, formally coined by crown lawyers in 1562 but largely forgotten by the end of her reign. It is unclear whether she saw her political body as gendered; Carol Levin has noted that Elizabeth often referred to herself as a prince and occasionally as a king. At the same time, her physical (if not her mystical) body remained female. Her second official state seal of 1584, more dynamic than its predecessor, portrayed England's monarch on horseback—but mounted sidesaddle.[17]

Throughout Elizabeth's reign, one important feature separates her from all of her female contemporaries and indeed from all of her female predecessors: she never married. Responding to her first parliament's request that she marry, Elizabeth referred to her coronation as a marriage to her kingdom, symbolized by the ring that she never removed. A few years later, a Scots diplomat, James Melville, described her motives more bluntly. "By taking a husband," he told her, "you would be merely a queen, but while remaining celibate you are both queen and king together, and you have too great a heart to imagine giving yourself a master." About this time she reportedly told a German ambassador who had come with his prince's marriage proposal that "I would rather be a beggar and single than a queen and married." Deflecting repeated public demands that she produce an heir during her potential childbearing years, Elizabeth maintained her decision to avoid marriage either to a foreigner, as her sister had done, or to one of her own subjects, as her famous father had done. As Melville said, her decisive consideration for avoiding marriage was the extent to which any husband, regardless of the limitations placed on him, would erode her personal authority. As early as 1561 she informed a Swedish diplomat, "I have the heart of a man, not a woman," and two years later she told her second parliament, "As I think [marriage] best for a private woman, so do I strive with myself to think it not meet for a prince."[18] Nevertheless, Elizabeth could not admit in public that she would never have children so she spun the issue of her possible marriage out for a quarter century, until she finally became too old to play the game convincingly. It is enlightening to compare Elizabeth's behavior with that of two male contemporaries, Sebastian of Portugal (r. 1567–78) and Emperor Rudolf II (r. 1576–1608), neither of whom ever undertook serious marriage negotiations during lengthy reigns. While today Elizabeth is considered a prodigious political success, despite ending her dynasty without naming a successor even on her deathbed, these two perennial bachelors have been generally considered, both then and now, as mentally unbalanced political failures: Sebastian led Portugal into disaster, while Rudolf's relatives finally forced him to retire.

As a female monarch ruling alone, Elizabeth possessed some advantages which she used to maximum effect. Several Renaissance princesses received good educations, including a mastery of Latin, but Elizabeth stands out as the one best prepared to rule. Her training was not only formal—when she took the throne, she claimed to know six foreign tongues better than English—but also practical because she had to survive several extremely difficult personal situations during the decade before her coronation. This combination equipped her superbly for the task of governing, for which she immediately acquired enormous enthusiasm. As she became entrenched in her position, Elizabeth attempted to fashion positive propaganda from her anomalous situation as a celibate Protestant woman ruler, even though Protestant theology avoided praising virginity. She cultivated a highly original political style which was simultaneously erudite to the point of affectation, nationalistic to the point of chauvinism, and parsimonious to the point of miserly. When Elizabeth traveled on progresses, she reversed the traditions of princely largesse; her hosts gave *her* presents. On the Protestant side, it played extremely well among foreign as well as domestic audiences for a very long time. As early as 1565 the sister of Sweden's king traveled to England in order to see this modern Queen of Sheba.[19] More surprisingly in an age of acute confessional conflict, Elizabeth later drew praise from several of her male Catholic peers for her skill at governing.

In her forty-five years as monarch, Elizabeth built nothing. Her greatest legacy to her kingdom was not physical but institutional: in a highly confessionalized age, she put her personal and extremely durable stamp on England's national Protestant church, restoring the basic worship services of her father and brother with several touches of her own. For her epitaph Elizabeth reportedly desired only "a line or two, which shall briefly express my name, my virginity, the years of my reign, the reformation of religion under it, and my preservation of peace."[20] Although her famous remark about not wanting to "put windows into men's souls" applies equally well to some of her female peers in Scotland and France, neither of them was "Supreme Governor" of an established national church to which everyone, in theory, owed obedience.

Elizabeth's piety was intensely personal. She infuriated Protestant zealots by keeping a small crucifix in her private chapel. Because she combined a superb classical Renaissance education with a genuine talent for foreign languages, Elizabeth preferred to express her religious beliefs in highly erudite ways. During her reign she composed some three dozen original prayers, few of them in English. The most revealing expressions of her peculiarly royal religious views come from two collections of these prayers, both printed privately early in her reign. The first, made in 1563, included seven Latin prayers accompanied by her commonplace book and lists of her major officials. Its prayer of thanksgiving included an element of self-congratulation which might have made even Louis XIV blush.

After listing the physical and intellectual deformities of many prominent people, some of royal blood, Elizabeth proclaimed, "I am
unimpaired in body, with a good form, a healthy and substantial
wit, prudence even beyond other women, and beyond this, distinguished and superior in the knowledge and use of literature and
languages, which is highly esteemed because unusual in my sex."[21]

A second collection, printed six years later, depicted her on its
frontispiece kneeling before an altar containing a prayer book with a
crown above it. Inside, Elizabeth flaunted her erudition with seventeen prayers in five foreign languages, including three each in
Spanish and Greek. This time her thanksgiving prayer (in French) is
modest. Ironically, her final Spanish prayer, taken from Psalm 37,
asked God to "give me strength so that I, like another Deborah, like
another Judith, like another Esther, may free thy people from the
hands of thy enemies," before concluding by unwittingly repeating
the motto of the Spanish Inquisition, "Lord, rise up and judge thy
cause." Around 1580, during serious matrimonial negotiations with a
French prince, Elizabeth made still another tiny and very private
collection of prayers in her own hand: two in English, separated by
one each in French, Italian, Latin, and Greek.[22]

Elizabeth's superb Renaissance education also enabled her to
act as her own foreign secretary, all the more necessary because no
foreign ambassadors at her court understood English. For the first
half of her reign, moreover, much of English foreign policy revolved
around Elizabeth's matrimonial negotiations, which she conducted
in foreign languages with unfailing flair and verve. Nevertheless,
some of her most impressive performances came late in her reign. In
1597, not long after telling the scholars of Oxford that she could
recall using her Latin perhaps thirty times in thirty-six years on the
throne, she burst into an impromptu tirade in Latin after an impertinent speech by a young Polish ambassador. Barely a month before
her death, she gave her last great diplomatic performance in greeting
the first Venetian ambassador to her court. After apologizing for her
rusty Italian, Elizabeth then used it to harangue his republican
employers for taking forty-four years to recognize her officially and
for their reluctance to treat female princes the same as males.[23]

The best-read female sovereign of Renaissance Europe even knew something about her medieval female predecessors. Defending her detention of Mary Queen of Scots to a French embassy in 1572, Elizabeth reminded them that "the Spaniards imprisoned Queen Urraca after stealing her kingdom"; she also cited two twelfth-century examples to prove that it was "no novelty to put children in charge of their mother's kingdoms after depriving them of its administration." Elizabeth then lectured the French that their own history was "full of examples of queens being imprisoned; it suffices to recall that three consecutive kings [the sons of Philip the Fair] imprisoned their wives" and warned them against such misplaced chivalry as their "unfortunate expeditions on behalf of the famous Joan of Naples."[24]

On becoming England's monarch, Elizabeth had prayed God to give her the grace to govern with clemency and without bloodshed. Although her reign was far less bloody than her father's or her sister's, after 1570 it produced about a thousand executions for sedition. It also included three major treason trials, which approximately trisected her reign: England's only duke was beheaded in 1572, Mary Stuart fifteen years later, and the Earl of Essex in 1601. Elizabeth long hesitated to sign the first two death warrants, especially the second, which she feared would damage her international reputation; as Catherine de Medici remarked, "It was never heard of that one Queen put another to death." In this case, a Protestant sovereign hid behind the confessional blood lust of her parliament, whose notables took the unprecedented supplementary precaution of signing a bond associating themselves with the execution.[25] Meanwhile, her victim tried to fashion herself into a Catholic martyr by disinheriting her son unless he abandoned Protestantism. In different ways, both women inflicted collateral damage on hereditary divine right royalty.

Even Mary Stuart's execution and celebrations of Elizabeth as a quasi-Christlike figure by Protestant extremists could not erase the respect many Catholic rulers expressed for Elizabeth's skill. "Were she only a Catholic, she would be our dearly beloved," exclaimed the outstanding late sixteenth-century pope Sixtus V in 1588, "just look at how well she governs!" When his comments reached her, Elizabeth mischievously suggested that perhaps they should get married. In 1594 a surprised English visitor to Florence noticed a portrait of her in the grand duke's palace and was told that he esteemed her for her many virtues. In France her subsequent execution of Essex earned praise from another Catholic ruler, King Henri IV, who commented, in standard male-gendered language, "Only she is a king; only she knows how to rule." Perhaps the ultimate compliment came from Philip II's daughter; in 1600, Isabel Clara Eugenia jested half seriously to her brother's favorite, the Duke of Lerma, that "the lady [Elizabeth] says she wants to consider me as her daughter; just imagine how much profit I would get from such a mother!"[26]

After an almost dowdy beginning, painted images of Elizabeth enhanced her increasing reputation. Early in her reign she showed surprising insensitivity about artistic propaganda, dismissing her sister's very capable court painter and naming no successor. The few portraits of her first dozen years, all by unknown artists, show Elizabeth in sober black and rarely contain any royal symbols. In the 1560s two politically savvy female regents, Margaret of Parma and Catherine de Medici, commented unfavorably about Elizabeth's negligence of this aspect of her public persona. But as her reign progressed, so did the number, scale, and especially the regal symbols on Elizabeth's portraits. In 1579, notes Roy Strong, "when it became virtually certain that Elizabeth would never marry, . . . the first elaborately allegorical portrait of the Queen was painted." By the final decade of Elizabeth's reign, her portraits had lost any pretense of realism. "Sometime about 1594," notes Strong, "a government decision was taken that the official image of the Queen was to be a legendary beauty, ageless and unfading." Color reproductions of such ageless "bejeweled icons" decorate the covers of an apparently inexhaustible series of Elizabethan biographies. Perhaps her single best-known image, the so-called Ditchley portrait of 1593, shows a young woman with her kingdom literally at her feet (see fig. 7). Near the end of her long reign, in her most triumphant image (*Eliza Triumphans*, 1601), a hidden wheeled conveyance transports a superbly dressed monarch under a canopy, supported on every side by well-dressed gentlemen and looking rather like a portable life-size relic. Smaller images were ostentatiously worn by English Protestant courtiers in much the same way that a nobleman at a Catholic court might wear an image of the Virgin Mary.[27]

However magnificently their heroine was dressed, Elizabethan representational strategies never infringed major gender taboos. No contemporary statues of her exist, nor did she sponsor any literature promoting female rule. Her few commemorative medals stress her kingdom's safety and security. In the mid-1580s the symbol of Noah's ark with the motto "safety through the waves" was copied from the Netherlands. Elizabeth's last medal, designed by her court painter after the defeat of the Armada, portrays a prosperous island honoring its prudent monarch but avoids allusions to a naval battle. It was England's Dutch allies who created mocking medals with sunken Spanish ships; one reportedly boasted an inscription from Virgil's *Aeneid*, "Done by a female leader."[28]

In 1597 a French ambassador remarked that Elizabeth's government "is fairly pleasing to the people, who love her, but it is little pleasing to the great men and the nobles," and he predicted that after her death "it is certain that the English would never again submit to the rule of a woman."[29] This was wishful thinking from a female-exclusionist kingdom. In fact, it took ninety-nine years before another female monarch ruled England; and despite having a husband, she tried to pattern herself on Elizabeth.

## Europe's Best-Prepared Heiress

In the century after Elizabeth I died in 1603, the number of autonomous hereditary kingdoms in Europe shrank to its minimum, and only one produced a genuine royal heiress. At the same time, no female king anywhere in Europe was ever more carefully groomed for her position than Christina of Sweden. Before departing to lead the Protestant cause in the Thirty Years' War, her famous father, Gustav Adolf, had left detailed instructions for raising his only child. After his death in 1632, his six-year-old daughter received a remarkably thorough and rigorous training, supervised by Sweden's five principal ministers of state, who introduced her to the business of government earlier than several male crown princes. Christina attended state councils before the age of thirteen and presided over them by the time she was eighteen, the same age as Europe's youngest female regent, Juana of Castile. As a monarch, Christina was fortunate. Most historians agree that Sweden attained the summit of its international prestige during the decade of her personal rule, which coincided with large territorial gains from the triumphant end of the long war in the Holy Roman Empire and with the arrival of internationally renowned scholars as well as many artistic treasures looted from central Europe.

Her posthumous reputation, however, is another matter entirely. Because of her abrupt abdication and repudiation of Sweden's national Lutheran church, Christina has never been especially popular in her native country, although no female monarch since Cleopatra VII has attracted so much scholarly interest outside her homeland. In 1966 the first major conference devoted to her, sponsored by the Council of Europe, presented her as "a personality of European civilization." During the past two centuries more than a dozen biographies of her have been published in German, English, and Swedish, followed closely by others in Italian and French. Some notable recent attempts still reveal a sense of bafflement about her significance, viewing her as "the restless life of a European eccentric," "the enigmatic Queen," and even "an exceptional king."[30]

In the history of female rule, Christina's reign has two peculiar distinctions. She was the only female monarch in Europe—and by far the youngest of either sex—to abdicate voluntarily after governing successfully for at least ten years. She also became the only dogmatically misogynist female monarch. These aspects converged when she first raised the possibility of abdication in 1651. Her councilors objected that "there is no like example on record anywhere in the world," and she herself could subsequently name only four men who had done so.[31] When persuading Sweden's diet (Riksdag) to make her designated successor a hereditary ruler, Christina also asked them to exclude his female descendants. Two reigns and a lengthy female regency later, Sweden reversed this policy, but

Christina continued to oppose any form of female rule in her private writings.

Her primary reason for abdicating seems clear in retrospect, even if Sweden's great chancellor Axel Oxenstierna admitted to the Riksdag in 1654 that "the Council of the Realm . . . does not know the reason for what has occurred." Her major biographers agree that it was Christina's desire to convert to Catholicism, which she had been studying secretly for over a year and would profess openly soon after leaving Sweden. Being the only child of Sweden's greatest Protestant hero and the head of a national Lutheran church in an age when confessional uniformity was normal in European monarchies, her decision to turn Catholic necessarily made her position politically untenable. She also offered other reasons. Christina argued to her councilors that a male ruler would give the kingdom "a champion who, when war threatened, could ride with his people to battle, while a woman could not." After they answered that "in Your Majesty's times we have fought enough wars . . . and God has granted us the greatest conceivable success," Christina dropped this pretext.[32] But the daughter of Gustav Adolf remained an enthusiastic admirer of military grandeur, which to her was not authentic unless a ruler commanded his army in person. She compiled extensive notes about Alexander the Great and despised her famous contemporary Louis XIV as a pseudowarrior.

From her early years Christina remained emphatically opposed to the idea of marriage. Sweden's Council had agreed in 1647 that, like England's sixteenth-century female rulers, she would retain full royal rights (*iura majestatis*) even if she married. Two years later she told them, "I declare quite definitely that it is impossible for me to marry." Europe's second unmarried female monarch differed from Elizabeth I in two important respects. First, Christina despised the diplomatic and courtly games of flirtation at which her English predecessor excelled. One can believe Christina's later comment that "there was no man in all of Sweden so bold as to talk about [marriage] to the Queen." Second, Elizabeth never named a successor, but Christina settled this problem long before her abdication. In 1649 she selected a German cousin whom she was widely expected to marry and then bullied the Riksdag into giving him hereditary rights. Christina later commissioned a medal that called her chosen successor, Charles X Gustavus, "King by the Grace of God and Christina" (*A Deo et Christinae Gratia Rex*) and commented, "This could be said with complete reason and truth."[33]

Throughout her life Christina felt profoundly royal but profoundly uncomfortable in her ascribed gender. At her coronation in 1650, the Swedish Royal Archives assert, Christina was proclaimed king (*konungh*), even specifying "not as Queen" (*nuu är drotningh*), and in the official royal genealogy she herself apparently crossed out the word *Regina* and substituted *Rex*. During her reign Christina adopted some typical masculine forms of heroic self-presentation. At first the girl monarch was shown on coins with her crown lying on a table. However, at the age of twenty-one, with her kingdom's armies victorious in the Thirty Years' War, she became Europe's first female monarch depicted on her coins wearing a triumphal laurel wreath instead of a crown (see fig. 9). She had more medals than Elizabeth, several of them with overtly militaristic associations. By 1648 they depicted Christina as Pallas, wearing a helmet crowned with laurel; she also became Minerva.[34]

The question of her sexual orientation and behavior pose problems for any biographer, despite (or because of) her own comments on the subject. When the Jesuits negotiating her conversion coded her male (as Signor Teofilo Tancredo), they simply copied their strategy of a century earlier with another strong-willed woman ruler, Juana of Castile. But Christina's male mimicry surpassed that of Europe's other female kings. A Jesuit concluded that "there is nothing feminine about her except her sex . . . her ways are all quite masculine." She was the first female ruler to commission a large-size portrait of herself on a rearing horse—although in it, as in real life, Christina rode sidesaddle (see fig. 10). The Spanish ambassador's chaplain noted, "Though she rides side-saddle, she holds herself so well and is so light in her movements that, unless one were quite close to her, one would take her for a man." Once released from the constraints of court life, Christina began her incognito wanderings under a male pseudonym and usually preferred to dress as a man. "From now on," notes Veronica Buckley, "she would be reluctant to wear women's clothes or a woman's hairstyle. She would appear in public wearing men's shoes, often boots, and frequently a sword; princes and popes would greet her with her legs showing and her feathered hat in her hand. Her speech would grow coarser . . . even her voice would deepen."[35]

Christina's royal and self-consciously masculine ego remained unaffected by her abdication. Despite her numerous disappointments and rapidly diminishing revenues, her sense of entitlement remained undiminished. She always insisted on receiving the full privileges of a reigning monarch, and her slogan "The Queen neither says nor does anything casually" testifies to how seriously she took herself. Nevertheless, Christina came to regret her early abdication and soon attempted to claim other crowns. In 1656 she sought French support for taking the kingdom of Naples. Four years later she hurried back to Stockholm when her chosen successor died, leaving a five-year-old son; much to Christina's annoyance, his widow became regent. In 1668 Christina became the Vatican's candidate for the throne of Poland after her Vasa cousin had imitated her by abdicating. This was the only occasion in the Europe before 1800 on which a woman actively sought elected office; but despite an extensive letter-writing campaign, Christina fared no better than other papal candidates for this position.[36]

In retirement Christina developed an ambitious but typically unfinished plan to commemorate the major events of her life and reign through a "metallic history" like that of Louis XIV: hers contained no fewer than 120 medals. The third depicted her famous father holding a child in his arms, with the legend, "She was worthy of her father's throne." In no. 28, the figure of Sweden kneels before its enthroned twelve-year-old monarch, "Sweden's Glory and Hope," offering her a scepter, crown, and sword. Nine consecutive medals (nos. 38–46) celebrated her military victories. A series on her abdication (nos. 71–74) ended with one inscribed, "All is vanity." The motto fits the entire project, since only eight reverse sides were ever engraved and only three complete medals were ever struck.[37]

Christina also used her leisure to rework no fewer than eighteen surviving drafts of her collection of lapidary maxims and a parallel series of slightly longer reflections. At her death in 1689 the maxims, finally entitled *The Fruit of Leisure*, numbered 1,139, and the *Sentiments*, 444. Consistent with her sense of self-importance, Christina also became the first monarch in Europe to compose an autobiography, which she dedicated, like St. Augustine, to God. Like several of her other major projects, it remained unfinished; the extant chapters barely cover the first ten years of her life. It concludes with a diatribe against women rulers that outdoes even Knox. "My feeling is that women should never govern," she began; "and if I were married, I would have doubtless removed any right of succession from my daughters, because I would love my kingdom more than my children. I should be believed about this all the more because I speak against my own interest." Three sentences later she remarked, "Everything I have seen about women who ruled or pretended to rule, both in histories and in the world, makes them seem ridiculous in one way or another. And," she added, "I do not exempt myself." Christina added, "The Salic law, which excludes women from the throne, is very just; women should never reign, and if there are examples, which I doubt, who did marvelous deeds on the throne, one should not count on this; these examples are so rare that no conclusions can be drawn from them."[38]

Despite her contempt for her female contemporaries, Christina admired some very early female predecessors. "With all their faults," she wrote, "Semiramis, Cleopatra, and many others deserve our esteem and admiration." Her ninety classically trained male pane-gyrists essentially agreed with Christina's assessment. Only one of their 112 Latin panegyrics situated Christina primarily among other well-educated women, but many compared her to other female rulers. Several of these were ancient, primarily Semiramis (10), the Queen of Sheba (9), and a classical warrior-queen, Zenobia (7); more recent female rulers such as Isabel of Castile (4), Christina's Scandinavian predecessor Margaret of Denmark (3), and Mary Tudor (2) suggested fewer parallels. However, comparing her to another relatively recent, equally scholarly and similarly unmarried female monarch seemed so obvious that it easily outnumbered those to any other woman ruler, ancient or modern; no fewer than 13 panegyrics compared Christina to Elizabeth I of England. As a child Christina had read William Camden's account of Elizabeth's reign; but throughout her later rants against the natural incapacity of women rulers, she constantly ignored this recent and illustrious predecessor. The comparison surely made her envious.[39]

Subsequent writers also noted the similarities between Europe's two best-known recent female monarchs. In 1718 the pairing of Christina with Elizabeth reappeared in David Fassmann's fourth *Dialogue of the Dead* (*Gesprach im Raum der Todten*). This Protestant polygraph avoided the controversial issue of their religious beliefs and instead constructed their discourse around the perils of physical love for women rulers. Christina began by denouncing love as causing women more pain than joy; Elizabeth basically agreed with her. Although Fassmann concludes his introductory section with both monarchs noting the markedly inferior legal standing of women in both Sweden and England, his dialogue is basically about sexual desire.[40]

## Europe's Last Crowned Female Figurehead

Christina lived just long enough to see a woman acquire a share of England's throne in 1689 and confirm her low opinion of female rulers. After the successful invasion of England by the Dutch prince William of Orange in 1688, his wife and first cousin, Mary, was jointly invested with official sovereignty early the next year in order to create a fig leaf of dynastic claims to hide their naked usurpation. Charles Beem omits Mary II from his discussion of England's female kings because she was not a genuine sovereign—nor, it should be added, a genuine heiress given that both her father and legitimate half brother were alive.[41] Politically, England's Glorious Revolution was a great leap forward into constitutional monarchy; although their coins proclaimed that they reigned by divine grace, William III and Mary II ruled by the grace of England's Parliament. At the same time, their reign represents a great leap backward dynastically to the medieval Navarrese pattern of joint rule, whereby the husband effectively monopolized royal power even when his wife was acting as regent. Coins and medals from their reign reflect this situation with didactic clarity. Their high-value coins adopt the parallel-profile presentation introduced in 1618 by Belgium's Catholic archdukes, with William's face overshadowing Mary's. Several commemorative medals from their reign depict William without Mary, but she appears only once without him—in order to commemorate her death. William III outlived her and became Europe's first jointly crowned royal widower to rule alone in more than 250 years. From the perspective of the history of female government, England after 1688 looks less like the dawn of modern liberalism than the last gasp of the Middle Ages.

Mary herself, through an unusually candid autobiographical source, provides the most persuasive evidence for considering her a political cipher, Europe's last crowned female figurehead. In the Netherlands she reviewed her activities at the end of each calendar year, paying primary attention to her religious obligations, and copies of these annual self-examinations from her last six years (1688–93) survive in Continental archives. They shed a curious light on her reactions to this so-called liberal revolution. In 1689, reunited with her husband in England, she recalled them "both bewailing the loss of the liberty we had left behind and were sensible we should never enjoy here." The very next day, "we were proclaimed and the government put wholly in the prince's hand. This pleased me extreamly, though many would not believe it"; as she added a bit later, "My heart is not made for a kingdom." Their joint coronation soon followed, with "so much pomp and vanity in all the ceremony that it left little time for devotion."[42]

Mary II's reluctance to exercise political authority and her preoccupation with her religious practices emerged even more clearly in the next year's reflections. When her husband departed and named her regent, she asked that he "would take care I should not make a foolish figure in the world, . . . being wholly a stranger to business. . . . I was in real fear for it," she concluded, "my opinion having ever been that women should not meddle in government." Moreover, "I have never given myself to be inquisitive into those kind of matters since I was married to him, since I saw him so full of it." She survived the experience, although "I had found how impossible it is to pray much when one has so much business." Subsequent years record her gradual accommodation to the duties of regency, noting fewer prayers and more quarrels with a younger sister who enjoyed a more affectionate marriage and even produced a male heir. Mary II died unexpectedly at the age of thirty-two, long before her asthmatic husband, provoking a veritable flood of funeral sermons and panegyrics in both English and Dutch. As Rachel Weil suggests, "The problems posed by Mary's possession of regal 'authority' without regal 'power' could be resolved more easily in poetic conceits than in legal terms."[43]

In 1693, with the self-effacing Mary II as England's official coruler, an Italian polygraph named Gregorio Leti published a laudatory biography of her Protestant predecessor Elizabeth I. Although never translated into English, this work became the most widely read life of a female monarch in Enlightenment Europe; it had nineteen editions in four languages before 1750, followed by a Russian version published a year before Catherine II died. The work offered a radically positive assessment of women's leadership capacities. "I do not know why men have conceived such a strange and evil opinion of women," Leti began his preamble, "as to consider them incapable of conducting important business . . . or carrying out great plans with vigor. If [men] see a person of that sex govern a state with prudence and success, they will inevitably take the glory away from her and attribute it to her favorites and ministers." Leti claimed women could master absolutely anything which they studied seriously, and even anticipated the great goddess theory by arguing that women had originally held political leadership before men usurped it. He then ridiculed the Germans, the French, and his fellow Italians for "consulting the barbarians and the Turks when establishing their laws regarding women" and concluded that "if we did not have many examples of women's marvelous success and extraordinary capacity for government, the sole example of Queen Elizabeth would suffice."[44]

Nine years after the first edition of Leti's biography of Elizabeth, Mary II's younger sister Anne became England's monarch. She did not need to read Leti in order to choose Elizabeth as her political model. Being already married, Anne could not finesse the problem of wifely subordination as her illustrious predecessor had done. Instead, she began a new trend by subordinating her husband.

# 6

## Husbands Subordinated
### The Era of Maria Theresa, 1700–1800

> She possibly considered this coronation less important than the two
> masculine crowns that she wore.
>
> —report on Maria Theresa attending her husband's imperial
> coronation, 1745

All four of Europe's eighteenth-century female monarchs were married when they acquired their thrones, but none ruled jointly with her husband. One of them, Ulrika Eleonora of Sweden (r. 1718–20), was considered little more than a puppet of her husband, but when her kingdom denied her request to allow her to rule jointly with him, she preferred to resign in his favor. The other three—Queen Anne of England (r. 1702–14), Maria Theresa, monarch of both Hungary (r. 1741–80) and Bohemia (r. 1743–80), and Maria I of Portugal (r. 1777–92)—exercised power while finding various ways to keep their husbands in politically useful but subordinate roles.

Once again, numismatics offers excellent illustrations of these political relationships. For the first time in several centuries, the coins of England's and Sweden's eighteenth-century female sovereigns omit any mention of their husbands. Those of Maria Theresa did likewise until her husband acquired his prestigious imperial title, after which the Austrian heiress ordered separate coins minted in his name. Far more of her coins than his have survived, reversing the only previous occasion when an heiress and her husband had separate coins in fifteenth-century Cyprus. The coins of Portugal's female monarch did name her husband, who was also her paternal uncle and had received an auxiliary coronation. But in an exact reversal of the coinage of England's William III and Mary II, Europe's most recent joint reign, this time Maria's name came first and her profile overshadowed that of her husband.[1]

Like Elizabeth I in the previous era, Maria Theresa became the central female ruler of eighteenth-century Latin Europe by virtue of the importance of her possessions combined with the length of her reign; she governed two sizable kingdoms and an archduchy for almost forty years, while the other three female monarchs combined for only twenty-eight years in power. But whereas her illustrious female predecessor finessed the issue of marriage, Maria Theresa adeptly exploited hers to her political advantage. She is still conventionally known through her husband's title (Empress) and her family dynasty is still officially known as the House of Habsburg-Lorraine, the first example in European royalty in which the wife's family name precedes that of her husband.

## Two Female Constitutional Monarchs

Like Mary II in England, her sister Anne and Sweden's Ulrika Eleonora have generally been perceived as political lightweights and have seldom been studied as rulers. Despite coronations making them sovereigns "by the grace of God" (this traditional phrase appears on their coins), they lacked the arbitrary authority of their early modern predecessors and of their eighteenth-century successors. The English Parliament presented its Declaration of Rights to its new sovereigns in 1689 before offering them the crown, and their successors ruled through Parliament. In 1718 Sweden's Riksdag proclaimed a similarly sweeping reduction in royal power before offering its new monarch her crown. Anne and Ulrika Eleonora are therefore Europe's first autonomous women rulers who can be considered constitutional monarchs since a beleaguered Mary of Burgundy signed a Great Privilege early in 1477 in order to preserve the core of her father's possessions.

The political roles of England's two Stuart sisters resembled those of the earlier pair of sisters occupying the same throne, Mary and Elizabeth Tudor; both times, the younger sister governed autonomously after a period of joint rule by the older sister and her foreign husband. Culturally, the Stuart sisters lacked the superb Renaissance educations of Henry VIII's daughters; English princesses still learned French, but they no longer learned Latin. Anne, shyer than her sister in public but more assertive in private, became eager to handle her public responsibilities after her brother-in-law totally excluded her from state affairs. "Discoursing her sufferings," the princess "often made a parallel between her selfe and Qu[een] El[izabeth]." Although married, Anne tried to model herself after an illustrious unmarried female predecessor who had governed alone. At her accession, Anne dressed herself from a portrait of Elizabeth and copied both her personal motto, "Always the Same," and her parochial boast that she was "entirely English" (both women had undistinguished mothers).[2]

Anne reacted to the political dominance of her sister's foreign husband by making certain that hers, also a foreign prince, would not be associated with her reign. Both a political and a military nonentity, George of Denmark became Europe's first royal husband since 1415 whose name never appeared on his wife's coins or on her commemorative medals. Deservedly called England's first prince-consort by Beem, his most important function was biological; like a traditional queen, he helped produce legitimate heirs to the throne while avoiding sexual scandals. His marital achievements were impressive: unlike her childless sister, Anne had seventeen pregnancies, but unfortunately most of them ended in miscarriages, and none produced an heir to the throne. The physical consequences contributed to making her a semi-invalid during much of her reign.[3]

Anne's rule provided various firsts for European female monarchs. Its most interesting novelty is the combination of her husband's political invisibility with the high political profile of two female advisers. The first and more important of these, Sarah Churchill, Duchess of Marlborough, held the major office of Groom of the Stole in the royal household. This witty, outspoken, avaricious, and deeply ambitious woman married an equally clever and ambitious man who became the greatest English general of his age; they died fabulously wealthy, owning an enormous palace larger than most royal residences. Queen Anne's political relationship with Lady Marlborough is documented through hundreds of surviving letters, written under the code names of Mrs. Morley (Anne) and Mrs. Freeman (Sarah). Only those from the queen survive; at her confidante's request, Anne dutifully burned all of Mrs. Freeman's letters.[4]

Their relationship generated all kinds of scurrilous gossip. After 1700 English political pamphleteering became an equal-opportunity profession; the cleverest and most virulent satires, including quasi-pornographic attacks on "Queen Sarah," were composed by Grub Street's first female hack, Delarivier Manley. After Lady Marlborough lost the queen's favor permanently and was forced to resign her court office in 1709, Anne was supposedly influenced most by a Lady of the Bedchamber, Mrs. Masham. This time the most scurrilous pamphlet was composed by a man and included insinuations about lesbianism, "stuff not fit to be mentioned of passions between women," as Lady Marlborough sniffed in her final letter to the queen. Anne herself had spread malicious political gossip by insisting that her half brother born in 1688 was a changeling and constantly referring to the baby as "it." This rumor was not finally laid to rest until more than twenty years later—far too late to improve the Stuart prince's chances of claiming the English throne.[5]

Throughout nearly all of Anne's reign English politics was dominated by a major European war against France in which neither its monarch nor her husband exercised any personal leadership. When it began, Anne was a premature invalid, sometimes unable to write unassisted and barely able to "walk a little with ye help of two sticks"; before it ended, she needed wheelchairs. Her husband, who died in the middle of her reign (1708), was militarily useless. Named generalissimo of all English land and sea forces at the outset of the war, Prince George never undertook active service (officially because of his health) and was given no administrative duties because of his incompetence. Without interference from either the monarch or her husband, the War of the Spanish Succession, still known in North America as Queen Anne's War, went gloriously for her kingdom.[6]

Because of this war Anne became Europe's first female monarch whose reign produced numerous medals. The vast majority often made on the Continent, celebrated British or allied victories on land and sea. Some portrayed this semi-invalid as a goddess of war hurling thunderbolts at her enemies, principally Louis XIV. The Sun King had long ago created a separate government office to make medals commemorating the glories of his reign, and his enemies relished the chance to mock him. Three medals carry the slogan *Ludovicus Magnus, Anna Maior* (Louis the Great, Anne the Greater). On one of these, made in Germany, Delilah (Anne) cuts Samson's (Louis XIV's) hair while on the reverse, Europe's greatest king tries to dance as Anne plays the tune (see fig. 11). In real life, neither ruler was so spry: Louis XIV sent Anne special wheelchairs (which they both used) during the peace negotiations in 1712.[7]

Edward Gregg has demonstrated that Queen Anne stubbornly made her own decisions and took a sustained interest in government, presiding over weekly cabinet meetings and attending key debates in the House of Lords. She was careful to exercise her prerogatives responsibly, trying to balance her kingdom's competing parliamentary factions when appointing bishops and creating peers. She demonstrated considerable diplomatic skill in dealing with Scotland during negotiations for its union with England in 1707 and also with representatives of her designated successors in Hanover, although one of them mistakenly assured Leibniz in 1705 that the queen was a political cipher. Anne was the last English monarch to exercise the prerogative of vetoing a parliamentary bill and the last to revive the custom of touching sufferers from scrofula, the king's evil. She was also the first in several centuries to avoid political executions, even after some prominent Jacobites were captured during an attempted invasion in 1708.[8]

The reign of Europe's next constitutional female monarch was brief but not uneventful. Following the plans of her ambitious husband, Frederick of Hesse, Ulrika Eleonora, already Sweden's regent during her unmarried brother Charles XII's frequent absences fighting abroad, successfully claimed the Swedish throne after his unexpected death, while her eighteen-year-old nephew, the son of her deceased older sister, was in Norway. Before being formally crowned in March 1719 (like Christina, as king), Ulrika Eleonora had to ratify a new constitution which greatly limited the monarch's power.[9]

Sweden's new ruler inherited a bleak international situation: her kingdom was mired in a long and increasingly unsuccessful war against both Russia and Denmark. Mediation by France and England ended the Danish conflict late in 1719, but Sweden had to sell off its two remaining possessions in western Germany. Ulrika Eleonora neutralized her nephew's supporters by creating 180 new noble families, more than any other monarch in Swedish history, in only fifteen months of rule (Anne had created thirty English peers in twelve years, only six of which represented new titles). Like Queen Anne, she had a close female confidante and adviser in Emerentia von Düben, her lady-in-waiting since 1707. But von Düben, unlike Sarah Churchill, was never accused of abusing her influence.

Ulrika Eleonora shared Christina's opinion that women were unsuited to govern a kingdom whose monarchs still led its armies into battle, something even England saw as late as 1743. In February 1720 she requested the Swedish Riksdag to follow the English example of William and Mary and make her husband joint monarch. When they replied that joint reigns had been forbidden in Sweden since the fifteenth century, she abdicated in Frederick's favor. However, the Riksdag stipulated that his title was purely personal: Ulrika Eleonora would return to the throne if he predeceased her, which he did not, and the crown was hereditary but restricted to *her* male descendants—she hoped until 1724 to have an heir but died childless. These events marked the third time in less than a century that Sweden had reversed itself on the issue of female succession, excluding women after both occasions on which they had experienced female rule. The Swedes would not change their minds again on this issue until 1980.

After her retirement Ulrika Eleonora lived far more quietly than her more famous Swedish predecessor. She served as regent while her husband was abroad in 1727 and 1731; on both occasions her image reappeared briefly on Swedish coins, in exactly the same subordinate position as Mary II had on English coins. In 1730 her spouse became the first king of Sweden to take an official mistress. Nevertheless, his wife continued to cooperate with him politically until her death in 1741.

## The Pragmatic Habsburg Succession

While the French Bourbons introduced the Salic law to Spain and Sweden returned to female exclusion, Europe's largest and most diverse block of dynastic possessions moved decisively in the opposite direction. The Habsburgs, while amassing a remarkable collection of territories, had usually possessed several legitimate male heirs. They had held the title of Holy Roman emperor since the fifteenth century, but this could not be inherited: a fundamental law of 1358 made it elective. Although this family lost the crown of Spain in the war which filled Queen Anne's reign, it retained a core of Austrian provinces, united as an archduchy, adjacent to two kingdoms, Bohemia and Hungary, which they had held since 1526. They also held parts of northern Italy and the southern Low Countries.

In 1713, shortly after abandoning a Spanish throne held by male Habsburgs since 1516, Emperor Charles VI summoned two dozen senior officials to promulgate a revised law of Habsburg dynastic succession, soon known as the Pragmatic Sanction. Its most important provision was to keep the various Habsburg territorial possessions forever indivisible, like a Spanish *mayorazgo* or an English entailment. Another significant provision extended the customary principles of European inheritance, masculinity, primogeniture, and legitimacy, to include the explicit possibility of a female Habsburg succession. "On the extinction of the male line, which may God be pleased to avert," these diverse lands would "come similarly undivided to [the emperor's] legitimate daughters, again according to the law and order of primogeniture." If this lineage failed, the succession, still undivided, went to the legitimate descendants of the daughters of his older brother, the previous emperor Joseph I; behind them came the legitimate descendants of the current emperor's sisters.[10]

The contents, Charles VI told his advisers, could be freely disseminated. But implementing them throughout his extremely heterogenous possessions proved both difficult and cumbersome. In 1719, when his only living child was a two-year-old daughter, Charles began at the marriage of his older brother's daughter Maria Josepha by obtaining her explicit renunciations of any hereditary rights, which her husband confirmed. Next, the emperor tried to ensure its official acceptance throughout his hereditary possessions. In the spring of 1720 he drafted a formula, or Rescript, which was obediently ratified by each of Austria's provincial assemblies and a few Italian possessions. It was then accepted by the three regional assemblies of the Bohemian crown in October 1720. The Prague diet recalled that in 1510 the future wife of their first Habsburg king had been declared Bohemia's "true and legitimate heir" if her brother died without heirs, which he did. Moreover, they also noted Ferdinand II's revised constitution of 1627, which included a provision that their "right to elect a king becomes operative only when . . . no heir of royal stock and blood, *male or female,* is in existence or to be expected."[11]

Negotiating its acceptance by the less docile diet of the kingdom of Hungary required more time and effort. Hungarians had forgotten that their kingdom had once experienced a female monarch in the late fourteenth century. Instead, in 1687 they had guaranteed "for all time . . . none other than the male heir in primogeniture" of the Habsburg emperor; but if the male Habsburg line died out, "the ancient and honorable prerogative of the Estates to elect and crown their kings [would] again apply." When Charles began pressuring the Hungarians, they worried less about female succession than about the indivisibility of their own kingdom, which included quasi-autonomous subsidiary regions like Transylvania and Croatia. Here too Charles got his way: his Pragmatic Sanction became Laws I and II passed by the diet of 1723. The last piece fell into place when the distant Italian-speaking city of Fiume, the Mediterranean port of the Hungarian crown, sent its ratification in November 1725; it ended by wishing the emperor a long life—and male descendants.[12]

Charles VI still faced the problem of obtaining international approval for this Pragmatic Sanction. No foreign power, no matter how friendly, was interested in guaranteeing the indivisibility of his sprawling inheritance because they had literally nothing to gain by doing so. International guarantees of a female successor became increasingly important in the 1730s, when it became apparent that Charles VI had two healthy daughters but was unlikely to have any legitimate male descendants. No daughter could acquire his title of Holy Roman emperor: only adult males could be elected. France, with its prohibition of female succession and traditional distrust of Austria, was guaranteed to make trouble. However, the only formal objection came from the elector of Bavaria, who accepted female succession but claimed a superior line of female Habsburg descent through a daughter of Charles VI's older brother.

Thus matters stood when Charles VI died in 1740, making female inheritance a reality for Europe's most prestigious ruling house. In such unprecedented circumstances, no one really knew how far the formal guarantees he had so laboriously obtained both within and beyond his multinational possessions would actually be observed in favor of his older daughter. In the event, the hereditary provinces of the Austrian archduchy fell into line immediately. A pro-Habsburg pamphlet argued that, as king of Bohemia, the heiress also had the right to cast a vote in the imperial electoral college, although no woman had ever done so.[13] However, the Bohemian kingdom, which had noted previous traces of female hereditary rights twenty years before, failed to confirm her, and the Hungarians, who had been completely oblivious to a possible female succession in 1687, hesitated. Internationally, the most blatant repudiation of the Pragmatic Sanction came from an unexpected direction: the new king of Prussia, whose father had agreed to respect it, immediately invaded Silesia, Bohemia's richest province, without even offering an official excuse. The ensuing War of the Austrian Succession, which lasted until 1748, became Europe's first major conflict since the Hundred Years' War to be fought over the issue of female inheritance. This time the heiress herself was the major protagonist, and she survived the experience to become the outstanding female monarch of central Europe and the only Germanophone woman to head a major government until 2005.

As Karl Vocelka noted, Maria Theresa is the only modern Habsburg ruler who has remained virtually immune from public criticism, except for a few polite whispers from Protestants and Jews who suffered discrimination under her religious policies. Anyone trying to appreciate her achievements immediately encounters the long shadow cast by a nineteenth-century Viennese archivist, Alfred Ritter von Arneth, who crafted two monuments to her. Von Arneth not only published a ten-volume biography of her, the largest project dedicated to any European monarch, male or female, but also designed the imposing statue of her, surrounded by her most important military and civilian officials, which still stands directly opposite the main entrance to the Hofburg, the old Habsburg palace.[14]

Maria Theresa also left monuments of her own in Austria. During the 1740s she constructed Schönbrunn, a great palace in the suburbs of Vienna whose magnificence rivaled that of Versailles. She lived here almost constantly during her widowhood, and her successors used it until 1918. Two other innovative creations named for her continue to serve some of their original purposes: the Theresianum, founded in 1746 in an unused Viennese palace, prepared the nobility for diplomatic careers; and the Theresian military academy, founded at Wiener Neustadt in 1751, trained noblemen to become, in her words, "capable officers and upright men." Both institutions outlived the Habsburgs and have been revived twice by twentieth-century Austrian republics. She was also the first woman ruler since the Low Countries regent Mary of Hungary to found a new settlement and name it for herself; Theresienfeld, a village she created in 1769 by building an irrigation canal near Wiener Neustadt, remains a small town today.[15]

Maria Theresa's most personal legacy to her successors was a lengthy memorandum which she dictated almost ten years into her reign. First published by von Arneth in 1871, it is generally known as her political testament, although she entitled it "Instructions drawn up from motherly solicitude for the special benefit of my posterity." Difficult to read because of Maria Theresa's idiosyncratic syntax and frequent Gallicisms (modern German versions require a glossary), it contains a moving account of how she survived the first years of her reign, although it is basically an explanation and justification of her reforms of 1749 in taxation and administrative centralization in her Austrian and Bohemian possessions. She began with "the unexpected and lamentable death of my father of blessed memory," who left her a magnificent inheritance. But she "was at the same time devoid of the experience and knowledge required to rule such extensive and various dominions, because my father had never . . . informed me of the conduct of either internal or foreign affairs. I found myself suddenly without either money, troops, or counsel," and just as important, "I had no experience in seeking such counsel." After giving brief portraits of her father's chief advisers, she explains how she decided "to undertake the business of government incumbent on me quietly and resolutely . . . making it ever the chief maxim in all I did and left undone to trust in God alone, Whose almighty hand singled me out for this position" and who would therefore make her worthy to fulfill her tasks properly. She protested that "I would instantly have laid down the whole government, . . . had I believed that in so doing I should be doing my duty or promoting the best welfare of my lands, which two points have always been my chief maxims. And dearly as I love my children, . . . yet I would always have put the general welfare of my dominions above them, had I been convinced in my conscience that I should do this, or that their welfare demanded it, seeing that I am the first and general mother of these dominions [*die erste und allgemeine Landesmutter*]."[16]

Maria Theresa learned what Louis XIV called the craft of kingship very quickly because she had no choice. The next sentence of her memorandum resumes, "I found myself in this situation, without money, without an army, without experience or knowledge and finally without advice . . . when I was attacked by the King of Prussia." Her ministers, "unable or unwilling" to believe he would do this, together with "my own inexperience and good faith," explain why Frederick II "was left free to overrun the Duchy of Silesia within six weeks." In this crisis she came to rely on a minister whom she had strongly disliked because of his policies at the time of her marriage four years previously. Looking back on the almost disastrous beginnings of her reign, Maria Theresa did not spare herself. Rivalries among her advisers "produced a deep enough split between ministers, services, and peoples which I did not notice early enough, and later, when it became very acute, I did not manage with sufficient resolution, because I was too good-hearted (and the situation was very delicate), but [I] only applied palliatives which made matters worse."[17]

It is instructive to compare her remarks, written in the winter of 1749–50, with the reflections of her "smooth-tongued" enemy Frederick II many decades later. A notorious misogynist whose personal antipathy to women extended to the point of virtually excluding them from his court, the young Prussian king had once exclaimed that "no woman should ever be allowed to govern anything," and his first important act as king had been to seize Silesia from its young Habsburg heiress. But decades of conflict taught this gynophobe never to underestimate her. In the preface to his *History of My Times,* published at Berlin in French, Old Fritz noted how "when it seemed that events presaged the ruin of the young Queen of Hungary [Maria Theresa], this princess, through her firmness and cleverness, escaped from such a dangerous corner and sustained her monarchy by sacrificing Silesia and a small part of the duchy of Milan; it was everything that one could expect from a young princess, who, scarcely arrived on her throne, grasped the spirit of government and became the soul of her council."[18]

## One Woman Ruling Two Kingdoms

Maria Theresa was the only woman in Europe to have official coronations in two kingdoms, although she lived in neither. Her experiences in becoming monarch were very different in each kingdom, and, while ruling both from Vienna, she treated them very differently throughout her long reign. Hungary, her favorite, she showered with all kinds of favors and privileges, while Bohemia was an unloved child, burdened with heavy taxes and reduced autonomy. As she said on her deathbed, "I have been a good Hungarian"; she tried to repay Hungarian support by preserving as many of their traditional liberties as possible, and Magyars, who seldom love their Viennese Habsburg overlords, remember her fondly as *mokuska,* or "little squirrel."[19] For Czechs, however, Maria Theresa's reign was a dark age when nothing could be printed in the national language. She left few footprints in Prague except a church near its great palace, although in 1777 she converted a former Jesuit church into Bohemia's national library, which it remains today. Unsurprisingly, since 1980 she has had three biographies in Hungarian and one in Czech.

Her acclamation as king by the Hungarian diet in 1741—they reportedly shouted, "We offer our blood and our lives for our king, Maria Theresa!"—was an essential early achievement that prevented a possible dismemberment of her inheritance. In order to accomplish it, she not only used the Latin she had learned as a girl for extensive personal negotiations with Hungarian magnates, but also learned to ride in masculine fashion for her coronation: the culmination of the ceremony required Hungary's new monarch to charge up a hill and point a sword to all four points of the compass. The event was commemorated by a medal and soon afterward in a painting, the first to depict a sword-wielding woman ruler galloping on horseback. Although Frederick II always called her the queen of Hungary, she was also its king. In 1745 in a Hungarian fortress a French antiquarian located the tomb of a female who had been buried with a crown and insignia of the House of Anjou. He announced to Maria Theresa that he was "sending the remains of the first King Mary of Hungary to Your Sacred Majesty, the second Mary also King."[20]

Throughout her reign Maria Theresa continued to shower favors on Hungary. She transferred the Serbian Banat district to Hungarian jurisdiction and rebuilt her official residences at Pressburg (now Bratislava), which remained Hungary's official capital, and at Buda. A minor Hungarian noble, Anton Grassalkovich, headed her treasury or *Hofkammer* from 1748 until 1771. Hungarian students had five equal-opportunity scholarships in her elite Viennese Theresianum; although the quota was rarely filled, no fewer than 117 Hungarians attended it between 1749 and 1774. A special unit of Hungarian royal bodyguards was created in 1760 for provincial nobles, including Protestants. In 1763 she founded an Academy of Mines in the kingdom's silver-mining center, Schemiz

(Selmecbanya). In 1777 she transferred Hungary's small university to Buda, its largest city and traditional capital, attaching to it a Theresian College, founded in 1767, which provided funds, including uniforms and meals, for sons of twenty magnates, twenty nobles, and ten officials to enter every year.[21]

Her other kingdom treated her very differently in 1740, and she treated it very differently afterward. Under military and diplomatic pressure from France, Bohemia's diet had chosen the elector of Bavaria, the son-in-law of the older brother of Maria Theresa's father, as their new king. The successful candidate then cast Bohemia's vote to help elect himself emperor, but he could not enjoy a traditional coronation at Prague because the Bohemian crown of St. Wenceslaus had long ago been taken to Vienna. After Maria Theresa had utilized her recently born son in her Hungarian negotiations of 1741, she then motivated her troops to expel the Bavarians from the province of Upper Austria by sending her commander a Madonna-like mother and child portrait accompanied by a stirring call to battle. Her soldiers chased the invaders out and proceeded to invade Bavaria, occupying its capital on the same day the Bavarian elector was being crowned Holy Roman emperor in Frankfurt. After making a truce that effectively abandoned Silesia to Frederick II, Maria Theresa sent her forces into Bohemia, and they soon drove the French from Prague.

On January 2, 1743, Maria Theresa celebrated the recapture of Prague with a truly original spectacle known as the Ladies' Carousel (*Damen-Karroussel*), which she commemorated with a large painting that still hangs in her palace of Schönbrunn. As the official newspaper reported, sixteen great noblewomen and court ladies, "despite having very little time to practice," paraded through Vienna arranged in four quadrilles, half of them on horseback and the other half in ornate carriages. Maria Theresa rode in the middle, wearing a tricornered hat and brandishing a dagger. All these great ladies carried weapons, including lances, darts, and daggers, and some even fired off pistols before they reached the Spanish riding school in the palace complex. There they held a mock tournament, ending with a jousting contest between Maria Theresa and Countess Nostitz in which both women, carrying lances, tried to knock off a "Turk's head" held by negro slaves.[22]

Her master of ceremonies noted that "the Queen [Maria Theresa was now queen of Hungary] rode like a woman," as did Countess Nostitz; but the other ladies, "both married and unmarried, rode in masculine fashion, which caused some remarks." Although Maria Theresa knew how to ride in masculine fashion, she used a sidesaddle at this all-female Viennese rodeo because she was then more than three months pregnant (she was pregnant almost half the time throughout the 1740s). Her bellicose celebration was a sublimated form of wish fulfillment. Looking back on her first eight war-filled years, she remarked in her political testament that "had I not been nearly always pregnant, no one could have stopped my taking the field against my perjured enemy [Frederick II]."[23] But on the battlefield, Prussia's soldier-king had to face only her male surrogates, her husband and her brother-in-law Charles of Loraine, and he proved more than a match for either of them.

Finally crowned at Prague amidst a wave of congratulatory pamphlets from her nervous new subjects and complaining that the heavy Bohemian crown looked like "a fool's cap," Maria Theresa displayed little respect for Bohemia's traditional liberties as she tried to apply her official motto, 'Justice and Clemency.' A special court set up to try the most prominent collaborators with the French and Bavarians eventually condemned six noblemen to death. Maria Theresa first exercised clemency by sparing the lives of all six, including one who had offered freedom to his serfs if they fought against the Austrians. Justice followed a few years later when she abolished Bohemia's separate chancery in Vienna and her major administrative and military reforms attempted to unify bureaucratic procedures within both her Bohemian and her Austrian possessions.[24]

Frederick II was politically correct in always referring to her as 'queen of Hungary' rather than empress, as she is conventionally known, because women could not rule the Holy Roman Empire. Nevertheless, after Charles Albert of Bavaria, the only European prince to reject the Pragmatic Sanction, had been elected emperor in

1741, the transfer of the imperial crown to her husband Francis Stephen, former Duke of Lorraine and Grand Duke of Tuscany, became the final major step in recovering her father's possessions. Although Maria Theresa was soon able to humiliate him militarily, she could do nothing about his imperial title as long as he lived. But his political misfortunes ruined his health, and Charles Albert died unexpectedly early in 1745, thus clearing the path for the election of Maria Theresa's husband. Her behavior when her husband was finally crowned emperor was noteworthy. Firmly opposing a separate coronation for herself, as the previous emperor had done for his wife, she used another pregnancy as an excuse for watching the ceremony from a balcony window, shouting an occasional *Vivat*. She explained to her chancellor that she valued this crown less than those of her two masculine coronations; this ceremony was merely "a comedy."

Nevertheless, imperial prestige mattered. An edict of February 1746 ordered that her titles on coins minted throughout her hereditary possessions (in eight different countries of today's European Union) now began with *R. Imp.Ge.*, Roman Empress of Germany. Moreover, half were now to depict the new emperor, whose face and titles had never appeared previously on Habsburg coins. However, evidence suggests that monetary parity was not actually observed. For example, during the next twenty years numismatists distinguish 129 types of silver thaler (the basic high-value Habsburg coin) bearing her name and only 82 with her husband's name—a ratio of more than 3:2.[25]

Politically, she now had it all. About the time she composed her political testament for her successors, Maria Theresa sat for a state portrait by Martin van Meytens that became the best-known image of her, apart from the millions of Maria Theresa thalers dated 1780 that are still produced. In Meytens's portrait, she wears a pink dress and holds a scepter; two crowns lie alongside her on a cushioned table, with a sword and a cornucopia resting on the fireplace behind her. But she was also very much a matriarch, and her numerous children crowd into several family portraits in which her husband is prominent but she invariably remains the center of attention (see fig. 13). Her titles were now far too numerous to be squeezed onto the circumference of any coin or medal, no matter how large. An official Austrian protocol from 1745, in Latin and German, began with six royal titles: Germany (as empress), Hungary, Bohemia, Dalmatia, Croatia, and Slavonia, followed by archduchess of Austria. Next came sixteen duchies, led by Burgundy, followed by two principalities, four burgraves (*markgrafen*), eight counties, and five simple lordships (*herrschaften*). A final formal honor arrived in 1758, when Pope Clement XIII restored the Hungarian title of Apostolic Majesty, not used since the eleventh century.[26]

In her political testament Maria Theresa mentioned none of her political titles and said little about her wars with Frederick II. She remained focused on explaining her major reforms, designed to ensure Austria's future military protection and to streamline its political decision making. A financial base sufficient to maintain an adequate standing army required much higher and more reliable annual payments from the representative bodies of her various provinces. Bureaucratic procedures were centralized by amalgamating the central Austrian and Bohemian court chancellories (but that for Hungary remained separate). As Emile Karafiol noted, Maria Theresa always remained "careful not only to respect traditional forms, but to preserve old institutions as much as she thought compatible with the essential needs of the state. . . . [O]nly by consultation, compromise, and piecemeal reform was she able to carry out extensive changes successfully and peacefully" because "she herself was part of the old order, accepting its assumptions even while unwittingly she undermined its foundations."[27]

Her early reforms concentrated on immediate and practical problems and adopted traditional forms wherever possible. For example, Maria Theresa called her comprehensive Austro-Bohemian census of 1753 a "description of souls" (*Seelenbeschreibung*) and entrusted it primarily to priests. It provided the ages of 6,134,558 of her subjects, including nobles and Jews, and also some street plans. Afterward, Habsburg bureaucracy continued its relentless march. Greater uniformity was introduced through parallel clerical and civil censuses in 1762.

Military reforms created a Conscription Patent in 1770 which omitted only her most remote Italian and Belgian possessions. A separate Jewish census throughout her possessions followed in 1776.[28] Despite its vast size, her state had a narrow summit; during her reign only seven great princely families, whose town palaces still adorn Vienna and Bratislava, effectively monopolized Hungary's major national offices.

Maria Theresa certainly did her part to increase Austria's population. When not preoccupied with mastering what her first mentor, the Count Silva Tarouca of Portugal, called "the ABCs of government" or pondering military strategies against Frederick II, she was producing a child almost every year until 1756. Overall, she gave birth to sixteen children, eleven of whom survived to adulthood—totals far exceeding those of any other reigning female monarch in Europe or elsewhere.[29] Her oldest surviving child, Maria Anna (1738–89), became an abbess in Prague. Reversing the normal pattern of primogeniture, her oldest son, Josef, inherited his mother's Austrian hereditary lands and her two kingdoms, while the second son, Leopold, inherited his father's Grand Duchy of Tuscany. One other daughter also became an abbess, while the remainder married various princes; most famously, her youngest daughter, Marie Antoinette, married the French crown prince who became Louis XVI. Her third son married the heiress to an Italian duchy, while the youngest boy became grand master of the Teutonic Knights and later archbishop of Cologne.

Maria Theresa played favorites with her children, as she did with her kingdoms. The daughter whom she loved best, the artistically talented Maria Christina, was allowed to marry for love, and the empress lavished wealth and honors on her dynastically disadvantaged husband, who had five older brothers. Maria Christina repaid her mother's favoritism by supervising her husband's magnificent art collection, which forms the nucleus of a great Viennese museum, the Albertina (her name provides its last four letters). No such sentimental considerations affected the marriages of any of Christina's sisters, especially the youngest, Marie Antoinette. Nor, for that matter, those of their oldest brother; Maria Theresa forced a disastrous second wedding on her heir and official coregent, Joseph.

In foreign affairs, Maria Theresa succeeded in making a durable alliance with Empress Elisabeth Petrovna of Russia, who gave her invaluable military assistance during two wars against Frederick II. After her greatest adviser, Prince Wenzel Anton von Kaunitz, persuaded her to ally with her old enemy France in 1756, only Elisabeth's death five years later prevented Maria Theresa from recovering Silesia from the Prussians during the ensuing Seven Years' War. When it broke out, she could draw well-trained officers from her new military academy. After Austria's first great victory over Prussia in this conflict, she celebrated by naming a new Habsburg honorary military order for herself. As Kaunitz noted, she had many Protestant officers in her service, so the Maria-Theresien-Orden rewarded exceptional bravery in combat without any religious or genealogical prerequisites. The statutes of the order were proclaimed by her husband as grand master and printed at Vienna in 1759, and it would last as long as the Habsburg empire.[30]

In 1764 her Hungarian chancellor persuaded her to restore a long-defunct honorary order named for Hungary's first Christian king, St. Stephen. Open to civilian officials as well as to soldiers, it was limited to highly aristocratic Hungarians. Emperor Franz Stefan, grand master of the new order bearing his wife's name, vehemently opposed this idea as needless and refused to attend when his wife, wearing Hungarian dress, officially proclaimed it at the opening of Hungary's diet in 1764. Instead, she herself became its grand master, having "acquired masculine quality through the legal fiction of the Pragmatic Sanction." When her husband died a year later, she quickly resigned in favor of her son.[31]

Maria Theresa accomplished most of her major political and military achievements before her husband's death in 1765, while they were celebrating the marriage of their second son. Her widowhood changed her lifestyle in various ways. After Joseph II automatically succeeded his father as Holy Roman emperor, his mother named him coregent; but Maria Theresa also announced that she would continue to rule "without however surrendering the whole or any part of our personal sovereignty over our states, which continue to be kept together, and moreover without the least actual or apparent breach of the Pragmatic Sanction." She also ordered new coins minted for her son, just as she had done for her husband twenty years before. Separate, of course, does not mean equal. Maria Theresa's highest value coins were worth ten ducats; those of her imperial husband never exceeded five ducats, and those of her equally imperial son never exceeded three ducats during his mother's lifetime.

Nevertheless, some things had changed. Like Catherine de Medici, Maria Theresa always dressed in black during her widowhood, and she always wore a traditional widow's cap both on her coins and in her few commissioned portraits. She designed a suitably majestic joint funeral monument for herself and her husband, which she apparently tested out before her death; it remains the most ornate tomb in the Habsburg dynastic vault, although somewhat upstaged by the starkly plain tomb of her son and successor alongside it. During her widowhood, administrative reforms became fewer and less fundamental. Except for her son's brief, inconclusive intervention in the Bavarian succession war (1778), there were no more military conflicts with Prussia. "Never lose sight of the fact," she advised him at that time, with her characteristic abrupt code switching between French and German, "that a mediocre peace is always better than a fortunate war."[32] Instead, she and her son gained much territory without bloodshed. In 1772 Kaunitz and Joseph II persuaded her to sign a treaty partitioning Poland with Russia and Prussia that produced the only important territorial increase in Habsburg possessions during her reign.

Maria Theresa spent much of those final fifteen years secluded in her palace of Schönbrunn. Michael Yonan has analyzed the most significant, although not the most popular, image of her during this period, Anton von Maron's large official portrait of 1773. It was commissioned to hang alongside a similar portrait of her husband in his redecorated bedroom at Schönbrunn; she liked the work well enough to ennoble Maron for these portraits, and her husband's portrait still hangs exactly where she intended it to go, but she never put hers beside it. Both spouses are depicted seated at desks beneath the same three figures symbolizing peace and prosperity; she even has olive branches over her head. Maria Theresa holds a printed view of Schönbrunn in one hand. Several books lie on her table; an inkwell symbolizes the large number of letters she wrote after 1765 "with maternal solicitude" to her various children; above her, an allegorical Peace bestows a specifically female crown.[33]

## Europe's Last Heiress of the Old Regime

Although few people noticed it, the coronation of Maria I of Portugal in 1777 marked the first time in over two centuries that Europe (now including Russia) had as many as three women monarchs ruling simultaneously. However, the last royal heiress of eighteenth-century Europe remains a somewhat shadowy figure with few biographers.[34] The most remarkable aspect of her reign was the complete, permanent mental breakdown she suffered after fifteen years on the throne. This situation required a prolonged regency until her death in Brazil twenty-four years later—the first occasion since Spain in 1516 in which a son had to rule in the name of an incapacitated mother.

Portugal's recurrent obsession with being absorbed by its larger Spanish neighbor had emerged whenever a woman claimed its throne. As early as 1383 much of its political elite feared being governed by the Castilian husband of its heiress. At its next dynastic crisis after its African disaster in 1578, one of the three candidates proposed at the Cortes of 1580 to succeed Portugal's dying king Henrique was a woman, D. Catarina de Braganza. She received one less vote than Philip II of Spain in Portugal's estate of nobility and tied with the illegitimate Prior of Crato, thus creating a stalemate. Unlike her male rivals, D. Catarina lacked military support. After 1640, Portugal ultimately resolved the issue of female rule through a patriotically motivated monastic forgery, purporting to be a ruling of 1143 that had remained completely unknown until 1632: it barred a woman from inheriting or transmitting the royal succession unless she was married to a Portuguese nobleman.

In the eighteenth century José I enjoyed a long reign and had six legitimate children, all of them daughters. Although his famous enlightened minister, the Marquis de Pombal, opposed endogamy, the king preferred to resolve the succession issue by marrying his oldest daughter to his younger brother Pedro. José I obtained a papal dispensation for this purpose in 1743, when she was nine and her uncle was twenty-six. Portugal's first generally acknowledged heiress received a solid education from a Jesuit tutor, Timoteo de Oliveira, until Pombal had him imprisoned in 1757. In 1760, when she was a spinsterish twenty-six, Pombal tried to arrange her marriage to an English prince; but when Charles III of Spain threatened to invade Portugal and suggested his own brother instead, José I secretly married her to her uncle.[35]

The tactic fulfilled its dynastic purpose: six children were born, half of whom survived infancy. The prompt arrival of a male heir in 1761 was celebrated in every major foreign capital except Madrid. As José I's regent during his final illness, his wife continued his endogamous politics by marrying this sixteen-year-old prince to her husband's youngest sister, who was exactly twice his age. Nothing this incestuous had occurred in the eighteen centuries since Ptolemaic rule in Egypt concluded with Cleopatra VII married to her two half brothers. Nevertheless, the end justified the means; Portugal now had native legitimate heirs, and after José I's death in 1777 its first female sovereign was acclaimed as D. Maria I, amidst an outpouring of literary congratulations.[36] At the age of forty-three, she was also Europe's oldest female monarch to have a coronation since Joanna II of Naples in 1419.

Her husband became Dom Pedro III. "Yesterday, in virtue of the fundamental law of this Monarchy," he wrote proudly to an Italian prince, "which has the same force in Portugal as the Great Charter in England, the Salic Law in France, the Golden Bull in Germany, or the Royal Law of Denmark, establishes that the husband of the Royal Heiress also becomes King, I have participated in this event, which is the first ever verified in this kingdom." But as their joint portrait illustrates, Portugal's heiress was its real sovereign, while Pedro III's position was closer to a consort than to a joint monarch. The official account of their coronation, printed in 1780 by the Royal Typographical Office, recorded the "memorable solemnities, pomp, and magnificence which exceeded anything seen previously" for "the eternal remembrance of the Portuguese nation and the incomparable Glory of its August Sovereign [*Soberana*]." The investiture and oaths of obedience were for Maria alone; her husband received separate *Viva!*s after hers. The gold coins celebrating their accession emphasize her preeminence, reversing the gender priorities of William III and Mary II ninety years earlier (see fig. 15).[37]

Maria I was a typical eighteenth-century monarch, genuinely preoccupied with the welfare of her subjects. Her numerous panegyrists celebrated the prudent moderation of her government. She exiled Pombal without repudiating the general direction of his reforms. She categorically opposed the death penalty before reluctantly allowing public executions of three Brazilian rebel leaders in 1790. In her fifteen years of rule, only four events, including the foundation of Portugal's Academy of Sciences in 1779, were deemed sufficiently memorable to merit medals. Nevertheless, much governmental business got accomplished. A new law code was planned in 1778, and six volumes were printed in 1786; the new United States of America was recognized in 1783 and new treaties made with Russia and Sardinia in 1787; a Royal Marine Academy was founded in 1778, followed by a Royal Academy of Fortification and Artillery in 1790 and a Royal Academy of Design in 1791. The sovereign's most important personal contribution lay in foreign relations: Maria I wrote several hundred private letters to her Spanish relatives attempting to maintain good relations with her kingdom's all-important neighbor.[38]

A personal tragedy, the death of her older son in October 1791, deepened into a national emergency three months later as Portugal's monarch slipped from melancholic depression into delirium and occasional frenzy. Political problems, most notably the increasing threat to monarchy in France and a serious revolt in Brazil, undoubtedly contributed to her collapse. A desperate call for help to Francis Willis, the English physician who had recently cured his insane monarch George III, proved both expensive and useless. Maria I would live until 1816, but she stopped ruling early in 1792. Like Juana la loca almost three centuries earlier, Maria *a louça* never forgot her official position ("I am always the queen of Portugal"). It seems symbolic both that the last divine-right female sovereign of Europe should be physically moved to a different continent in the Napoleonic era and that her corpse returned home under a constitutional monarchy.[39]

Although Maria I had claimed her inheritance without a struggle, in some important ways her diligent and maternal reign before her incapacity in 1792 resembled that of Maria Theresa, but in miniature; the Portuguese heiress had many fewer subjects, many fewer children, and many fewer major political achievements. Like Maria Theresa, Maria I gave her eldest and secular-minded son (but not her husband) a public role in government in 1785. Her husband had already created a new palace for them at Queluz, on the outskirts of Portugal's capital, to which she added a wing after his death. Five centuries of female monarchy in western Europe concluded with this unremarkable reign. However, the real end of Europe's divine-right female rulers came not in Lisbon in 1792 but in St. Petersburg four years later, and the last woman standing was undeniably remarkable.

# 7

# Ruling Without Inheriting
## Russian Empresses

Russia offers a unique historical example: the same century has seen five or six women reigning despotically over an empire where women were previously slaves of male slaves.

—Charles-François-Philibert Masson, *Mémoires secrets sur la Russie* (1800)

Despite Russia's reputation of being semioriental, its Westernizing eighteenth-century governments experienced the longest period of female rule anywhere in Europe. Between 1725 and 1796, four tsarinas and a female regent governed it for all but three and a half years. Like the four heiresses of Latin Europe during the same century, the combined reigns of these Russian women total almost seventy years, with one woman being responsible for half of each total. But essential differences also separate the Russian from the Latin Christian cohort of eighteenth-century female rulers, and historians have yet to analyze the Russian phenomenon adequately in either national or international contexts. Russia's leading eighteenth-century expert, Evgeny Anisimov, reduced the subject to a series of disconnected biographical sketches, although these women's political situations abound in shared experiences.[1]

Three peculiarities distinguish the Russian cluster of female rulers. First, although all five were related to male tsars either by blood or marriage, three (both empresses named Catherine and the eighteenth-century female regent) had changed their names after converting from Protestantism to Russian Orthodoxy. Second, none of the four empresses, unlike the married heiresses of Latin Europe, had husbands at any time during their reigns. Third and most important, none of Russia's female autocrats inherited her throne. Instead, for the first time in European history, four women, including a regent, acquired autocratic power through coups by the elite guards regiments created by Peter the Great; and immediately after her proclamation, a fifth woman used these regiments for a constitutional coup to restore absolute rule. So while Russia was indeed Westernizing during this period, it experienced female rule under conditions utterly different from those elsewhere in Europe.

Although Peter the Great (r. 1689–1725) is justly famous as Russia's great Westernizer, his numerous female successors, beginning with his widow, were intimately connected with the successful implementation of his policies. Their role begins with the location of Russia's capital. In 1727 his young grandson returned it from Peter I's newly built "window on west" to its traditional home in Moscow, which remained the location for Russian coronations. However, by 1732 his female successor had returned it to her uncle's new Baltic seaport of St. Petersburg, and her female successors kept it there. They built, remodeled, and rebuilt all of the numerous European-style imperial palaces in and around Russia's new capital. The most famous of these, their downtown Winter Palace, now known as the Hermitage, ranks among the world's greatest museums; it was constructed by Peter the Great's daughter and furnished magnificently by her successor.

As rulers, these women became increasingly autonomous and autocratic. If Russian tsarinas were not the only eighteenth-century female rulers to be portrayed riding horses in masculine fashion (a few of Maria Theresa's medals used this pose in the 1740s), only Russian women wore men's hats and even an officer's uniform while riding. Considering their collective achievements, it is perhaps not coincidental that only in the mid-eighteenth century, after a longer delay than in any other non-Muslim country, including China, did chess-loving Russians finally put an extremely powerful woman on their boards alongside the king.² It would be more appropriately Russian to create a *Matrushka* doll commemorating its women rulers, with a gaudy Catherine II on the outside concealing Elisabeth, who conceals Anna, who conceals Catherine I; its ultimate figure would be a tiny Sophia, the female regent who preceded them.

## Before and After Peter the Great

Few of Peter I's numerous biographers notice that his personal reign (1689–1725) was both preceded and followed by the earliest examples of female rule in Russian history. Both situations were also unparalleled in any major state for many centuries. Peter's predecessor was the first female regent to claim formal sovereignty since Irene of Athens usurped the throne of Byzantium almost nine centuries previously; his successor was the first former concubine of humble birth to govern a major state since Egypt's Shagarrat al-Durr in 1250. If Peter's half sister Sophia was officially only a coruler with her brother and himself in 1686–89, his widow Catherine I became Russia's first full-fledged empress (*Imperatritsa*) in 1725–27. Both women exercised sovereignty in customary ways, issuing decrees and putting their faces and titles on Russian coins. Neither was married, and both conducted government business through a male favorite with whom they worked closely.

Sophia's regency began as literally the power behind the throne when a dynastic dilemma was resolved in 1682 by the joint rule of her younger brother Ivan, who by all accounts could not rule unaided, and their half brother Peter, who seemed very competent but was underage. Until April 1686 she remained simply "the great Sovereign Lady, Pious Tsarevna [tsar's daughter] and Great Princess Sophia Alekseevna," and her name invariably followed those of her male siblings. As Lindsay Hughes notes, not until the political and diplomatic success of this odd Russian troika reached its peak did Sophia reinvent her title by moving the key term *autocrat* (*samoderzhitsy*) to follow her name instead of preceding it. Under the leadership of a great Westernizer, Prince Vasily Golitsyn, Russia's joint rulers had already begun a new land survey and conducted an extremely active foreign policy, sending ambassadors to several

European countries and making treaties, including an Eternal Peace with Poland in 1686.[3]

The three years following Sophia's full association as joint ruler were dominated by Golitsyn's unsuccessful war in the Crimea against the Ottoman Empire. These military adventures coincided with Sophia's expanding political ambitions. In the 1680s eulogies addressed to her outnumbered those honoring Russia's nominal sovereigns; after 1686 her image decorated the reverse of Russia's gold coins, with the co-tsars on the front, and her first overtly secular European-style portraits appeared. These seem realistic; unlike previous Western portraiture of female rulers, none displays any flattering physical features, and all foreign chroniclers considered Sophia remarkably ugly. By 1687 she was contemplating a separate coronation for herself; portraits depicting her with imperial regalia circulated both in Russia and abroad. The most daring, an anonymous oil painting that was not published until 1895, placed her, crowned and holding imperial regalia, within a double-headed imperial eagle.[4]

After the failure of Golitsyn's Crimean campaign became apparent in 1689, Sophia's downfall was sudden and complete. Peter I, now seventeen, opposed her publicly, stripped her of all state titles, and shut her in a Moscow convent. Nine years later, compromised in an abortive revolt of palace guards (*strel'tsy*) while Peter was in Europe, Sophia was interrogated. An Austrian diplomat claimed that Peter threatened her with the fate of Mary Stuart, executed "by command of her sister [*sic*] Elizabeth."[5] Instead, Sophia was forced to become a nun, taking the name Susanna, while the corpses of rebel leaders were hung on the convent walls where she could see them. But an oil portrait of Sophia within the double-headed eagle was also preserved in the same convent, perhaps in the same rooms where Peter I later lodged his repudiated first wife, who outlived him.

Peter's second wife, Catherine I, a Baltic Protestant servant named Marta Skavronsky who had been taken by a Russian officer in 1702, followed him on the imperial throne. Europe's only illiterate female ruler, she also offered its best example of female promotion based on political merit. While bearing several children to the tsar, she also accompanied Peter on several military campaigns and greatly impressed him with her courage and judgment during his most desperate emergency in 1711. Afterward, Peter honored Catherine in special ways, first by marrying her in 1712. Two years later, celebrating a naval victory over Sweden, Peter created a new honorary order bearing her name and made her its grand master. It became Russia's second-ranking order behind that of St. Andrew, which Peter had previously created. Women were prohibited from becoming members, but every eighteenth-century empress, beginning with Peter's widow, immediately put on the order's blue sash and declared herself its head. The most extraordinary honor Peter bestowed on Catherine was to crown her as empress in May 1724, an unprecedented event which began Russia's "uncharted and unplanned journey towards female rule." Peter himself put the crown on her head while she knelt in prayer. A peculiar coronation sermon omitted both scriptural citations and historical precedents; as the inscription on its commemorative medals proclaimed, this event was entirely the "work of God and Peter the Great."[6]

Because the Guards trusted her to continue Peter's policies, his widow rather than any of his relatives became his successor. Governing in association with Peter's closest adviser, Alexander Menshikov, who had employed her and converted her to Russian Orthodoxy before introducing her to the tsar, Catherine's two-year reign was relatively uneventful. Its most important achievement was to inaugurate Russia's Academy of Sciences, chartered before Peter's death but not opened until 1726. All of its members were foreigners. In 1727 the dying empress named her husband's eleven-year-old grandson as her successor, with Menshikov as regent. This arrangement lasted only six months, until Russia's old aristocrats persuaded young Peter II to alter his grandfather's policies and return the capital to Moscow.

Two years after Catherine I died, a German journalist named David Fassmann paired her with Zenobia in his 129th *Dialogue in the Land of the Dead*. Because both women had accompanied a husband or son into battle, it highlighted their wartime experiences. Zenobia complains about being insulted by men, Catherine about Russian soldiers needing brandy before battles. The author knew the ancient ruler of Palmyra better than he knew Catherine; Fassmann thought Catherine came from minor nobility (a great exaggeration) and wasn't certain of her birth year. Zenobia boasted of her descent from Cleopatra but acknowledged that Catherine's achievement was unprecedented for a woman of her rank. After Peter's death, "there was no man who was in the smallest degree capable of ruling." Only the Turks expressed amazement at her rule and refused to send ambassadors to a land governed by a woman.[7] One year after this dialogue appeared, Catherine's stepgrandson died unmarried, leaving Russia once again without a male tsar.

## An Underrated Empress?

The next woman to rule the Russian Empire, Anna Ivanovna, remains an ugly duckling: an undeniable coarseness permeated her ten-year reign. Although England's Bloody Mary and even Spain's Juana the Mad have now found academic defenders, this empress continues to resist positive evaluations. Russia's leading historian has shown no desire to rehabilitate her reign, while her best-known biography in English comes from a ballet expert unable to read Russian. Disdain for this large, unusually strong, and physically unattractive female monarch began early. Soon after her accession, a Russian nobleman commented that "although we are confident of her wisdom, high morals, and ability to rule justly, she is still a female and thus ill-adapted to so great a number of duties." When the same ecclesiastical dignitary who had preached at Catherine I's coronation in 1724 undertook the same task for Anna Ivanovna's, his sermon avoided discussions of female exceptionality and, astonishingly, he never even mentioned the new empress by name. Many charges have been leveled against her: an "absolute nonentity" in government; a shallow, coarse woman, devoid of introspection and cruel to the point of sadism. Several female rulers of early modern Europe enjoyed hunting, but only Anna Ivanovna had the results recorded when she gunned down a thousand small animals and a few wild boars during a single summer.[8]

Like her recent female predecessor, Anna Ivanovna called herself an autocrat but governed through an all-powerful male minister. A crucial difference was that Anna's principal minister, Ernst Biron, whom she made Duke of Courland in 1737, was a minor Baltic German noble rather than an upstart Russian like Menshikov. Russians have never forgiven her for imposing a "German tyranny" for which they invented a special term, *bironshchina*, that combines notions of brutality, corruption, and foreign rule. Russia had experienced many brutal regimes—Peter the Great's was especially noteworthy—and corrupt officials permeate its history; what made bironshchina so intolerable was a quasi-colonial foreign domination that employed such brutality and profited most from the corruption.

However, Europe's two greatest German-born eighteenth-century rulers, both writing in French, showed considerable respect for Anna's political record. In 1746 Frederick the Great, who acquired Prussia's throne shortly after Anna's death, wrote that her reign "was marked by many memorable events, and by some great men whom she was clever enough to employ; her weapons gave Poland a king. In 1735 she helped Emperor Charles VI by sending 10,000 Russians to the edge of the Rhine, a place where this nation had been little known. Her war against the Turks was a succession of prosperities and triumphs" in which "she dictated terms to the Ottoman empire." Anna did more than wage war. "She protected the sciences in her capital," Frederick continued. "She even sent scientists to Kamchatka to find a shorter route for improving commerce between Muscovites and Chinese. This princess had qualities that made her worthy of the rank she occupied; her soul was elevated, her mind firm; she repaid service liberally and punished with severity; she was good by temperament, and voluptuous without disorder." But Frederick had little praise for her chief minister, who had once been expelled from Prussia's university. Biron, "the only one who had a noticeable ascendancy on the spirit of the Empress, was naturally vain, crude and cruel, but firm in business and not intimidated by vast undertakings." He possessed "some useful qualities, without having any that were good or agreeable."[9]

In her private sarcastic dialogue the *Castle of Chesmé*, Catherine the Great preferred Anna's rule to those of her successor Elisabeth and her predecessor Catherine I. Here Anna tells Elisabeth, "I liked authority as much as you, but I didn't waste it on frivolities." Challenged about who had made better use of her authority, Anna replies, "My reign showed more nerve than yours," to which Elisabeth retorts, "What some people call nerve, others call cruelty." When Catherine I interrupts them by remarking that Elisabeth was always her favorite, Anna retorts tartly, "We noticed that more than once" and asks, "Didn't she sign your name to Prince Menshikov's orders?" However, Catherine II's greatest praise for Anna comes later, when young Peter II tells her, "I loved you because your firm and masculine spirit made me suppose that you were further removed than any of my female kin from trivial bickering."[10]

Anna Ivanovna's selection as empress seemed fortuitous. With no male Romanovs available, Russia's aristocrats decided that a widowed and childless niece of Peter the Great, who had been ruling a small, poor Baltic principality for nineteen years as a Russian protectorate, would be more manipulable than her sisters or Peter's daughter. They imposed constitutional limitations which she signed unhesitatingly and then tore up publicly as soon as she had been proclaimed (the torn original remains in Russia's state archives).[11] Anna moved quickly to secure her position by creating a new guards regiment, commanded by Biron's brother. Too old to have children, she resolved the succession issue by bringing her older sister's German-born daughter to court to be raised as a Russian. Anna's most important early decision was to return Russia's capital to St. Petersburg, where it would remain until 1917.

Some of her other early decisions proved equally permanent. In 1731 Anna created a ruthlessly efficient secret police bureau. It quickly expanded the definition of high treason through the notorious phrase "by word or deed" (*slovo i delo*) and except for a six-month abolition in 1762 it endured under various titles at least as long as the Russian Empire. In 1732 Anna also created an elite training school for Russian military officers, the first founded by a woman ruler (Maria Theresa began one more than twenty years later). Housed in Menshikov's former palace, the Cadet Corps endured until 1917, benefitting Russia's cultural as well as its military history. During Anna's reign it participated in Russia's nascent theatrical tradition, and five years after her death its printing office produced the first useful maps of Russia's empire. Another durable creation of Anna's reign was the ballet school founded in 1736 to train young Russians of both sexes.

Anna's propaganda preferred to celebrate other achievements. The ice palace which she had constructed in the bitter winter of 1740 and opened to the public is notorious today as the site of a bizarre and sadistic icy wedding of court dwarfs, but at the time it was presented as both a scientific and an artistic triumph. Peter the Great introduced the custom of striking medals glorifying the ruler's achievements; Anna was the first tsarina to imitate him. Commemorations of her coronation were in Russian, while one in Latin celebrated her liberation of the Don River basin from the Tartars in 1736 for a European audience. Three medals, two in Russian, commemorated her peace treaty of 1739 with the Ottoman Empire. It gained land for Russia in the same region where her illustrious uncle had been defeated in 1711, and the Latin version proclaimed "Peter Great, Anna Greater" (*Petrus Magnus, Anna Maior*).[12] Soon after her death, a life-sized bronze statue, the first that celebrated a modern woman ruler, depicted her accompanied by a small child (see fig. 12).

Many blemishes offset Anna's successes. A state bank of 1733 soon failed, while taxes increased and other reforms were stalled by wars over the Polish succession (1733–35) and against the Ottoman Empire (1735–39) which filled much of her reign. A general survey to resolve disputes about landownership was announced in 1731 but stagnated after its guidelines were drafted in 1735. Her restored capital suffered a serious famine in 1733 and a devastating fire in 1737. Her government pursued religious dissenters with considerable brutality: a Jew was burned alive in St. Petersburg in 1738 for converting a naval officer, who was burned along with him. Both state persecution of Russia's Old Believers and state attempts to convert Muslims through bribes long outlasted Anna's reign. In failing health, Anna named the newly born son of her own

Russianized niece as her heir, passing over Peter I's daughter. On her deathbed, a "positive declaration" signed by 194 Russian dignitaries named Biron as regent instead of the baby's mother.

After her death, another German *Dialogue in the Land of the Dead* paired Empress Anna with Elizabeth I of England. A woodcut of both women bore the legend, "The heart of a courageous hero in a woman's breast frightens enemies and brings joy to others," and its subtitle promised to assess both women's "wise and successful governments." Inside, Anna's achievements were overshadowed by those of England's long-dead monarch, who receives twice as much space as the newly arrived Russian empress who sought her out. At its end, Elizabeth learns that Anna's testament named her newly born great-nephew as her heir, but with her favorite Biron as regent rather than her niece. Elizabeth immediately predicts a bitter struggle between them, and a messenger bursts in to announce that Biron has been overthrown.[13]

Biron's regency lasted exactly three weeks before he was replaced by Russia's second female regent, Anna Leopoldovna, who held power in her son's name for exactly a year. Known before her conversion in 1733 as Elisabeth Katharina Christine von Mecklenburg-Schwerin, she had married a German prince related to both Russian and Austrian royalty. Her husband's role remains mysterious, apart from procreating children: the regent gave birth to a daughter in 1741. The combination of Anna Leopoldovna's unimportant husband and her exceptional closeness to a female companion, Julia Mengden, makes her regency resemble the reign of England's Queen Anne. Its strangest incident was the arrival of a Persian embassy seeking to marry the shah to the daughter of Peter the Great, bringing as gifts fourteen elephants: nine for the infant tsar, four for the intended bride, and one for the regent (they were still alive when the future Catherine II arrived). Its most important act was Russia's endorsement of Austria's Pragmatic Sanction supporting Maria Theresa's claims, a policy which provoked France's traditional ally Sweden to declare war on Russia. After the regent's army, commanded by two English Jacobite exiles, won a victory in Finland and before Anna Leopoldovna could proclaim herself empress, French diplomacy helped organize a coup that overthrew the regent and replaced the baby tsar with the last surviving child of Peter the Great, his daughter Elisabeth.[14]

The most remarkable aspect of Anna Leopoldovna's one-year regency is the extent of its erasure from official Russian memory. The fate of the infant who had been proclaimed Tsar Ivan VI is extraordinary even by Russian standards: he was taken to a remote fortress and left to rot for more than twenty years as "Nameless Prisoner Number One," until his guards killed him because someone tried to liberate and restore him. Meanwhile, in 1745 the acts of his mother's regency were officially expunged from Russian records, and no state document could contain the name or title of Ivan VI. Coins issued in his name were recalled and melted down, although a few have survived. Even books describing his reign, whether in Russian or European languages, were ordered to be collected by the secret service and locked up in the Academy of Sciences. However, like the charter so ostentatiously torn up by Empress Anna in 1730, Russia's state papers from the year 1740–41 were preserved and finally published in the 1880s.

Even though the new empress categorically opposed capital punishment, the personal fate of her immediate predecessors was severe. After an abortive plot to restore them was discovered in 1743, the ex-regent and her husband were transported to a remote Arctic village, while two high-ranking noblewomen were whipped and banished permanently to Siberia. In 1746 the former regent died in childbirth; she received a state funeral, at which no mention was made of the cause of her death. Her husband survived in the Arctic for another thirty years. Not until 1780 did Catherine II permit their four surviving children to move to Denmark, where Anna Leopoldovna's last child finally died in 1807.

## Peter the Great's Daughter

Russia's third female autocrat and fourth woman to rule its empire in sixteen years, Tsarina Elisabeth would remain on her throne for twenty years, the longest female reign since her English namesake died in 1603. She was also the third woman ruler, after Elizabeth I and Christina, who never married. Yet she has always been eclipsed by her flamboyant successor Catherine II, who composed autobiographical memoirs describing most of her predecessor's reign in rather sly fashion. For such reasons, Elisabeth's best recent foreign-language biography is subtitled "the other Empress."[15]

The cultural distance between Elisabeth's reign and her mother's seems greater than the eighteen years which separated their coronations. In early 1742 an entourage of twenty-four thousand people and nineteen thousand horses left the new capital for a five-day trip to Moscow. Elisabeth made her formal entry through four triumphal arches. The first, erected by the city government, included images of the biblical Judith and Deborah in addition to her parents and herself. The second featured a deliberately unfinished statue of her father, with an effigy of his daughter wielding the equipment needed to finish it and an epitaph urging her to "Act with firmness and courage." Her carriage was drawn by eight Neapolitan horses, and behind her, in a carriage drawn by six horses, rode her young orphaned nephew and designated heir. Eighty-five cannon salvos saluted her entrance to the cathedral. The archbishop's sermon struck an old-fashioned note by greeting Elisabeth as a regent for a grandson of Peter the Great, who sat in the place traditionally reserved for the tsar's wife.[16]

But at her coronation ceremony eight weeks later, the same archbishop saluted her as "all-powerful Empress and Autocrat of all the Russias" after she had placed the crown on her own head. The new empress then entered the sanctuary, strictly reserved for priests, and took communion in both kinds. The accompanying festivities included an Italian opera, *La clemenza di Tito*; it was performed before five thousand spectators, with court nobility and military cadets playing minor roles and a Ukrainian choir singing from a libretto whose Italian words were transcribed phonetically into Cyrillic. Three years later these events were artfully massaged in a pamphlet published for foreign consumption by the Academy of Sciences.[17]

In an age when protocol mattered greatly, Elisabeth devoted considerable attention to diplomacy, and gaining formal acceptance of Russia's imperial status throughout Europe became her first objective. In 1721 her father had proclaimed himself Emperor (*Tsar*) of All the Russias, thus giving Russia equal standing with the Holy Roman Empire and putting it ahead of all European kingdoms, but neither France nor Austria had acknowledged this new title. In 1725 France also rejected Peter's proposal that its young king marry Elisabeth. A memorandum argued that the Romanovs were unworthy of such an alliance because they ignored both primogeniture and the Salic law. Elisabeth used the War of the Austrian Succession to make early progress toward international recognition of her imperial rank. In 1743 Frederick II gave Russian diplomats precedence at the Prussian court, while his enemy Maria Theresa, acting as monarch of Hungary, recognized Elisabeth's imperial title later in 1743, and the king of Poland followed in 1744. But the Holy Roman Emperor Charles VII, elected instead of Maria Theresa's husband, evaded the issue, while his French allies stubbornly refused to entitle her empress. In 1745 France botched the issue so badly that Russia broke off diplomatic relations for a decade, and a rupture with France's ally Frederick II soon followed. From this point on, the female Russian autocrat became a firm ally of the female Habsburg heiress against the misogynistic Prussian king.[18]

As part of her diplomatic offensive Elisabeth produced commemorative medals intended primarily for foreign consumption; in 1772 Prussia owned eleven of these with Latin inscriptions but only four with Russian inscriptions. Elisabeth's Latin medals celebrated her domestic achievements: freeing prisoners (1741), opening a canal begun by her father (*Perfecit Parentis Opus*, 1752), and proclaiming a tax rebate (1753). Several were struck in 1754: for founding a national university in Moscow, declaring a tax rebate for twenty-three years, and creating a town called New Serbia; but her most remarkable medal that year celebrated the birth of her nephew's son. It depicts the empress offering incense to the gods, but the baby's father is not shown, and his mother is never mentioned. The final medal from her reign, in Cyrillic but featuring Russian soldiers dressed as ancient Romans, celebrated two victories over Prussia in 1759.[19]

Although interested in her reputation abroad, Elisabeth was notoriously lazy about conducting domestic political business. She never signed into law the most important political initiative of her reign, a much-needed revision of Russia's legal code of 1649. Containing such interesting features as denying special treatment to nobles, it had been prepared in 1755 by the capable and versatile Peter Shuvalov, who would soon turn his talents to war finance and military engineering. Why Elisabeth refused to sign it will remain unknown, the most charitable explanation being that it retained capital punishment, a practice she consistently opposed. She was Europe's first eighteenth-century ruler who never permitted public executions, well before such enlightened policies became fashionable.[20]

Elisabeth's lengthy reign was generally prosperous both for herself and her subjects. Its first fifteen years saw no foreign wars, Russia's longest such respite in two centuries, and the population rose from 15.6 million in 1723 to 23.3 million in the census begun at Elisabeth's death. Foreign trade also increased dramatically: by the mid-1740s the average number of ships, primarily English, trading in Russia's new capital had more than doubled from Anna's reign. Elisabeth's personal prosperity increased after 1744 through income from new silver mines in the Urals that were managed for her private use; significant amounts of gold were also produced there after 1748. Thus she could afford elaborate displays of conspicuous consumption at court while proclaiming measures of tax relief in 1753 and 1754.[21]

During her reign, Russia began replacing imported leadership in military and cultural affairs. In the early 1740s most Russian generals were still foreigners, but Anna's cadet school was now producing high-quality Russian officers. Elisabeth's brief military intervention in western Europe in 1748 was a failure, but after 1757 native officers performed far better during the long, difficult war against Frederick the Great. However, Russian naval officers never matched its infantry commanders. Culturally, the Academy of Sciences in St. Petersburg remained a foreign enclave, but Russia's first European-style university was founded at Moscow. Russian music progressed: in 1753 the brother of Elisabeth's vocally talented lover Alexis Razumovsky formed a forty-man orchestra that played in her capital, while the empress ordered an opera to be composed and sung in Russian. A French director trained the first generation of Russian painters in her Academy of Fine Arts, created in 1757 under the patronage of Elisabeth's next important lover. Something similar happened with architecture, in which by 1760 young Russians had begun to compete with famous foreigners.[22]

Elisabeth's private life could not have been more different from that of her sixteenth-century unmarried English namesake. Instead of a pretense of virginity, the empress preferred a simulation of marriage to Razumovsky, who soon became known in Russia as the Nocturnal Emperor. No dashing noble courtier, he was the son of a Ukrainian peasant and had attracted Elisabeth's attention through his exceptional singing voice. The enormous social gulf between them resembles that between Elisabeth's own parents, with the sexes reversed. Although proud of his honorary title as count of the Holy Roman Empire (1744), Razumovsky never displayed any interest in Russian political questions. In a reversal of the conventional double standard, he had no known mistresses, but she had several brief affairs. The last half of Elisabeth's reign saw a prolonged liaison with Ivan Shuvalov, a man eighteen years younger than herself who also became a major political adviser. Like a queen-consort dealing with her husband's most important mistress, Razumovsky remained on good terms with his young successor and maintained an apartment immediately adjoining Elisabeth's throughout her reign.

Tsarina Elisabeth displayed a bewildering variety of moods about gender codes. She rode astride horses, even wearing a man's hat, but forbade other women from doing so. She also enjoyed dressing as a man, appearing as a French musketeer or Dutch sailor at court masquerades where she required both sexes to cross-dress. At the same time, she acquired prodigious numbers of dresses, changing them at least once a day while threatening beatings and exile to Siberia for any woman who deliberately imitated her hair-style or her dress. She was also so terrified of mice that she hired a man to supervise thirty giant castrated cats in order to keep her palaces free of them.

The last part of Elisabeth's reign is dominated by her military alliance with her female colleague Maria Theresa. Rarely has Europe seen two major female sovereigns so close in age (Elisabeth was eight years older) whose reigns coincided for twenty years. The Russian empress and the Habsburg heiress overcame their early mutual wariness to remain close diplomatic allies after 1748, even though their religious traditions were different and their states had not been traditional allies. Although their political portraits reflected completely different domestic situations (Maria Theresa was frequently portrayed amidst her numerous children, while Elisabeth was never painted together with her nephew and heir), the similarities between these women seem important. Both refused to put vanquished political enemies to death in the 1740s. Both constructed huge residential palaces which still delight tourists today, and both did so while engaged in an enormously expensive war against Prussia. Both even expressed a desire to fight the famous soldier-king Frederick II in person. As we have seen, Maria Theresa blamed her inability to do so during the early 1740s on her continual pregnancies. A dozen years later, Russia's pleasure-loving, childless tsarina, now well into middle age and overweight, similarly contemplated commanding her army in person and told her attendants, "My father [Peter I] went; do you believe that I am stupider than he?" They reportedly replied, "He was a man; you are not."[23]

Elisabeth and her chancellor understood clearly the relationship between diplomacy and warfare, that only through large-scale successful military intervention in European dynastic wars could the Russian Empire become a major player in European power politics. When the next major conflict erupted in 1756, Russia jumped in with a large army. Austro-Russian collaboration raised occasional difficulties. Shuvalov exhibited his versatility by creating a conical long-range howitzer, but only after Frederick II captured some of them and exhibited them at Berlin in 1758 did Shuvalov compose a letter to Maria Theresa, in excellent French, explaining how to make them. The two female sovereigns came very close to destroying the famous soldier-king and his no-longer invincible armies, as Maria Theresa's troops raided Berlin, while Elisabeth's even occupied it for three days. In March 1760 their last treaty contained a secret clause proposing "mutually and in most solemn fashion" a somewhat premature division of Frederick II's possessions: the Austrian heiress reclaimed all of Silesia, while the Russian empress remained in possession of those parts of the kingdom of Prussia that are "presently conquered by the armies of Her Imperial Majesty of all Russia." Their common enemy escaped humiliation only through Elisabeth's death. No other prolonged military alliance between two major women rulers has been recorded in the annals of European war and diplomacy.[24]

Russian occupation of eastern Prussia lasted three years before Elisabeth's Prussophile nephew immediately returned it to Frederick II, demanding nothing in exchange. Old Fritz admitted in private that the bears had behaved themselves quite well, and the extent of Prussian collaboration with the occupying forces so annoyed him that he never visited the region again. The Russian National Library preserves eulogies of Elisabeth printed at Königsberg in 1760 and 1761, and the empress used her private silver hoard to make high-quality coins bearing her image for use in Prussia. Now a forgotten Russian exclave, the oblast of Kaliningrad still contains a Stalin-era statue of Elisabeth dressed in her Guards uniform.[25]

## Catherine II: Greatness and Female Rule

The volume and variety of information both by and about Europe's only female ruler generally known as the Great are simply overwhelming. In the first years of her reign, hyperbole was confined to such phrases as "the most praiseworthy, most powerful Empress and lady Catherine, autocrat of all the Russias, our God-sent most gracious Mother of the Country." But official adulation soon escalated; in subsequent decades she was routinely called simply the Great. A recent French series profiling great statesmen points out that both Voltaire and the Prince de Ligne used the masculine form *le Grand* to describe her. Catherine herself apparently preferred to have it both ways: on the exterior was a charming, gracious woman, while inside were the mental habits of a man—and, one might add, more disciplined energy than all but a very few men or women have possessed.[26]

Her coup d'état of 1762 could only have happened in a state already long accustomed to seeing women seize power in this manner. Her political perils before acquiring the throne recall those of Elizabeth Tudor in England or Isabel la Católica in Castile, but Catherine II's acquisition of sovereign power was far more remarkable than theirs because of the total absence of any hereditary claim. Hers was not Europe's longest period of female rule—Catherine II was nearly a decade older than these illustrious predecessors when she seized power—but it undeniably ranks among the most transformational. She became Russia's second major Westernizer, Peter's political heir, whose task and glory were to fulfill his dream. Her most enduring monument, Étienne-Maurice Falconet's equestrian statue of Peter the Great, which inspired Aleksandr Pushkin's "The Bronze Horseman," still occupies a central location in her capital city. Its dual inscriptions, four simple Russian and Latin words, proclaim it a gift to Peter the First from Catherine the Second. If Peter's biological daughter transformed her father's simple log house into a pilgrimage shrine, his German-born admirer totally eclipsed her when it came to commemorations.

The sheer number of written public documents surviving from Catherine's reign necessarily makes any brief summary unsatisfactory. Perhaps only Louis XIV or Philip II ever read and annotated more papers. As she remarked in an epitaph she wrote for herself in 1788, "Work was easy for her." Catherine composed almost 10,000 letters, in both French and Russian (with occasional phrases in German), and signed about 14,500 decrees, by far the largest totals for any prerevolutionary Russian ruler. She also wrote incessantly about an amazing variety of subjects, ranging from the nascent study of comparative languages to numerous plays, educational manuals for her grandchildren, and a great deal of Russian history; she even began the first translation of the *Iliad* into Russian. Before the Revolution of 1917, many of her most essential state papers were published by the Russian Historical Society, and twelve volumes of her personal works also appeared between 1901 and 1907. But because the Soviet regime long ignored her, both series remain incomplete. In particular, the preparatory drafts and memoranda that preceded Catherine's major decisions remain widely scattered and hard to assemble. A senior Russian archivist calculated in 1996 that updating these source publications will require "more than one generation of historians."[27]

Since 1917 more biographies of Catherine II have appeared in west European languages, especially English, than in Russian. The title Great is more often attached to her on foreign titles, whereas a thousand-page-long Russian anthology from 2006 discusses Catherine II *pro et contra*. Nevertheless, most Russian scholars agree that the most important recent study of her reign was published in England by Isabel de Madariaga, the daughter of an exiled Spanish statesman. Catherine would have enjoyed the flurry of commemorative conferences for the bicentennial of her death in 1996. In Russia, an enormous gathering at her capital (once again named St. Petersburg) presented no fewer than 128 papers, subsequently published only in Russian summaries later that year. Meanwhile, other commemorations were held at her coronation site (Moscow), her German birthplace (Stettin), the seat of her father's tiny patrimony (Zerbst), the home of both her mother and her husband (Holstein), and elsewhere in Germany (Mainz). Another international commemoration in Paris coincided with the opening at Amsterdam of a major exposition of treasures from her reign in the Hermitage Museum.[28]

Even if coups d'état by women were becoming a Russian tradition, Catherine's displayed unusual daring. Voicing his habitual misogyny, Frederick II subsequently claimed that "neither the honor nor the crime of this revolution can be justly credited to the empress," but it is undeniable that her audacity reached levels never imagined by her recent female predecessors: at her coup, Catherine named herself a colonel of the guards and led them on horseback, dressed in one of their traditional uniforms. She took great pride in commemorating this feat with a very large canvas, one that still hangs in the largest room of the palace where she received her husband's surrender (see fig. 14).

Why did it succeed? In only six months her husband, Peter III, had first alienated public opinion by abandoning conquered

Prussian territory with no visible advantages. He then alienated the elite Russian guards by making them wear Prussian-style uniforms and terrified the Orthodox church by secularizing many of its properties. At the same time, he made two popular changes, freeing the Russian nobility from Peter I's obligation to serve the state either militarily or bureaucratically for twenty-five years and abolishing the much-feared secret police, thereby greatly reducing the risks to plotters. Peter III also affected an eighteenth-century aristocratic nonchalance about his wife's pregnancy by another man. But it was a serious mistake because the father, Grigory Orlov, was a popular Guards officer with four well-placed brothers. After Catherine gave birth to her second son, the Orlovs and their friends provided the muscle for her coup. Frederick II heard about their plot and tried to warn his great admirer Peter III, but, as Old Fritz put it, the tsar abdicated "like a child being sent to bed"—and conveniently died a few days later while under the supervision of one of Orlov's brothers. Because she had absolutely no hereditary claim to govern, several plotters believed Catherine would become regent for her eight-year-old son. After rewarding the Guards and reassuring the church, the new empress skillfully finessed this option. She refused to ratify her husband's shameful peace with Prussia and created commissions to study the problem of abolishing the service requirement for nobles and the fate of church lands.[29]

Many political questions were sorted out during the next two years. Grigory Orlov was put in charge of the artillery; like Elisabeth's Nocturnal Emperor, he took no official part in Russia's government. Very few high-ranking officials who had served Peter III were dismissed; some were transferred, but none was exiled. Peter III had recalled Anna's former chief minister, Biron, now seventy-three years old, after twenty years in Siberia, and Catherine II restored him as Duke of Courland, a title he had held since 1737. An important piece of old business was resolved in 1764 when Nameless Prisoner Number One, the former baby Tsar Ivan VI, was killed by his guards during a botched attempt to liberate him. The conspirator was executed, the first such public event in over twenty years, while Ivan's actual killers received secret but tiny rewards. Meanwhile,

Catherine began tidying up Russia's finances and modernizing its administration. She increased the number of officials, doubled their salaries, and appointed an incorruptible chief investigator who prosecuted bribery vigorously.

After using them as pretexts for overthrowing him, Catherine began implementing her husband's changes in both foreign policy and church affairs. Abroad, she signed a treaty with Frederick II in 1764 that became the cornerstone of her foreign policy for sixteen years. Prussian support helped Catherine to seat one of her former lovers, Stanislas Poniatowski, on the Polish throne after it became vacant in 1763 (Biron became one of his vassals). Besides abandoning Elisabeth's alliance with Maria Theresa for her husband's Prussian alliance, Catherine quietly accepted two of Peter III's major changes in domestic affairs. She confirmed his highly popular abolition of the service requirement for nobles and resumed his controversial policy of transferring church peasants to state control. She ruthlessly silenced an arrogant and eloquent prelate who also supported the claims of Ivan VI. After ordering his arrest at a synod, the new empress attended his interrogation and deprived him of his offices. When he remained obstinate, she ordered him defrocked and shut in an Estonian fortress, where his guards spoke no Russian and knew him only as Andrew the Liar.[30] Catherine did reverse one of Peter III's reforms: within a few months she quietly reinstated the secret police, while attempting to eliminate their use of torture.

Catherine II believed that "true talent is usually modest and hidden away somewhere on the periphery" and that "true valor . . . never strives for recognition, never displays greed, and never advertises itself."[31] She searched diligently for these qualities. Once she had located reliable collaborators for sensitive positions, the empress tended to keep them in office indefinitely. Even her love life settled down after a period of promiscuity in the 1750s, one which continues to perplex her biographers over the paternity of the crown prince, Grand Duke Paul. Orlov was undoubtedly the father of the boy born in 1762 and raised as Alexander Bobrinskoy, and he remained Catherine II's lover for twelve years, the longest tenure of any holder of this particular position. Some key civilian officials served for at least thirty years; A. A. Vyazemsky, her incorruptible prosecutor, remained in this capacity until his death in 1792, while Stepan Sheskovsky, the reliable head of her secret police, also held his position for thirty years. So did a third important official. Her husband had named George Browne, an eccentric Irish Catholic soldier with a distinguished record in the Seven Years' War, to command the army for his proposed invasion of Denmark. Instead, Catherine named him governor of her two Baltic provinces with German nobility, Estonia and Livonia, and kept him in office until he died in 1792 at the age of ninety-four.[32] South of him, old Biron, who died in his Italianate palace built during Anna's reign at the age of eighty-two, and his son Peter ruled Courland as reliable Russian clients until it was surrendered to Catherine at the third Polish partition in 1795.

Catherine II's early political program culminated with the convening of Russia's unprecedented legislative convention of 1767, which accomplished little beyond increasing her stature outside Russia. Reforms were sidetracked in 1768 by a war declared by Turkey, which Catherine excitedly claimed had "aroused the sleeping cat and . . . now they [in Europe] will talk about us."[33] It lasted six years, produced some remarkable victories, provoked Emelyan Pugachev's rebellion, and ended with minor but strategic territorial acquisitions in the south. Meanwhile, the Russian Empire also gained large amounts of territory in the west through the first partition of Poland, about which Catherine boasted even less than Maria Theresa. During the later years of her reign, when Russian armies seemed invincible, imperial aggrandizement through both military and diplomatic aggressions became increasingly naked. Russian hegemony in Moldavia and Georgia encountered little opposition, but Russian usurpation of the supposedly autonomous Crimea provoked a second major Turkish war in 1788–91, accompanied by a largely naval war with Sweden in 1789–90. Huge territorial acquisitions followed the abolition of the Polish–Lithuanian Commonwealth after the partitions of 1793 and 1795.

Under Catherine II, foreigners no longer commanded Russian armies, but Russia's native naval officers continued to lag far behind its infantry generals, and at one point the empress even hired the naval hero of the American Revolution, John Paul Jones. When he died in 1788, her greatest naval hero, Admiral Samuel Grieg, an old Scot, belonged to no fewer than five Russian chivalric orders, including two created by Catherine II: the Order of St. George, established during her first major war in 1769, and the Order of St. Vladimir, created in 1782 to celebrate her twentieth anniversary as empress.[34]

Less gloriously, Catherine II's reign confronted the last and largest popular rebellion in imperial Russia, Pugachev's revolt of 1773–74. Catherine's counterfeit husband and his main collaborators exhibited unusual panache by creating not only a counterfeit court but also a counterfeit government that issued printed and sealed decrees in the name of Peter III. A rebel nobleman conducted the illiterate Pugachev's official correspondence in French and German, while two literate Tatars did likewise in Arabic, Persian, and Turkish. Both its so-called College of War and the adopted names of principal rebels directly mimicked Russia's real court and government, including Catherine's lover, Count Orlov. Pugachev himself abandoned his family to marry the daughter of a Yaik Cossack, who was then addressed as Her Imperial Majesty. The real empress attempted to liquidate these affronts to her prestige as rapidly, efficiently, and completely as possible. Once the revolt was broken and the rebel leader himself captured, Catherine II concentrated her efforts first on avoiding torture, which she said always obscured the truth and had thus far proved unnecessary, and then on ensuring a minimum of bloodshed. "As regards executions," she informed her chief prosecutor, "there must be no painful ones, and only three or four people."[35] She took special care to discover whether Pugachev had coined money, who had painted his portrait, and what medals he had granted his followers. The artist turned out to be an icon painter who had painted Tsar Peter III over a likeness of the empress captured from a government office; no coins had been minted, but captured silversmiths had made about twenty medals for him. At his execution, Pugachev's counterfeit seal was broken in his presence. Then, to the bitter disappointment of the Moscow crowd, he was beheaded before traditional barbarities were inflicted on his corpse. Catherine's final objective was to obliterate all memory of this revolt by erasing the names of key places and persons connected with it. Pugachev's house was destroyed, and his village was renamed after one of her generals. The main village of his rebellious Yaik Cossacks likewise had its name changed, and the Yaik River became the Ural. Even Pugachev's brother, who had not taken part in the revolt, had to change his surname.

Pugachev was the most important of several men claiming to be Peter III, but he was not Russia's strangest impostor. This dubious distinction belongs to his immediate successor, the first and only documented female royal pretender in European history. Her real name remains unknown, but she became known in Russia as Tarakanova (literally, "of the cockroaches"). Accompanied by an entourage of Polish exiles and French agents who claimed she was the daughter of Empress Elisabeth, she was astutely kidnapped in 1775 at the Adriatic port of Ragusa with the help of British diplomats. Together with two Polish aides and six Italian servants, she was sent to St. Petersburg for interrogation, in French because she spoke no Russian. In captivity, she spun a series of fairy tales and wrote a letter to the empress which Catherine furiously noted "extended her insolence to the point of signing herself as Elisabeth." This "rank scoundrel," who died of natural causes after six months in prison, inspired several romantic novels and a very early silent French film.[36]

Domestically, Catherine's first major achievement was to summon Russia's earliest elective assembly in December 1766; it would also be the last until 1905. When it opened in July 1767, it contained 29 deputies representing government institutions, including the Orthodox church, 142 deputies from the provincial nobility, 209 deputies from Russian towns, and 200 peasant deputies, including 54 from non-Russian tribes. Catherine's final document began by asserting that "Russia is a European power" and claimed in a burst of Enlightenment optimism that "Peter the Great, on introducing European manners and customs among a European people, found such facility as he himself never expected." Its next article boasted that "the Empire of Russia contains 32 degrees of latitude and 165 of longitude on the terrestrial globe"—and Catherine II later extended its western and southern limits considerably. Article 9 asserted, "The Sovereign is absolute, for no other than absolute power vested in one person can be suitable to the extent of so vast an Empire." She borrowed a great deal from Montesquieu's *Spirit of the Laws* but finessed his assertion that the law of succession was the most fundamental of any country, because she could not devise one that would retrospectively justify her seizure of power.[37]

Her leading biographer, Isabel de Madariaga, asserts that Catherine's *Nakaz*, or Instruction, to the assembled deputies constituted "one of the most remarkable political treatises ever compiled and published by a reigning sovereign in modern times." It was also widely disseminated across Europe. A deluxe edition of 1770 was printed in Russian, Latin, French, and German, and a luxurious bilingual Russian–Greek edition followed in 1771. An English translation appeared in 1768, followed by Italian, Dutch, and Polish versions. French censorship guaranteed its notoriety by banning the work. Her famously misogynist ally Frederick the Great complimented her legislative efforts as a "masculine, nervous performance, and worthy of a great man." Comparing the Russian autocrat to Semiramis, Elizabeth I of England, and their peer Maria Theresa, the Prussian king remarked, "We have never heard of any female being a lawgiver; this glory was reserved for the Empress of Russia."[38] The assembly attempted to honor her with the title of Mother of the Fatherland, which she refused after their proposal had entered the official record.

Although no general law code for the empire ever emerged from these discussions, many of its central provisions were incorporated into subsequent legislation, especially the major administrative reforms which followed the end of her first Turkish war (Maria Theresa's greatest administrative reforms also followed the end of her first major war). With her usual energy, Catherine II and her advisers made six drafts, including more than six hundred worksheets written in her own hand, before the "Statute for the Administration of the Provinces [*gubernyi*] of the Russian Empire" was promulgated in November 1775. Its key provisions, carried out under Catherine II's constant close personal supervision, divided her empire into twenty-five major units of approximately equal population and multiplied the number of courts, schools, almshouses, public buildings, and subaltern officials in each. By 1785 further conquests and treaties had increased the number of imperial gubernyi to forty-one; they had reached fifty when she died in 1796. As these reforms were implemented, the cost of Russia's local government mushroomed from 1.7 million roubles in 1774 to 5.6 million by 1785; by her last year, they had nearly doubled again to 10.9 million. De Madariaga notes that the share of Russian state income devoted to military expenses declined considerably throughout her reign, while civilian administration ate up more than half of the budget by the time she died, and asserts that "the demilitarization of administration and society was the corollary of the presence of a woman on the throne."[39]

The sharp increase in numbers of gubernyi indicates the scale of Catherine II's territorial acquisitions at the expense of the Polish–Lithuanian Commonwealth and the Ottoman Empire. From the commonwealth she claimed to have liquidated only the Slavic part, the former grand duchy of Lithuania, while leaving the Catholic Poles to her German partners in crime; in fact, she took only slightly less than Joseph Stalin would after 1945. Her southern acquisitions from the Turks gave Russia permanent control of the Black Sea. Such huge gains merely whetted Catherine's appetite for the fantastic Greek project of her old age, which envisioned destroying the Ottoman Empire completely and installing her younger grandson Constantine in the ancient Byzantine capital of Constantinople.

Catherine II was Europe's only female ruler to consciously promote her political greatness, and she closely supervised the production of various forms of durable propaganda to perpetuate her achievements. At her coronation, 850 commemorative medallions were struck in gold and silver for the most distinguished guests, 2,000 more in bronze for lesser notables, and about 30,000 small copper pieces were thrown to the crowd. To celebrate her tenth anniversary in power, she put her accession medal of 1767, depicting her as a helmeted Minerva, on snuffboxes for her closest associates. At the same time, she reinforced her credentials as a Russian patriot by ordering a series of 57 medals representing every previous Russian ruler from tenth-century Rurik to Tsarina Elisabeth (omitting, of course, Ivan VI and Peter III).

Catherine II used medals far more extensively than any previous female ruler. That same year, 1772, her Prussian allies gave her a printed pamphlet listing every Russian medal in their possession. In the first decade of her reign this German-born Westernizer had issued far more of these in Russian than in Latin, mainly commemorating such new institutions as a Foundling Hospital (1763), an Academy of Fine Arts (1765), the Carousel Theater (1766), Russia's Legislative Assembly (1767), St. Isaac's Cathedral (1768), and the Economic Society (1768). More recent medals celebrated Russia's success in its ongoing war with the Ottomans; one, with a beautiful map, commemorated Alexis Orlov's naval victory over the Turks. However, Prussia did not possess all of Catherine II's early medals. Two more, both with Latin inscriptions, went to British physicians to celebrate the introduction of vaccination (1768) and "Liberation from Plague" (1770). A large collection subsequently acquired by France included medals in Russian commemorating an expedition to Kamchatka (1762), her foundation of the Smolny Institute for girls (1764), her new honorary military order of St. George (1769), the transportation of the pedestal for her great equestrian statue of Peter I (1770), and Grigory Orlov's actions in plague-ridden Moscow (1771).[40]

Across the next decade, Catherine II maintained a steady stream of political accomplishments, also commemorated by medals. By 1781 she proudly enumerated no fewer than 492 notable political achievements throughout her burgeoning empire: 29 provinces reorganized, 144 towns organized and built, 30 foreign treaties, 78 military victories, 88 memorable edicts, and 123 edicts for ameliorating the general welfare of her subjects. Only a few of these deserved medals, while some of her most famous but insufficiently glorious political events of the 1770s were not commemorated in this way— for example, the suppression of Pugachev's revolt and the first partition of Poland, in which Catherine, unlike Maria Theresa, did not reclaim provinces lost many centuries earlier. Nevertheless, both

London and Paris possess Russian medals from this decade
commemorating such events as her renovation of the Kremlin
(1773); the marriage of Crown Prince Paul (1773); her peace treaty
with Turkey and her victorious general, Prince Peter Rumiantsov
(both 1774); her creation of new provincial governments (1775); the
second marriage of Crown Prince Paul (1776); the fifty-year jubilee
of Russia's Academy of Science (1776); the birth of her first
grandson, Alexander (1777), depicting the empress but not the
father; homage from her new Greek subjects in the Crimea (1779);
and the birth of her second grandson, Constantine (1779).

In 1782 a whole series of medals celebrated the unveiling of
Falconet's statue of Peter the Great, with tokens thrown to the crowd
as at a coronation; others celebrated the strengthened Russian navy
and Russia's new Imperial Academy of Language, headed by Princess
Ekaterina Dashkova. In 1783 medals celebrated Potemkin's conquest
of the Crimean peninsula, including a superb map; formal Russian
annexation of the Crimea, also with a map; and Russia's new client,
the king of Georgia. The next year produced one celebrating the
creation of a free port at Theodosia (present-day Sebastopol). Those
from 1788 celebrated Potemkin's victory over the Turks at Ochakov,
including a diagram of the battle; another marked the death of
Russia's naval hero Admiral Greig, for whom Catherine personally
composed an epitaph in Tallinn's Protestant cathedral (and ensured
that the inscription tells us so). A year later she also composed the
inscriptions for three more medals honoring Potemkin. The empress
did not overlook older events: in the 1780s she planned a new series
with 235 motifs from Russian history, of which 94 were eventually
struck. Another cluster of medals were struck in 1790 to celebrate
both a land victory over Sweden and the subsequent peace treaty;
Marshal Alexander Suvorov's victories over the Turks; and laws guaranteeing the security of private property. Catherine II's medals were
so numerous that they were occasionally exported in bulk. Complete
sets in silver and bronze went to Vienna in 1767 and again in 1790,
by which time their number had increased to 188; numerous medals
were also given to King Gustav III of Sweden during his state visit in
1777. By the end of her reign, two engravers—one doing designs of

the empress while his partner engraved the subject—had together created no fewer than 250 medals.

Here, as in much else, Catherine II surpassed nearly all of her male predecessors, and her numismatic legacy goes beyond her medals. A Swedish expert has shown how Catherine II's coinage reflected both Russian territorial expansion and the cost of war. After 1774 Russian-made coins replaced Moldavian coins, and Russianized Georgian coins employing imperial double eagles were minted during the last fifteen years of her reign. New mints were opened in Siberia and at the old Genoese port of Kaffa in the newly conquered Crimean peninsula. Paper banknotes were introduced in 1769 during Catherine II's first Turkish war, but they fell rapidly in value and were supplemented by very large and unwieldy copper roubles, which lost half of their face value by the end of her reign. However, Russia's silver coins never diminished in value throughout her entire reign.[41]

To a greater extent than her female predecessors, Catherine II aided other capable women. Maria Theresa did as much as Catherine II to educate schoolgirls (and more to teach them music), and Russian policies on coeducational primary education adapted her Austrian models. Catherine II did more for women's secondary education. Early in her reign she adapted the French model developed by Louis XIV's second wife to create two boarding schools in St. Petersburg, one for girls of noble descent, which lasted until the Bolshevik Revolution, and one for nonnobles. The major statue honoring Catherine II on Nevsky Prospect in St. Petersburg surrounds her with prominent figures from her reign; unlike Maria Theresa's otherwise similar *Denkmal* in Vienna, Catherine II's group includes another woman, Princess Dashkova.

Despite being the sister of Peter III's mistress, Dashkova was a close collaborator at Catherine's coup of 1762, and offers the best example of a talented woman being entrusted with important official positions by a female ruler. After two decades of often strained personal relations, during much of which Dashkova lived abroad as a widow raising her son, Catherine II named her to head the Academy of Sciences in 1782. On first hearing of her appointment, Dashkova wrote a protest that "even God, in making me a woman, has dispensed me from being employed as director of an Academy of Sciences." But she took the oath of office in a cold sweat and served for twelve years in a position that no woman has held since. In 1783 the empress also named Dashkova president of the newly founded Russian Academy of Letters. Like its French prototype of 1635, it was responsible for producing an official dictionary of the Russian language. Under Dashkova's energetic direction a complete six-volume Russian dictionary appeared between 1789 and 1794.[42]

Dashkova reputedly sought even less conventional posts. "It is well known," asserted the notorious memoirist Charles-François-Philibert Masson in 1800, "that [Dashkova] long ago petitioned Catherine to make her a Colonel of the Guards, a task which she doubtless would have filled better than most of those she exercised; but Catherine was too suspicious of a woman who boasted so much of placing her on the throne to offer her such a post. However," Masson concluded sourly, "one more female reign, and we would have seen a girl as an army general and a woman as minister of state." After Catherine II's death, Dashkova defended her patron against such detractors, considering her far superior to Peter I, a "brutal and ignorant tyrant" obsessed by "the ambition to change everything without distinguishing the useful and good from the bad."[43]

Catherine's patronage also benefited Europe's outstanding eighteenth-century woman sculptor, Marie-Anne Collot. The first Frenchwoman to master this art, she worked in St. Petersburg in 1766–78 as an assistant to the French sculptor Falconet, then creating the famous equestrian statue of Peter the Great. Collot's greatest talent lay in sculpting heads (Falconet's weakest point), and in 1770 she made Peter's head. She also did portraits. The empress invited her to court balls and gave her numerous commissions. In 1767 Russia's Academy of Fine Arts made Collot a foreign member. Her work in marble was copied in plaster, terra cotta, and bronze, and a bust of the empress she made in 1768 is in the Hermitage. Collot's portrait of Catherine II with a laurel wreath, celebrating a victory over the Turks in 1769, was copied for medals. A marble bust of the empress in an informal pose with a veil, sculpted from life, was intended as a gift for Voltaire. "Without Catherine II," concludes a recent study, Collot "would never have been able to exhibit her talents as a portraitist, nor her artistic genius."[44]

Catherine II lived very well indeed. In a letter of 1790 to her old friend Baron Frederick Grimm, she described her surroundings in her Winter Palace: "My collections, not including the pictures and Raphael's *Loggia*, consist of 38,000 books, four rooms filled with books, prints, 10,000 engraved stones, about 10,000 drawings, and a natural history section housed in two large rooms; all this is accompanied by a charming theatre . . . to go to and from my room takes three thousand paces, there I walk among a mass of things I like and enjoy, and these winter strolls are what keeps me healthy and active"—she forgot to mention her 16,000 coins and medals.[45] She had already published a three-volume catalogue of her paintings in 1785, which contained information about 2,658 items, including 58 by Rembrandt and 87 by Rubens. A truly attractive side of Catherine II emerges from her rules of conduct for visitors to this palace, which can still be found there (now in Russian and English). They begin with "Leave your rank at the door." Her self-confidence extended to the point of having herself painted in traditional Russian headgear, and even as a casually dressed old lady out walking in her garden with one of her dogs (see fig. 16). One cannot imagine a greater departure from the idealized late portraits of her most illustrious female predecessor, Elizabeth I.

Catherine II's panache extended even to her tableware. Her Green Frog Wedgwood service for fifty people took its name from its original destination, a minor palace outside Petersburg, a place whose Finnish name meant "frog marsh" (Catherine called it *La grenouillière*). Shipped from England to Russia in 1774, it included a 680-piece dinner service and 264-piece dessert service; the decoration of each piece contained both a green frog and a view of some English subject. Wedgwood's plates also had practical advantages: lacking heavy gilding or ornaments, they were surprisingly light and stacked well. Most of them have survived: the Hermitage still holds 1,025 of the original 1,222 views.[46]

As is all too well known, Catherine II's love life kept pace with her other forms of acquisitiveness, even (or especially) in her old age. She was the first female monarch since Urraca in the early twelfth century to acknowledge an illegitimate son, and, like Urraca, she neither disowned him nor showered him with privileges. The two most important men of her reign followed the same pattern as that of her immediate predecessor, Elisabeth: first, a handsome man her own age with little interest in affairs of state (Orlov), then a brilliant younger man full of political advice (Potemkin). But Orlov managed some important public tasks—his service in Moscow during the plague of 1771–72 was exemplary—and Potemkin's record as a statesman completely dwarfs Shuvalov's. Catherine II's reputation for promiscuity rests largely on the officially acknowledged bedmates who followed Potemkin in relatively rapid order; on average, they were almost thirty years younger than she.[47] Her most illustrious female predecessor, Elizabeth I of England, spent all but two of her last sixteen years acting out a romance with a man thirty-three years younger than herself.

Catherine's most important official by far, Potemkin, was also a former lover whom, as noted earlier, she may well have secretly married in 1774. But Potemkin, accompanied by a small harem that included some of his married nieces, exercised his vast responsibilities as a de facto viceroy at the opposite end of the Russian Empire from the woman in St. Petersburg whom he called his mother-sovereign. None of Catherine's other sexual partners exercised any political influence except the last one, Platon Zubov, and her leading biographer suggests that his "rapid rise is the measure of Catherine's own decline."[48]

Catherine's fear and loathing of revolutionary France also darkened the final years of her reign. An enormous distance separates her discussions with Denis Diderot during Pugachev's revolt from the loyalty oath she imposed on all French subjects in her empire twenty years later. She persecuted enlightened critics ruthlessly and urged unified action by European monarchs against revolutionary France but never committed Russia's formidable army to this cause. She also remained sufficiently acute to predict in 1794 that "France could be reborn more powerful than ever if some providential man, adroit and courageous, arose to lead his people and perhaps his century."[49] A few years after her death Napoleon seized power, and the French repaid her by publishing various legends about her sexual behavior.

Before then, the unprecedented turbulence of the French Revolution inspired the last notable eighteenth-century dialogue of the dead, composed by an unidentified French émigré and printed in southern Germany in 1797.[50] As it opens, Charon ferries Catherine II's shadow across alone because she was "a colossus in a century of pygmies" who risked sinking his boat—something he says has happened about twenty times in the previous six thousand years with the very greatest poets, scientists, and statesmen. Catherine II was already called the Semiramis of the North. But in 1797 her semilegendary predecessor, here called the Catherine of Asia, had a positive reputation; as Charon told Catherine, "Semiramis . . . effaced [her usurpation of power] by forty consecutive years of glory." Upon arrival, Catherine, "with the title of a great king," is taken to a special space reserved for sovereigns, where she converses first with Peter the Great. When he asks if his "barbarous and Asiatic subjects have become civilised Europeans," she replies, "At least they now have its laws and will soon have its manners." She boasts, "I have reigned as a woman of genius" and, echoing the author's view of Semiramis, says, "Thirty-four years of clemency and justice are the only abuse I have made from one day of hope and audacity." Omitting Pugachev, she concludes by listing her political and cultural achievements, noting that "one or two of the pages I have furnished to history I would like removed one day." The dialogue's agenda emerges after Catherine II upbraids Louis XVI for seeking approval from his subjects and even offers grudging praise for revolutionary France: "It is impossible to defend a worse cause with more energy and sometimes with more talent." Her dialogue with Frederick II, whom Charon also ferried across alone, mixes astute remarks about flattery with analysis of Europe's current situation. Catherine tells Frederick, "I fear it is we who have prepared all this disorder."

Seventeen years earlier, Catherine herself had composed a more original dialogue of the dead that said a great deal about modern female monarchs. The central hall and ten surrounding rooms of one of her palaces (renamed Chesmensky in commemoration of Russia's great naval victory over Turkey) contained portraits of all reigning European royalty as well as marble bas-reliefs of all Russian rulers from Rurik to Tsarina Elisabeth, as usual omitting Peter III and Ivan VI. Inspired by this setting and informed by personal experience and her vast reading, in 1780 Catherine composed a wickedly malicious private satire mocking both her fellow west European monarchs and her Russian predecessors through imaginary dialogues between their representations.[51]

It began with Maria Theresa complaining to her son Joseph II about the scandalous behavior of her daughters, among whom Marie Antoinette was far from the worst. The Habsburg matriarch then complains that Catherine II's palace "needs a crucifix. My old eyes are accustomed to always having one around, and I've always put my entire hopes in the miracles of Christ Jesus." Joseph II, with whom Catherine got along much better, comments, "Yes, mom, but nevertheless we've still lost Silesia. All we need is money, troops, and a good general to work the miracle that will get it back for us." His antique mother then comments, "I want to die in peace. Another war would be a burden on my conscience, and I can't decide anything without asking my confessor. Besides, my good friend Empress Elisabeth is no longer on earth, except as a medal." On this cue, Catherine II's predecessor remarks, "And this medal, I believe, is as unflattering as every other extant portrait of me." Their dialogue spins along, with Elisabeth remarking, "Empress is a title that includes the privilege of doing whatever you like without being bothered by it," to which Maria Theresa responds, "That's just what I've often thought, but I only said so in secret." Elisabeth is then mocked by her predecessor Anna for wasting her authority on trivialities. Catherine concluded the satire by mocking her illustrious contemporary Frederick II, to whom she had previously admitted that she felt herself inferior as a ruler.[52] Her distant Russian predecessor St. Alexander Nevsky tells Frederick II, "I never undertook any unjust wars." When Frederick insists, "Let's see more closely how much merit hides behind your beard," St. Alexander replies,

"My dear colleague, it's not enough to be clever," adding that the Prussian philosopher wastes his time composing mediocre French poetry and doesn't know him "any better than you know German literature." Catherine II also dropped hints about Frederick's rumored homosexuality. She expected, correctly, that these remarks would remain unknown for a century after her death.

Catherine II always managed several projects simultaneously, and some were left unfinished because of her death. Militarily, a Russian army commanded by the brother of her current lover was at Baku, preparing to invade Persia. Domestically, she had been constructing a building to house the newly created Imperial Public Library on the widest boulevard of her capital, close to its busiest shopping complex. Pace Shakespeare's Julius Caesar, the evil that women rulers do need not live after them, nor is the good interred with their bones. After Catherine II's death Russia's army was immediately recalled from Persia, while both her shopping center and her national library continue to fulfill their original purposes on Nevsky Prospect. Catherine II was also the only female ruler of Europe who kept all government business out of the hands of her son and heir. Rumors abounded that the old empress wished to pass over Grand Duke Paul in favor of her beloved older grandson Alexander, whom she had trained from infancy to be a model ruler; but for once Europe's customary rules of succession held firm in Russia. Paul's first public act was to rebury his father at a solemn state funeral and place his bones next to his mother's, where they rest today. Another of his early acts was to decree a law of succession that explicitly barred any woman from ever inheriting Russia's throne. An era ended in 1796: Europe would not see another woman governing a major state for almost two centuries.

# 8

# Female Rule After 1800
## Constitutions and Popular Culture

Republics are as detrimental to [women's] ambition as monarchies are favorable to them.

—Alexandre-Joseph-Pierre de Ségur, *Women, Their Condition and Influence in Society*

## What Happened to Female Rule in Europe After 1800?

The most important change to female rule in Europe after 1800 is that opportunities for women to control governments—the essential thread of this story—ceased for a very long time after Catherine II died. At the same time, revolutionary France, the enemy of all monarchs, succeeded in durably smudging the posthumous image of the last and most spectacular female ruler of the old regime—not by denying her political accomplishments, but by depicting her as a sexual monster even more depraved than the daughter of Maria Theresa whom they had guillotined. The greatest damage was inflicted by a Swiss writer named Charles-François-Philibert Masson, who had served in Russia during the final decade of Catherine II's reign before being expelled soon after her death. When his *Secret Memoirs on Russia* first appeared anonymously at Paris, the author (now a French citizen) had just published a long and deservedly ignored epic poem praising the military prowess of democratic Switzerland. However, his *Secret Memoirs* enjoyed great notoriety. Rapidly translated into German, English, and Dutch, it had several reprintings after Masson had been exposed as the author, and it laid the groundwork for Catherine's durable posthumous reputation as sexually insatiable.[1]

Masson began by praising Catherine II as "the most powerful and most famous woman who has occupied a throne since Semiramis" and predicted that "her sex, giving a new context to the great qualities which she deployed on her throne, will put her above any comparison in history." Catherine, he thought, had surpassed even Europe's best-known male absolutist: "The dazzle of her reign, the magnificence of her court, her institutions, her monuments, her wars, are for Russia what the century of Louis XIV was for Europe." But her achievement was greater because "the French made Louis glorious, while Catherine made Russia glorious." Masson's preface ended with the assessment that "she astonished the world by her various talents, wrote like a sage, and reigned like a king." However, the prevailing atmosphere in France at this time was extremely hostile both to autocracy and to women in politics, and the author's praise for her vanished quickly, never to return. Refusing to decide "if she was truly great," he expressed grave reservations about Catherine II's place in history. "Usurping a throne which she wished to keep," he continued, "she was obliged to protect her accomplices, who bought impunity through their crimes. A foreigner in the empire where she reigned, she tried to identify herself with the nation by adopting and even flattering its tastes and prejudices. She sometimes knew how to reward but never knew how to punish, and it was only by letting her authority be abused that she was able to conserve it. She had two passions," Masson continued, "her love for men, which degenerated into libertinage, and her love for glory, which degenerated into vanity." The first, he admitted, "never dominated her, although she often prostituted her glory and her body," while the second "made her undertake things which were rarely accomplished."[2]

Masson devoted his next chapter to examining Catherine's sex life. Although "all the Russian empresses and the majority of women

with genuine independence have all had male favorites and lovers
. . . only Catherine II, realizing the ancient fables of a queen who
subordinated the love, sentiment, and modesty of her sex to her
imperious physical needs, profited from her power to give the world
a unique and scandalous example." Behaving rather like Louis XIV
(but with the sexes reversed), she "had the impudence to make
[sexual service] into a specific court function with an official apartment, titles, honors, prerogatives, . . . and of all the offices at court,
this one was fulfilled most scrupulously." Masson concluded by
trying to make her a lesbian: "At the end of her life, Catherine
became so masculinized that she required women: her tribadism
with Dashkova, Protasova and Brantiska was known everywhere,
and the last favorite only served to hold the candles."[3] Despite such
grotesque exaggerations, some of Masson's mud stuck, pushing
Catherine II's posthumous reputation from panegyrics toward
pornography.

After 1800 Catherine the Great had no female successors for
the simple reason that Europe's principal autocratic states now
excluded women from ruling. The Russian Empire remained autocratic until 1917 (and Russia remained so long afterward), but
Catherine's son ensured that it now had its own version of female
exclusion. The second German Empire also adopted female exclusion at its creation in 1871, influencing its imperial Japanese ally to
act similarly in 1889. Meanwhile, nineteenth-century western Europe
preferred constitutional monarchies, dominated by representative
assemblies which denied electoral rights to women. This situation
prolonged the record of Europe's old republics, including Venice, the
Swiss Confederation, and the Dutch, all as totally masculine as the
College of Cardinals or the Arab Ulama. Writing at the same time as
Masson, the Vicomte de Ségur observed that republics were far more
detrimental to politically ambitious women than monarchies; two
centuries later, academic scholarship confirms that republics
continue to restrict female political participation significantly more
than constitutional monarchies.[4]

As monarchs ceased to govern arbitrarily, women's dynastic
position was at first unclear. In 1830 a new west European constitu-

tional monarchy, Belgium, adopted the French Salic law; but in the same year, Spain's Bourbon monarch replaced his kingdom's version of it with a Spanish Pragmatic Sanction. During the next decade three young women inherited European monarchies. Unlike their youthful medieval predecessors, each of them had at least nine children, but, like nearly all of their youthful medieval predecessors, they did not govern their kingdoms. Their fates differed greatly. Queen Victoria of Great Britain reigned far longer than any of her female predecessors, while Maria II of Portugal died at thirty-four and Isabel II of Spain was compelled to flee abroad at the age of thirty-eight.

At her father's death in 1833, Isabel II, the three-year-old heiress, became "by the grace of God Queen of Castile, León, Aragon, the Two Sicilies, Jerusalem, Navarre, Granada," and much else, including "the Eastern and Western Indies and the Islands and Lands of the Ocean." Four years later, during a civil war against the adherents of her paternal uncle, who opposed female inheritance, Spain acquired a constitution, and its child monarch became "Queen of the Spains by the grace of God and the Constitution of the Spanish monarchy." In 1843 Isabel II was declared of age and required to marry a first cousin, who proved personally disastrous and politically useless. Finally forced into exile in 1868 after bearing many children of dubious paternity, she abdicated in 1870 and died at Paris in 1904. Maria II of Portugal, born in 1819, was twice made a constitutional monarch by her father. Restored to her throne in 1834, she became Europe's first female monarch since the fourteenth century to die from postnatal complications after giving birth to her eleventh child in 1853.[5]

The better-known and better-educated contemporary of these two monarchs, Victoria, inherited the British monarchy at the age of eighteen in 1837 and lived until 1901. Hers was the longest female reign in European history, and during it she became Europe's first female monarch promoted to the rank of empress (of India, in 1876). However politically astute she was, Victoria possessed much less personal authority than her constitutional predecessor, Queen Anne, who could still veto legislation and exercise supernatural powers by touching her subjects for the king's evil. Moreover, provisions of German Salic law removed Britain's last continental possession by preventing Victoria from inheriting the kingdom of Hanover, which had been united with the English crown for over 120 years. Like Isabel II, Victoria married her first cousin—with the significant difference that Victoria chose him herself. Like Maria II, Victoria found an extremely satisfactory consort by marrying a nephew of King Leopold I of Belgium, who was also Victoria's uncle and her first political mentor. Victoria survived five assassination attempts in the first dozen years of her reign and had nine children. A recent poll ranked her as Britain's eighteenth most popular personality.

Women's inheritance rights in Europe's constitutional monarchies have increased steadily after the ten-year-old Wilhelmina became queen of the Netherlands in 1890. In this part of the former Low Countries, three women have now reigned continuously for more than 120 years, which probably constitutes a world record. A more revealing example is Luxembourg, the only grand duchy in the European Union, which detached itself from personal union with the Netherlands in 1890 by claiming to be subject to Salic law. But when its first autonomous grand duke had six daughters and no sons, Luxembourg amended its succession rules seventeen years later, and two sisters ruled it from 1912 to 1964. The process has accelerated recently. Sweden approved female succession to its crown (for the third time) in 1980. Belgium repealed its version of the Salic law in 1991. Spain's restored monarchy adopted male-preference primogeniture in 1978 but changed to gender-free primogeniture in 2005. In 2009 Denmark, whose current female monarch is its first in more than five centuries, voted 85 percent in favor of genderless royal primogeniture. Nowhere in present-day Europe do royal inheritance laws discriminate against women, although the other three traditional guidelines—legitimate birth, direct descent, and primogeniture—remain in place.

Unlike their divine-right predecessors, Europe's constitutional monarchs do not govern. Its modern governments are parliamentary and elective, and long after their twentieth-century enfranchisement throughout Europe women rarely hold leadership positions within them. Nor do they in the rest of the world. Although the world's first democratically elected female prime minister would govern Sri Lanka more than once after 1960, and a few others have followed, no woman made a serious presidential bid in the United States until 2008 and no woman headed any European government between the death of Catherine II and the election of Britain's Margaret Thatcher. If women increasingly occupy cabinet positions in European governments, old prejudices persist against entrusting them with responsibility for military matters; a sample of 371 women holding ministerial portfolios between 1968 and 1992 in fifteen European parliamentary countries put defense at the very bottom of the list (under 1 percent), below even prime ministers (1.3 percent).[6]

Can one find any similarities between absolutist female heads of government before 1800 and their democratic female successors after 1960? Although the type of evidence normally used by historians makes it difficult to obtain insights into personal and intellectual styles, an interesting similarity appears if one compares the autobiographical writings of two women who exercised the ordinarily male task of kingship, Christina of Sweden and Catherine II (something none of their male counterparts ever did with comparable candor), with the autobiographical sketch submitted by Europe's first female prime minister to *Who's Who*. Even though Catherine II's father had been a political nonentity and Christina had repudiated her father's deeply cherished religion, both female autocrats of the old regime retrospectively idealized their fathers, with whom they had had relatively little personal contact. On the other hand, both of their mothers got short shrift and tended to be seen as obstacles to their political development. Centuries later, Thatcher mentioned her father's rather modest political achievements but never even named her mother.

Beyond this example, other possible similarities emerge by juxtaposing some of Catherine II's more candid self-evaluations with Blema Steinberg's elaborately calibrated psychological profiles of three twentieth-century female prime ministers. One is that both the eighteenth-century autocrat and her recent female epigones were formidable workaholics. In composing a brief epitaph for herself at the age of fifty-nine, Catherine II mentioned, as noted, that "work was easy for her," and there is a paper mountain of corroborative evidence. Steinberg found similarly exceptional capacities for sustained and focused effort among her political subjects. On the other hand, however exceptional their political careers, neither the autocrat of the old regime nor her twentieth-century successors could be described as deep thinkers. In a letter written at the age of sixty-two, Catherine II, who had already dabbled in more different intellectual pursuits than any other ruler, male or female, remarked, "I have never believed that I have the creative spirit" and added, "I have come to know many people in whom I perceived, without envy or jealousy, considerably more intellect than I have." Steinberg reached the essentially similar conclusion that none of her three women possessed creativity or originality.[7]

These are not the only possible similarities which might be extrapolated backward from evidence emerging in recent times. For example, the behaviors by which women who exercise supreme authority have cultivated loyalty from their closest male subordinates do not seem to have changed much over the past few centuries. Neither has the rapid decisiveness with which female heads of government react when confronted with dangerous opposition changed much since Mary Tudor learned about Jane Grey's coronation or Catherine II learned about Pugachev's impersonation of her dead husband.

## Modern Cultural Perceptions of Female Rulers

Cultural ambivalence about whether a successful female ruler could exhibit appropriate female behavior persisted far into the post-1830 constitutional era. Designing an educational program for his kingdom's ten-year-old heiress Maria da Gloria in 1829, a Portuguese reformer noted that "a princess who must reign by herself is a female in fact but a male in law, so her education must offset nature and diminish as far as possible the *woman* in order to form the *Queen*." Not long afterward, Queen Victoria observed, "We women . . . are not fitted to reign" and characterized her most famous predecessor, Elizabeth I, as a good queen but a bad woman.[8]

Successful women rulers from Hatshepsut to Thatcher have been rulers first and women second. However, popular representations of them have always reversed these aspects because romance sells infinitely better than political power in female hands. The cultural reduction of female rulers to women driven more by passion than by political ambition has a long history. Even Zenobia of Palmyra, for whom love interests had to be invented, became the tragic heroine of a French play by 1647 and of a Venetian opera by 1694.[9] When seeking historical subjects, Neapolitan composers avoided their native city's colorful fourteenth-century female ruler Joanna I, whose career furnished material for several plots, in favor of safely distant ones with romantic potential. During four years in Russia at the invitation of Catherine II, Domenico Cimarosa composed an opera about Cleopatra and Marc Antony which premiered at St. Petersburg in 1789.

It was a safe choice, as no other early historical woman ruler can begin to rival Cleopatra VII's enduring popularity. Mary Hamer's assertion that through her appropriation by Augustan Rome "the status of Cleopatra [is] a founding myth in Western culture" hits close to the mark. In 1907, in a survey that not only preceded film but also overlooked cycles of tapestries celebrating her, a German scholar recorded that since 1540 Europeans had created no fewer than seventy-seven plays, forty-five operas, and five ballets about her.[10] Regardless of the cultural medium, Cleopatra is almost invariably depicted as devoting her entire attention to her romantic relationships with two famous Roman men. Although she had four children, she is rarely shown as a mother, and she is almost never shown performing her basic task of governing Egypt. The power of Roman propaganda has ensured that, after more than two thousand years, there is still only one image showing Cleopatra simultaneously as both mother and monarch. It was almost certainly Cleopatra herself who had it put on the wall of an Egyptian temple.

Medieval Georgia's golden age heroine, Queen Tamar, provides a less familiar but equally instructive example of the modern cultural reduction of a highly successful female ruler to a *femme fatale*. After Russia had absorbed her old kingdom, Mikhail Lermontov, a major

Russian poet fascinated by the "exotic" Caucasus, composed a poem about Tamar in 1841, pasting her onto an old Georgian legend about a destructively seductive princess living in the mountains. Although Lermontov's depiction of the Georgian queen was pure fantasy, it inspired a nineteenth-century Austrian author, J. P. Fallmerayer, to call her the Caucasian Semiramis. In 1903 Knut Hamsun, a Norwegian playwright and future Nobel laureate, twisted Lermontov's portrait into a commentary on the new woman of the 1890s. Nine years later the *Ballets russes* restored Lermontov's temptress in a lavish French production with Tamar and her entourage decked out in Oriental costumes. Outside of her remote native land, no one remembers her as a saint.

A century ago a new art form, cinema, began to provide what has become the most influential source of public images of bygone female rulers. Most films about Europe's female monarchs, often starring famous actresses, were produced long before any woman had reemerged at the head of a European government. Two short early dramatic films about Europe's best-known female monarchs came from France, the pioneer of female monarchical exclusion. The first, in 1909, featured Catherine the Great and the female impostor known as Tarakanova; three years later, with Sarah Bernhardt in the title role, another film retold Elizabeth I's affair with Essex. In addition to featuring in many later films, since the 1960s female rulers have also been subjects of a closely related genre, television miniseries. As in operas built around legendary or authentic female rulers, the need for dramatic effect has usually prevented a comfortable fit between history and cinema or, subsequently, television. The primary rule governing popular depictions of female rulers in Western culture continues to apply: royal romance is endlessly marketable, but women shown exercising political power can make audiences uncomfortable.

Cleopatra VII continues to inspire more artistic portrayals in various genres than any more modern European female ruler. Films about her began in America in 1912 and have inspired some of the most spectacularly lavish productions. The second, made in 1917, ranks among Hollywood's most expensive early films, reportedly costing half a million dollars and employing two thousand people. The star, the famous vamp Theda Bara, wore several fantastic costumes, but because some of them were considered too obscene to be shown after the mid-1920s only a few fragments now survive. Another large-budget Hollywood version was made by Cecil B. De Mille in 1934. An even more elaborate version, made in 1963 and starring Elizabeth Taylor, remains one of the most expensive films ever made. Cleopatra VII remains culturally polyvalent: a South Indian Tamil film about her was made in 2005, and a Brazilian film followed in 2007.

Ranking just behind Cleopatra in cinematic Orientalism is a female ruler who remains nameless. Four years after Hollywood's first big-budget *Cleopatra* came *The Queen of Sheba*, by the same director but with a different leading actress. It reportedly boasted 671 scenes, a cast of thousands, and 500 camels; long before *Ben-Hur*, it even had a thrilling chariot race—between two women wearing skimpy costumes. No known copies of any reel from this film survive. No major remake occurred until 1959, another lavish production with little cultural depth. Unlike Cleopatra, this anonymous female monarch has been featured in two well-researched television documentaries in 1998 and 2002.

Some films about non-European women rulers were not intended for Western audiences and seem more authentic, not only because their historical subjects were genuine but also because both their producers and leading actresses came from the original countries. Yet *authentic* must not be confused with *historically accurate*. Within this subgroup, Wu Ze-tian of China deserves special mention. The first film about her, a black-and-white Chinese version made in 1939, was followed by others made in Taiwan (1960) and Hong Kong (1963). However, her most spectacular filmed reincarnations have appeared serialized on television, which seems better adapted for depicting the most durable early woman ruler (counting her years of regency, Wu Ze-tian ties Elizabeth I at forty-five years) and the only one who began as a low-ranking concubine. For such reasons, a televised series about her made in 2003 runs over twenty hours.[11]

Both thirteenth-century Muslim women rulers have also been commemorated cinematically because the states they governed developed flourishing film industries in the twentieth century. In

India, a black-and-white film from 1924 entitled *Razia Begum* preceded *Razia Sultana* in 1961. A more recent Hindi film, *Razia Sultan* (1983), offers a typical Bollywood plot based on her imaginary love affair with an Ethiopian-born court official. In Egypt, a production from 1935 entitled *Chagarrat al-Dorr* starred a Lebanese actress.

Because of the need for a romantic focus, some of Europe's more important early female kings, including its first important late medieval royal heiress, Joanna I of Naples, and the best-known and most politically successful among them, Isabel of Castile, have never inspired either feature films or lengthy television documentaries. However, their most significant early modern successor, Elizabeth I, has inspired several of both and undeniably enjoys an optimal fit between history and film. Her biography offers a rare mixture of political authority, exercised with exceptional wit and flair, and romance without marriage, thereby offering an irresistible role for actresses to exhibit their talents in apparent conflicts of interest between love and political duty, interspersed with scenes of straightforward political leadership at dramatic moments—although they nearly always include a face-to-face meeting with her rival, Mary Queen of Scots, something that never happened.

As in her biographies, Elizabeth I has been portrayed in cinema and on television, mainly in her own country. After Sarah Bernhardt, Bette Davis played her twice in Hollywood films (1939 and 1955) before Cate Blanchett did so more recently (1998 and 2007). Elizabeth I has also been commemorated in opera: in 1953 Benjamin Britten updated Rossini's version for the coronation of England's second Elizabeth. England's film industry has been supplemented by high-quality public television, the BBC giving Elizabeth I an early television debut in 1968. The present century has seen another BBC television miniseries about her. Major award-winning productions, most recently starring Helen Mirren (2007), continue to feature her.

Elizabeth's immediate female predecessor, Mary Tudor, remains politically incorrect, putting England's first autonomous female monarch off-limits for British film and television producers, whereas Elizabeth's easily romanticized Scots cousin Mary Stuart, generally considered a political failure, has received considerable media attention. But Mary Queen of Scots consistently follows her English cousin in media treatments. An American playwright, Maxwell Anderson, wrote a play about her in 1933, three years after writing one about Elizabeth; Mary Stuart's featured BBC television debut (1971) similarly came three years after Elizabeth's.

Only one noteworthy film has been made about Europe's other unmarried female king, when Hollywood cast its greatest Swedish actress, Greta Garbo, as Christina in 1933. Significantly, although the historical Christina utterly lacked Garbo's dazzling beauty, *Queen Christina* was a romantic comedy, a genre avoided whenever English-speaking filmmakers tackle England's Queen Bess. In the film Garbo not only portrayed a highly intelligent woman who devoted considerable time and effort to the task of ruling her kingdom, but even wore male clothing and high boots in many early scenes. The Hollywood plot then reduced Christina's attraction to Catholicism, the principal reason for her early abdication, to an accidental encounter with a handsome Spaniard. Their affair dominates the film's last half, with Garbo changing into female dress. In this way the film stood history on its head, since the probably bisexual Christina habitually wore male clothing only *after* her abdication.

Europe's most important female monarchs who enjoyed both satisfactory marriages and politically successful reigns have resisted cinematic treatments because patriotic epics cannot expect to draw large audiences if they star women with several children. Only the extraordinary local popularity of Maria Theresa explains why Austria's greatest twentieth-century actress, Paula Wessely, once made a film about her. In 1951, trying to restore a public image badly tarnished by Nazi collaboration, Wessely used her own studio and whatever authentic locales and opera costumes were available in occupied Vienna to produce and star in a film entitled *Maria Theresa*. As it opens, viewers see a middle-aged matronly empress governing the Habsburg Empire for several minutes before its plot develops around her husband's only known extramarital affair.

The worst fit between the film industry and female rulers afflicts Russia's eighteenth-century empresses. Their reigns offer abundant material for many cinematic plots, but they have become stateless because postrevolutionary Russia's deservedly famous film industry ignored them. By default, therefore, only foreign actresses have portrayed them in various cultural distortions of the Westernization of Russia, and the worst situation of all affects the most important Westernizer, Catherine II. The cinematic career of the Semiramis of the North has been as extensive (although not as expensive) as that of the Semiramis of the Nile. Between the Bolshevik Revolution and the end of the twentieth century, Catherine II has played a more or less central role in at least twelve films, none of them made in Russia. This German-born princess has been interpreted by two famous German actresses, Marlene Dietrich (1934) and Hildegard Knef (1963), and by America's Bette Davis. The American comedienne Mae West had the screenplay from 1934 rewritten as a stage play that ran for 191 Broadway performances in 1944–45 but was never filmed. Given Catherine's widespread reputation as a nymphomaniac, it seems inevitable that she also became Europe's only woman ruler to be featured in a pornographic film.[12]

By far the best filmed interpretation of Catherine II has been provided by British television, with excellent historical commentary from such leading experts as Isabel de Madariaga. Nevertheless, precisely because Catherine II offers such an extraordinary and extreme combination of political and sexual liberation, her potential as a major authority figure for Western women has yet to be adequately tapped by commercial media. This woman achieved supreme rule by overthrowing and imprisoning her husband shortly after giving birth to an illegitimate child—and later wrote the basic account of her coup herself!—and she exited public life thirty-four glorious years later after publicly flaunted sexual affairs with a series of handsome men some thirty years younger than she. The personal history of Catherine II so far exceeds conventional parameters of appropriate behavior for politically ambitious women that even the most adventurous producers, directors, and actresses dare not confront either the beginnings or the end of her reign. At least with respect to women as heads of state, twenty-first century modernity lags behind eighteenth-century reality.

# Notes

Chapter 1. *Early Female Sovereigns in Global Perspective*

1. Jean Blondel, *World Leaders: Heads of Government in the Post-War World* (London, 1980), 116.

2. Jacob Lassner, *Demonizing the Queen of Sheba: Boundaries of Gender and Culture in Postbiblical Judaism and Medieval Islam* (Chicago, 1993).

3. Anna Maria Capomacchia, *Semiramis: Una femminilità ribaltata* (Rome, 1986), 13.

4. Quotes from Joan R. Piggott, "The Last Classical Female Sovereign: Koken-Shotoku Tenno," in Dorothy Ko, JaHyun Kim Haboush, and Joan Piggott, eds., *Women and Confucian Cultures in Premodern China, Korea, and Japan* (Berkeley, 2003), 48; Richard Stoneman, *Palmyra and Its Empire: Zenobia's Revolt against Rome* (Ann Arbor, 1992), 6, 119; Gavin R. G. Hambly, "Becoming Visible," in Gavin Hambly, ed., *Women in the Medieval Islamic World* (New York, 1998), 9; and Abou'lkasim Firdousi, *Le livre des rois,* trans. Jules Mohl (Paris, 1838–78), 7:337.

5. Götz Schregle, *Die Sultanin von Ägypten: Sagat ad-Durr in der Arabischen Geschichtschreibung und Literatur* (Wiesbaden, 1961).

6. Duane Roller, *Cleopatra: A Biography* (Oxford University Press, 2010), 106–7, 179–83; also Jonathan Williams, "Imperial Style and the Coins of Cleopatra and Mark Antony," in Susan Walker and Sally-Ann Ashton, eds., *Cleopatra Reassessed* (British Museum, 2003), 87–94.

7. Pat Southern, *Empress Zenobia: Palmyra's Rebel Queen* (London, 2008).

8. Suggested in December 689 by a high-ranking official, the son of one of her cousins, Zetian characters were required for official documents throughout the empire and remained in use during her personal reign but were abandoned immediately after her abdication. Estimates of the number of new ideographic characters involved range from twelve to nineteen, and the first change affected Wu's own name: see R. W. L. Guisso, *Wu Tse T'ien and the Politics of Legitimation in T'ang China* (Bellingham, Wash., 1978), 221–22; useful examples adorn chapter headings in Jonathan Clements, *Wu: The Chinese Empress Who Schemed, Seduced and Murdered Her Way to Become a Living God* (Stroud, UK, 2007).

9. Judith Herrin, *Women in Purple: Rulers of Medieval Byzantium* (Princeton, 2001).

10. Firdousi, *Livre des rois,* 7:340–43; Jenny Rose, in Hambly, *Medieval Islamic World,* 43–45; Antonio Panaino, "Women and Kingship: Some remarks about the enthronisation of Queen Boran and her sister Azarmigduxt," in Josef Wiesehöfer and Philip Huyse, eds., *Eran und Aneran. Studien zu den Beziehungen zwischen dem Sasanidenreich und der Mittelmeerwelt* (Stuttgart, 2006), 221–40; H. M. Malek and V. S. Curtis, "History of the Coinage of the Sassanian Queen Boran (A.D. 629–31)," in *Numismatic Chronicle* 158 (1998), 113–29.

11. Fatima Mernissi, *The Forgotten Queens of Islam* (Cambridge, 1993), 115–38; Farhad Daftary, "Sayyida Hurra," in Hambly, *Medieval Islamic World,* 117–30. No coins are known.

12. After Suiko (Tenno 33), Tenno 35 ruled for three years, Tenno 37 for six-plus years, Tenno 41 for eleven years, Tenno 43 for eight years, Tenno 44 for a few months, Tenno 46 for nine years, and Tenno 48 for six years: see Joan R. Piggott, *The Emergence of Japanese Kingship* (Stanford, 1997).

13. Piggott, "Koken-Shotoku Tenno," 47–74, esp. 52–54.

14. It still stands in her old capital of Gyeongju in South Korea: Nha Il-Seong, "Silla's Cheomseongdae," in *Korea Journal* 41 (2001), 269–81.

15. Yung-Chung Kim, ed., *Women of Korea: A History from Ancient Times to 1945* (Seoul, 1976), 25–30.

16. David Lang, *Studies in the Numismatic History of Georgia in Transcaucasia* (New York, 1955), 22–27, 28–33; Stephen H. Rapp, "Coinage of T'amar, Sovereign of Georgia in Caucasia," *Le Muséon* 106 (1993), 309–30. In Europe, no coin of joint rulers placed the wife's name first until 1566.

17. Antony Eastmond, *Royal Imagery in Medieval Georgia* (University Park, Penn., 1998), 93–184; M. Canard, "Les reines de Georgie dans l'histoire et la légende musulmanes," *Revue des Etudes islamiques* 42 (1969), 3–20.

18. Minhaj Siraj Juzjani, *Tabakat-i-Nasiri,* ed. and trans. H. G. Raverty, 2 vols. (London, 1881–87), 1:637–38; Peter Jackson, "Sultan Raddiya bint Iltutmish," in Hambly, *Medieval Islamic World,* 181–97; for her coins, Stan Goron and J. P. Goenka, *The Coins of the Indian Sultanates* (New Delhi, 2001), 26–27, 153–54.

19. It is approved by 'Ismat ad-Din, the title on her coins: printed by Schregle, *Sultanin von Ägypten,* 161–65.

20. Peter Jackson, *The Seventh Crusade, 1244–1254: Sources and Documents* (Aldershot, 2007), offers the best recent introduction to these events.

21. Ibid., 153. A Victorian expert noted that "the inscriptions [on her coins] are unparalleled in Oriental numismatics": S. Lane Poole, *The Coinage of Egypt (AH 358–922)* (London, 1879), xvii–xxi.

22. Jackson, *Seventh Crusade,* 216.

23. Hambly, *Medieval Islamic World,* 18; Mirnissi, *Forgotten Queens,* 99–100.

24. G. Gyorffy, *King St. Stephen of Hungary* (Boulder, 1991), 45; Miriam Yalom, *Birth of the Chess Queen* (New York, 2004).

25. Therese Martin, *Queen as King: Politics and Architectural Propaganda in Twelfth-Century Spain* (Leiden, 2006), 198–207 (at 199).

26. Maria del Carmen Pallares Mendez, *La Reina Urraca* (San Sebastian, 2006), 12, 105–7; Elena Lobato Yanes, *Urraca I: La Corte Castellano-Leonesa en el siglo XII* (Palencia, 2000), 126; Martin, *Queen as King,* 29.

27. Marsilio Cassotti, *D. Teresa: A primeira rainha de Portugal* (Lisbon, 2008).

28. Charles Beem, *The Lioness Roared* (New York, 2006), 25–62. On her seal and charters, see Elizabeth Danbury, "Queens and Powerful Women: Image and Authority," in N. Adams, J. Cherry, and J. Robinson, eds., *Good Impressions: Image and Authority in Medieval Seals* (London, 2008), 18.

29. Joyce Tyldesley, *Hatchepsut: The Female Pharaoh* (London, 1996), 103–4.

30. Antonino Forte, *Political Propaganda and Ideology in China at the End of the Seventh Century* (Naples, 1976), 204, 268 (quotes). Two authentic accounts from Wu's time, now in the British Library, were finally identified as such after World War II.

On Wu's use of this sutra, compare Guisso, *Wu and the Politics of Legitimation,* 37–46, 66–68, with Clements, *Wu,* 134–37. Three centuries later an official Chinese history would claim that Wu had it fabricated: see Nghiem Toan and Louis Ricaud, *Wou Tsö-T'ien d'après le texte du Nouveau livre des T'ang* (Saigon, 1958–59), 117.

31. Cynthia Herrup, "The King's Two Genders," *Journal of British Studies* 45 (2006), 493–510; Louis Montrose, *The Subject of Elizabeth* (Chicago, 2006), 201–3, 234–5, 245–6.

## Chapter 2. Europe's Female Sovereigns, 1300–1800

1. Leslie P. Peirce, *The Imperial Harem* (Oxford, 1993), 274. The British Museum has over two dozen of Sati Beg's coins from several mints; see Stephen Album, *Checklist of Islamic Coins,* 2d ed. (Santa Rosa, Calif., 1998), 108; Fatima Mernissi, *The Forgotten Queens of Islam* (Cambridge, 1993), 85–6, 107–10.

2. This section summarizes my article "Gendered Sovereignty: Numismatics and Female Rule, 1300–1800," in *Journal of Interdisciplinary History* 41 (spring 2011): 533–64.

3. Alphonse de Witte, *Histoire monétaire des Comtes de Louvain, Ducs de Brabant et Marquis du Saint-Empire Romain,* 3 vols. (Antwerp, 1894–99), 1:156. As late as 1498 another female ruler of a (temporarily) autonomous duchy, Anne of Brittany, issued equally daring gold coins depicting her seated and enthroned.

4. Maximilian's name nowhere appears on the 92 gold and silver coins from her five-year reign in the Belgian Royal Library, or on any of her more than 150 silver coins from four of her provincial mints possessed by the American Numismatic Society (ANS); her annual averages surpass those of either her male predecessor or her male successor.

5. The ANS holds over 90 coins from their joint reign (1598–1621), but only 28 of them are silver and only one *albertin* (named for her husband) is gold.

6. Margaret and her successors kept Norway's mints closed for a century after 1387; Danish coins had apparently resumed by 1400.

7. 1507–15 and 1518–30, 1531–55, 1559–67, 1598–1633, 1725–41, and 1780–93. Maria Theresa's younger sister also governed it jointly with her new husband for much of 1744 before dying in childbirth. Jonathan Israel, *The Dutch Republic 1477–1806* (Oxford, 1995), 981–83, sketches the government of the region's most obscure female regent, Maria Elisabeth, an older sister of Emperor Charles VI.

8. David Chambers, *Discours de la legitime succession des femmes aux possessions de leurs parens et du gouvernement des princesses aux Empires et Royaumes* (Paris, 1579), 16.

9. Isabel de Madariaga, *Russia in the Age of Catherine the Great* (reprint, London, 2002), 153 (emphasis added).

10. See page 82 for a fuller discussion.

11. Her candidacy generated 267 letters, now preserved in France; Waclaw Uruszczak, *Polonica w korespondencji królowej szwedzkiej Krystyny w zbiorach Bibliothèque Interuniversitaire w Montpellier* (Cracow, 2001).

12. Simone de Beauvoir, *The Second Sex,* trans. H. M. Parshley (New York, 1953), 130.

13. Alison Weir, *Mary, Queen of Scots and the Murder of Lord Darnley* (London, 2003), 77, 99, 388.

14. Albertus Magnus, *Quaestiones de animalibus,* book 10, q. 4.

15. At her formal entry into Ghent in 1599, the sovereign archduchess Isabel Clara Eugenia was girded with a traditional sword: see Ruth Betegón Diez, *Isabel Clara Eugenia: Infanta de España y soberana de Flandes* (Barcelona, 2004), 99.

16. Tarsicio de Azcona, *Isabel la Católica: vida y reinado* (Madrid, 2002), 181; Christian Steeb, "Kaiser Franz I. und seine ablehnende Haltung gegenüber der Stiftung des königlich ungarischen St.-Stephans-Ordens," in H. Dikowitsch, ed., *Barock–Blütezeit der europäischen Ritterorden* (St. Polten, 2000), 35: *per fictionem juris virtute pragmaticae sanctionis die qualiatem masculinam anererbet hat.*

17. Louis Montrose, *The Subject of Elizabeth* (Chicago, 2006), 231.

18. Later in his sixty-year reign, George III suffered a major breakdown and was replaced by his heir from 1810 until 1820.

19. John H. Elliott, ed., *The World of the Favorite* (New Haven, 1999), includes Elizabeth I and Leicester.

20. For analogous reasons, this consideration helps explain why no French king or Holy Roman emperor married one of his own subjects.

## Chapter 3. Difficult Beginnings

1. Armin Wolf, "Reigning Queens in Medieval Europe: When, Where, and Why?" in John Carmi Parsons, ed., *Medieval Queenship* (New York, 1993), 169–88. The 1:8 ratio also holds between 1600 and 1800 among the far fewer but larger monarchies permitting female successions.

2. Charlotte of Cyprus bequeathed her claims to her husband's Savoyard relatives; Blanca of Navarre bequeathed hers to her ex-husband, Enrique IV of Castile; and Juana *la Beltraneja* of Castile bequeathed hers to her long-dead husband's Portuguese heirs.

3. S. Herreros Lopetegui, "Navarra en la órbita francesa," in *Historia de Navarra* (Pamplona, 1993), 1:193–208.

4. The relevant document is the only one of seventeen surviving from his reign in Navarre written in French rather than Latin: M. D. Barragán Domeño, ed., *Fuentes documentales medievales del Pais Vasco: Archivo General de Navarra, I: Documentación Real* (San Sebastian, 1997), 18 (#6).

5. There is now a considerable body of scholarship on the so-called Salic law; see especially Eliane Viennot, *La France, les femmes et le pouvoir, vol. 1, L'invention de la loi salique (V–XVIe siècle)* (Paris, 2006).

6. Béatrice Leroy, "A propos de la succession de 1328 en Navarre," in *Annales du Midi* 82 (1970), 138–46. On their reign, see Fermín Miranda García, *Felipe III y Juana II de Evreux,* 2d ed. (Pamplona, 1994), 53–65. Their successors, escaping from Spanish invaders in 1512, carried Navarre's official invitation back to France; with twenty-one of its original eighty-seven seals still attached, it is now in the departmental archives at Pau, E 517.

7. Archivo General de Navarra, *Catalogo de la Sección de Comptos, I (842–1331)* (Pamplona, 1952), 380–81 (# 879, 883).

8. Barragán Domeño, *Documentación Real,* 55–62, esp. 58.

9. Ibid., 64–70, 78–86.

10. Philippe Charon, "Les chanceliers d'origine française des rois de Navarre, comtes d'Evreux au XIVe siècle," *Principe de Viana* 60 (1999), 119–44; Miranda García, *Felipe III y Juana II de Evreux,* 113–14, 136–38, 84 (quote). The couple drew far more income from their French possessions than from Navarre; most of the money spent at their coronation came from their French domains.

11. Barragán Domeño, *Documentación Real,* 71–301 (#45–180).

12. Nancy Goldstone, *The Lady Queen: The Notorious Reign of Joanna I* (New York, 2009), 79.

13. This section relies heavily on Elizabeth Casteen, "The Making of a Neapolitan She-Wolf: Gender, Sexuality and Sovereignty and the Reputation of Johanna I of Naples" (Ph.D. diss., Northwestern University, 2009), and on Goldstone's *Lady Queen.* Contrary to the assumption of many writers, including Boccaccio, Robert the Wise gave Joanna's fiancé no titles and none of his lands except a principality that he and his fiancée already shared. Compare a reproduction of one of her earliest state seals (1346), <http://commons.wikimedia.org/wiki/File:Segell-joana-I-napols–1346-comtessa-provença-plom.jpg> with a later one, <http://commons.wikimedia.org/wiki/File:Joan_I_of_Naples.jpg>.

14. Matteo Villani, *Cronica,* ed. G. Porta (Parma, 1995), 1:9: *maestra, e donna del suo Barone, il quale come marito dovea essere suo signore.*

15. Emile-G. Léonard, *Les Angevins de Naples* (Paris, 1954), 402–3.

16. Boccaccio, *Famous Women,* ed. V. Brown (Cambridge, 2001), 467, 471, 473. Boccaccio's much-studied feminist critic, Christine de Pizan (1365–1430), avoided any mention of Joanna in her writings and excluded her from the *City of Ladies.*

17. Matteo Camera, *Elucubrazioni storico-diplomatiche su Giovanna Ia, regina di Napoli e Carlo III di Durazzo* (Salerno, 1889), 262 n. 1; Henri Rolland, *Monnaies des comtes de Provence, XIIe–XVe siècles* (Paris, 1956), 145–68, 221–37, esp. figs. 89–92 (231–34).

18. Etienne Baluze, *Vitae paparum avenionensium,* 4 vols. (Paris, 1914–27), 2:646: *volebat corrigere et emandare reginam, et quod regnum fuerat male rectum et gubernatum a magno tempore per feminam.*

19. Jean-François de la Harpe, *Jeanne de Naples: tragédie en cinq actes et en vers: représentée par les Comediens français le 12 décembre 1781 au palais des Tuileries et à Versailles devant Leurs Majestés le 20 du même mois* (Paris, 1782).

20. Vivian Etting, *Queen Margrete I (1353–1412) and the Founding of the Nordic Union* (Leiden, 2004), xvii, 22, 58–59, 61, 148.

21. Ibid., 55–56 (emphasis added), 58. Her privy seal from the early 1390s can be seen at <http://commons.wikimedia.org/wiki/File:Dronningmargrete1ssekret.jpg>.

22. Full text of her instructions in Etting, 146–50.

23. Her most recent biographer, Alessandro Cutolo, *Giovanna II* (Novara, 1968), judges her most detailed biographer, Nunzio Federico Faraglia, *Storia della regina Giovanna II* (Lanciano, 1904), to be excessively indulgent.

24. Another female royal succession could have taken place in Castile in 1369, after its king was murdered by an uncle of illegitimate birth; but the killer ascended the throne while the dead king's two unmarried daughters sought sanctuary as far away as England. Both women married English princes and founded so-called Lancastrian

lineages that played a major role in Iberia, especially Portugal, for many centuries. Illegitimacy was also no barrier to succession in fourteenth-century Italian principalities: see Jane Fair Bestor, "Bastardy and Legitimacy in the Formation of a Regional State in Italy: The Estense Succession," *Comparative Studies in Society and History* 38 (1996), 549–85.

25. Her documentary trail vanishes after 1418: César Olivera Serrano, *Beatriz de Portugal* (Santiage de Compostela, 2005), 495 (#45).

26. The ANS possesses coins from the reigns of the sisters who inherited Hungary and Poland but none bearing the names of their husbands, who ruled these kingdoms for thirty years after their deaths. Maria of Sicily and her husband each have one coin. Only four silver coins with the name and image of Beatrice of Portugal are known to exist. Samples of Maria of Hungary's coins at <http://commons.wikimedia.org/wiki/File:MarieUhry_penize.jpg>.

27. Maria Rita Lo Forte Scirpo, *C'era una volta una regina: Due donne per un regno: Maria d'Aragona e Bianca de Navarra* (Naples, 2003), 44, 67. Maria's crudely printed signature is reproduced as fig. 7.

28. Compare Serrano, *Beatriz,* with the Portuguese version: Salvador Dias Arnaut, *A crise nacional dos fins do seculo XIV* (Coimbra, 1960).

29. Oscar Halecki, *Jadwiga of Anjou and the Rise of East Central Europe* (Boulder, 1991), 150–51, 156, 164–66, 194–95, 226–27 n. 47. For her state seal, see <http://commons.wikimedia.org/wiki/File:Jadwiga_Andegaweńska_seal_1386.PNG>.

30. Ibid., 247–48, 262; Jadwiga's name never appears in the foundation charter. On her beatification and canonization, see Boleslaw Przybyszewski, *Saint Jadwiga–Queen of Poland 1374–1399* (Rome/London, 1997), 83–95.

31. On female regency government in the fifteenth-century crown of Aragon, see Theresa Earenfight, *The King's Other Body: Maria of Castile and the Crown of Aragon* (Philadelphia, 2009). On Blanca, see Lo Forte Scirpo, *C'era una volta una regina,* 133–262; Laura Sciascia, "Bianca di Navarra, l'ultima regina: Storia al femminile della monarchia siciliana," *Principe de Viana* 60 (1999), 293–310; Eloisa Ramirez Vaquero, *Blanca y Juan II* (Pamplona, 2003); and Florencio Idoate, "La coronación de unos reyes navarros en 1429," in his *Rincones de Historia de Navarra* (Pamplona, 1954), 17–20.

32. Ramirez Vaquero, *Blanca y Juan,* 112. Two versions survive: the original at Pamplona (AGN, Casamientos y Muertos Reales, Leg. 1, carp. 18) and a copy at Pau (AD Pyrénées-Atlantiques, E 563).

33. Miguel Ibañez Artica, "Acuñacones de Blanca y Juan II (1425–1441–1479) y de Carlos, Principe de Viana (1441–1461)," in *La moneda en Navarra* (Pamplona, 2001); Elena Ramirez Vaquero, *Blanca, Juan II y el Príncipe de Viana* (Pamplona, 1986), 286–87; and her *Juan II, Leonor y Gaston IV de Foix, y Francisco Febo* (Pamplona, 1990), 303–5.

34. Figures calculated from Alvaro Adot Lerga, *Juan de Albret y Catalina de Foix, o la defensa del Estado navarro (1483–1517)* (Pamplona, 2005), 301–11; as in the case of their fourteenth-century predecessors, the king issued more documents alone (sixty-seven) than the proprietary queen (forty-two). See also R. Anthony and H. Courteault, eds., *Les testaments des derniers rois de Navarre* (Toulouse/Paris, 1940), 62–90.

35. Ferdinand's heirs never explicitly renounced this district, but it made no payments to them after 1525 and began acknowledging the traditional House of Navarre in 1528: Susana Herreros Lopetegui, *Las tierras navarras de Ultrapuertos (siglos XII–XVI)* (Pamplona, 1998), 138–45.

36. The standard account remains Sir George Hill, *A History of Cyprus,* vol. 3: *The Frankish Period, 1432–1571* (Cambridge, 1948). There is a notable lack of biographies of the Greek female ruler of Cyprus, but several of her Italian successor. See also a French version of the great Cairo chronicle of Taghiri-Birdi: M. Tahar Mansouri, *Chypre dans les sources arabes médiévales* (Nicosia, 2001), 89–95, 123–27.

37. See Latin sources summarized in Hill, *Cyprus,* 555–57.

38. George Bustron, *Chronicle 1456–1489,* trans. R. M. Dawkins (Melbourne, 1964), 35 (#113).

39. Marilyn Yalom, *Birth of the Chess Queen* (New York, 2004), 191–211; Barbara Weissberger, *Isabel Rules: Constructing Queenship, Wielding Power* (Minneapolis, 2004), 148–53.

40. Compare Peggy K. Liss, *Isabel the Queen,* 2d ed. (Philadelphia, 2004), 67–8, with Tarsicio de Azcona, *Isabel la Católica: Vida y reinado* (Madrid, 2002), 124.

41. The tale of Isabel's procession with an uplifted sword, repeated by many biographers, was actually fabricated by one of Fernando's partisans: see Ana Isabel Carrasco Manchado, *Isabel I de Castilla y la sombra de la ilegitimidad* (Madrid, 2006), 23–37. On Isabel's niece, see Tarsicio de Azcona, *Juana de Castilla, mal llamada la Beltraneja* (Madrid, 2007); on Ferdinand's position, compare Liss, *Isabel the Queen,* 113–18, with Azcona, *Isabel,* 147–55 (*en lo camp fom iurat, recebut, elevat per Rey en aquestes Regnes*). Both agreements of 1475 were printed by Diego José Dormer, *Discursos varios de historia* (Saragossa, 1683), 295–305 (quote, 304).

42. During the war, Ferdinand and Isabel stripped silver from churches in order to produce their coins (Azcona, *Isabel,* 176–78). Juana's official seal survives in a single Spanish municipal archive, but several of her coins are extant (Azcona, *Juana,* 125–27); on Isabel's propaganda, see Carrasco Manchado, *Isabel y la ilegitimidad,* 176–95. Almost a century ago a facing set of both women's identical facsimile royal signatures ("I the Queen") was published in Spain: J. B. Sitges, *Enrique IV y la Excelente Señora* (Madrid, 1912), 40.

43. Richard Kagan, *Clio and the Crown* (Baltimore, 2009), 48. Isabel holds books in more than one of her portraits: see Elisa Ruiz García, *Los libros de Isabel la Católica: Arqueología de un patrimonio escrito* (Madrid/Soria, 2004), 247–49.

44. E. Harris Harbison, *Rival Ambassadors at the Court of Queen Mary* (Princeton, 1940), 211–12.

45. An obvious starting point is the twenty printed volumes of the *Registro del Sello* summarizing the Castilian chancery's official actions between 1480 and 1500. Some useful comments in Carrasco Manchado, *Isabel y la ilegitimidad,* 469–75.

46. In 1485 the *Registro del Sello* recorded 357 joint decrees, plus 104 signed by Ferdinand alone and 73 by Isabel alone. Thus 70 percent were joint, with a 6–4 ratio between husband and wife. The former ratio is slightly below Navarre's 80 percent, the latter identical (see n. 34 above). In 1480 Isabel approved five legitimations and Ferdinand none; in 1485–6, Ferdinand approved twenty-one legitimations,

Isabel none. In 1485–86, twenty-four *escribanos públicos* were named jointly by both sovereigns, but thirty-seven more by Ferdinand alone and only three by Isabel alone. Compare Azcona, *Isabel,* 201, and Liss, *Isabel the Queen,* 213.

47. Azcona, *Isabel,* 181, 551–52.

48. On Isabel's reponsibility, compare Liss, *Isabel the Queen,* 191–92, with Azcona, *Isabel,* 262–63. Henry C. Lea, *A History of the Inquisition of Spain,* 4 vols. (New York, 1906–10), 1:289–92, notes that "there is absolutely no evidence in [Ferdinand's] enormous and confidential correspondence that he ever used it for political purposes" (291); but compare Beatrice Perez, *Inquisition, pouvoir, société* (Paris, 2007), 92–94, 107–10.

49. On the size of her inheritance, see Monika Triest, *Macht, vrouwen en politiek 1477–1558: Maria van Burgondië, Margreta van Oostenrijk, Maria van Hongrije* (Louvain, 2000), 44–45 (with map). Her plea to officials in Dijon apparently never reached its destination: Georges-H. Dumont, *Marie de Bourgogne* (Paris, 1982), 160–61. On Dutch linguistic autonomy in 1477, see Peter Burke, *Toward a Social History of Early Modern Dutch* (Amsterdam, 2005), 13–14.

50. Her seal is reproduced in Christine Weightman, *Margaret of York, Duchess of Burgundy 1446–1503* (New York, 1989), 133; the medal by Bernd Kluge, *Numismatik des Mittelaters* (Berlin/Vienna, 2007), 419 (#1101).

51. The official Burgundian version of this ceremony in Jean Molinet's *Chroniques,* 2:538–44, agrees with accounts from foreign observers: see Nancy B. Warren, *Women of God and Arms* (Philadelphia, 2005), 1–4.

52. Bethany Aram, "La reina Juana: nuevos datos, nuevas interpretaciones," in Maria Vitoria López-Cordón and Gloria Franco, eds., *La Reina Isabel y las reinas de España: realidad, modelos e imagen historiográfica* (Madrid, 2005), 101–3.

53. Bethany Aram, *La reina Juana: Gobierno, piedad y dinastía* (Madrid, 2001), 234, 278–80; Walter de Gray Burch, *Catalogue of Seals of the Department of Manuscripts in the British Museum* (London, 1900), 6:630 (#23,077); M. J. Rodríguez-Salgado, *The Changing Face of Empire: Charles V, Philip II and Habsburg Authority, 1551–1559* (Cambridge, 1988), 129.

54. José Maria de Francisco Olmos, "Las primeras acuñaciones de Carlos I (1517): Un golpe de estado monetaria," in Carmen Alfaro, Carmen Marcos, and Paloma Otero, eds., *Actas del XIII Congreso Internacional de Numismática* (Madrid, 2003), 2 vols. (Madrid, 2005), 2:1471–76; on coins of *Juana y Carlos* minted at Naples in 1516–19, see Philip Grierson and Lucia Travaini, *Medieval European Coinage . . . in the Fitzwilliam Museum, Cambridge, 14 (Italy III)* (Cambridge, 1998), 424–30.

55. Dormer, *Discursos,* 303–5 (*mucho mayor sinrazón y más injusto y deshonesto fue lo que pretendieron las Reynas Juanas de Nápoles, que escuyeron algunos de sus maridos del nombre y regimento del Reyno*).

### Chapter 4. Female Regents Promote Female Rule, 1500–1630

1. Helmut G. Koenigsberger, *Monarchies, States Generals and Parliaments: The Netherlands in the Fifteenth and Sixteenth Centuries* (Cambridge, 2001), 91.

2. Dagmar Eichberger, *Leben mit Kunst, Wirken durch Kunst: Sammelwesen und Hofkunst unter Margrethe van Osterreich, Regentin der Niederlands* (Turnhout, 2002).

Her palace at Mechelen – the first ever built by a female regent in Europe – can be viewed at <http://commons.wikimedia.org/wiki/File:Mechelen_gerechtshof_01.jpg>.

3. Margaret was painted twice together with her brother, and one of these was certainly sent to Spain during negotiations for their marriages: see Dagmar Eichberger, ed., *Women of Distinction: Margaret of York/Margaret of Austria* (Louvain, 2005), 142 (#48), 118–19 (#19–20), 83–85 (#18–19, 21).

4. Marguerite Debae, *La bibliothèque de Marguerite d'Autriche, essai de reconstitution d'après l'inventaire de 1523–1524* (Louvain/Paris, 1995); Susan G. Bell, *The Lost Tapestries of the City of Ladies: Christine de Pizan's Renaissance Legacy* (Berkeley, 2004), 72–95; Jean Lemaire des Belges, *Oeuvres,* ed. J. Stecher, 5 vols. (Louvain, 1891), 4:69–70.

5. H. C. Agrippa, *Declamation on the Nobility and Preeminence of the Female Sex,* ed. Albert Rabil Jr. (Chicago, 1996), 19–21 and nn. 38, 84–85, 88. Agrippa's unorthodox stances on various topics explains why this was among his first works to be printed. By 1544 this work had appeared in French, German, English, and Italian translations.

6. Letter of March 15, 1526, in Orsolya Rethelyi, ed., *Mary of Hungary: The Queen and Her Court 1521–1531* (Budapest, 2005), 216.

7. Quote from Pierre de Brantôme, *Recueil des Dames,* ed. E. Vaucheret (Paris: Pléiade, 1991), 510. On their respective levels of authority, see Laetitia V. G. Gorter-van Royen, *Maria van Hongrije, regents der Nederlanden: een politieke analyse op basis van haar Regentschapsordonannties en haar corrrespondentie met Karel V* (Hilversum, 1995), 326–39. Gorter-van Royen and J.-P. Hoyois have begun to publish Mary's state correspondence; the first volume, *Correspondence de Marie de Hongrie avec Charles Quint et Nicolas de Granvelle* (Turnhout, 2009), covering the year 1532, includes over 150 letters to her from the emperor and over 100 of hers to him.

8. Brantôme (Pléiade ed.), 510–11, 516. On Mary's hunting, see Christoph Niedermann, "Marie de Hongrie et la chasse," in B. Federinov and G. Docquier, eds., *Marie de Hongrie: Politique et culture sous la Renaissance aux Pays-Bas* (Mariemont, BE, 2008), 115–23; on her military knowledge, see Pieter Martens in ibid., 90–105.

9. Mary intended it for the main hall of her new palace at Binche, alongside an identical statue of her nephew and successor Philip II; both are now at the Prado in Madrid (both reproduced in Federinov and Docquier, *Marie de Hongrie,* 176). On Mary of Hungary's portraits, see Bob van den Boogert and Jacqueline Kerkhoff, eds., *Maria van Hongrije: Konigin tussen keizers en kunstenaars* (Zwolle, 1993), esp. 142 (#104), 324 (#222), and 329 (#227); on her musical patronage, see Glenda G. Thompson, "Mary of Hungary and Music Patronage," in *Sixteenth Century Journal* 15 (1984), 401–18; on her library, Claude Lemaire, "La bibliothèque des imprimés de la reine Marie de Hongrie, régente des Pays-Bas, 1505–1558," in *Bibliothèque d'Humanisme et Renaissance* 58 (1996), 119–39.

10. I use the English translation of her letter of resignation in Jane de Jongh, *Mary of Hungary, Second Regent of the Netherlands* (London, 1958), 263–66; see also Gorter-van Royen, 9.

11. Thierry Wanegffelen, *Le pouvoir contesté: souveraines d'Europe à la Renaissance* (Paris, 2008), 156.

12. Reprinted in full by Gorter-Van Royen, 340–49.

13. Ibid., 343–44, 345, 346, 347, 348 (my translations).

14. Antonio Villacorta Baños-Garcia, *La Jesuita* (Barcelona, 2005), 183–85, 225.

15. Ibid., 226 n. 28, 249–50, 309–10, 335–37; Archivo General de Simancas, Estado, Leg. 103, fol. 310 (20/9/1554).

16. Villacorta Baños-Garcia, *La Jesuita,* 217–22, 226–29.

17. Ibid., 379. On her portraits, see Annemarie Jordan Gschwend, "Los retratos de Juana de Austria posteriores a 1554: la imagen de una Princesa de Portugal, una regente de España y una jesuita," in *Reales Sitios* 39 (2002), 42–65. The 'hunting-dog' portrait is available at <http://commons.wikimedia.org/wiki/File:Infanta_Juana_of_Spain1. jpg>. In 1562, the female court artist Sofonisba Anguissola placed Juana beside a little girl; contrast <http://commons.wikimedia.org/wiki/File:Sofonisba_Anguissola_-_ Portrait_of_Juana_of_Austria_with_a_Young_Girl,_1561.jpg>.

18. Ana Isabel Buescu, *Catarina de Austria (1507–1578): Infanta de Tordesillas, Rainha de Portugal* (Lisbon, 2007), 251–53, 258, 327–48 (also reproduces both of Mor's portraits between 128 and 129).

19. Maria do Rosario Themudo Barata de Azevedo, *As regencies na Menoridade de D. Sebastião,* 2 vols. (Lisbon, 1992). On her policies toward new Christians, see Francisco Bethencourt, *The Inquisition: A Global History, 1478–1834* (Cambridge, 2009), 326, 328.

20. Ruy Gonçalves, *Privilegios e praerogativos que ho genero femenino tem por Dereito commum, e Ordenaoens do Reino, mais que o genero masculine* (Coimbra, 1557); see the facsimile edited by Elisa Maria Lopes da Costa (Lisbon, 1992).

21. See bibliographical essay; Leonie Frieda, *Catherine de Medici* (New York, 2005), 117; Thierry Wanegffelen, *Catherine de Médicis: le pouvoir au féminin* (Paris 2005), 230–35. Her seal is reproduced in Wanegffelen, *Pouvoir contesté,* 461.

22. J. Boutier, A. Dewerpe, and D. Nordman, *Un tour de France royal: Le voyage de Charles IX (1564–1566)* (Paris, 1984), 238, 241–46; Wanegffelen, *Catherine,* 302.

23. Frances Yates, *The Valois Tapestries* (London, 1959); Clarice Innocenti, ed., *Women in Power: Caterina and Maria de' Medici: The Return to Florence of Two Queens of France* (Florence, 2009).

24. Bernard Cottret, *La royauté au féminin: Elisabeth Ie d'Angleterre* (Paris, 2009), 125–26.

25. Eliane Viennot, *La France, les femmes et le pouvoir,* vol 1: *L'invention de la loi salique (Ve–XVIe siècle)* (Paris, 2006), 575–87; Brantôme, *Receuil des Dames,* 134–35.

26. Compare François Hotman, *Franco-Gallia,* ed. and trans. Ralph Giesey and J. H. M. Salmon (Cambridge, 1972), chap. 26, esp. 483, with David Chambers, *Discours de la legitime succession des femmes aux possessions de leurs parens et du gouvernement des princesses aux Empires et Royaumes* (Paris, 1579) (its dedicatory letter was dated August 21, 1573). The copy in the British Library bears the royal bindings "E.R." Although the principal source on this enemy of England (whose surname is spelled variously as Chalmers and Chambers) is his police file in the papers of Lord Burghley, and although he published nothing in England, Constance Jordan puts Chambers at the conclusion of her classic article "Women's Rule in Sixteenth-Century British Political Thought," *Renaissance Quarterly* 40 (1987), 445–50.

27. Chambers, *Discours,* 14–15v, 16v, 18–19v.

28. Ibid., 24v, 25v, 32v–33.

29. R. J. Knecht, *Catherine de Medici* (London, 1998), 99. Catherine also suffered from confessional solidarity between female Protestant monarchs. When a third French religious war broke out in 1568, Elizabeth not only loaned money to Jeanne III of Navarre but also sent a hundred so-called volunteeer cavalrymen, including a very young Walter Raleigh, to assist her Huguenots against the French king; see William Camden, *The History of the Most Renowned and Victorious Princess Elizabeth, Late Queen of England,* abridged ed., Wallace MacCaffrey, ed. (Chicago, 1970), 124.

30. Portraits: Joanne Woodall, *Anthonis Mor: Art and Authority* (Zwolle, 2007), 390 (#139), 398 (#146), 403 (#148). Medal: Luc Smolderen, *Jacques Jonghelinck: Sculpteur, médailleur et graveur de sceaux (1530–1606)* (Louvain-la-Neuve, 1996), 287–92.

31. Geoffrey Parker, *Philip II* (Boston, 1978), 195–96. Original documents in *Colección de documentos inéditos para la historia de España,* 42:218–22 (Philip II's donation), 42:225–28 (Philip III's ratification); seal reproduced in Smolderen, *Jonghelinck,* plate CIX.

32. On their government, see Geoffrey Parker, "The Decision-Making Process in the Government of the Catholic Netherlands under 'the Archdukes,' 1596–1621," in his *Spain and the Netherlands 1559–1659: Ten Studies* (London, 1979), 164–76; on their coinage, see André Van Kermuylen, ed., *Monnaies des Pays-Bas méridionaux d'Albert et Isabelle à Guillaume Ier* (Brussels, 1981), 1–64. Magdalena Sanchez argues that she had "greater powers than those held by any previous Spanish governor in the Netherlands, including her late husband": see "Isabel Clara Eugenia and Power," in Anne J. Cruz and Mihoko Suzuki, eds., *The Rule of Women in Early Modern Europe* (Urbana, 2009), 72–73.

33. Ruth Betegón Diez, *Isabel Clara Eugenia: Infanta de España y soberana de Flandes* (Barcelona, 2004), 158–60.

34. Ibid., 205, 212; Francis Van Noten, "The Horses of Albert and Isabella: Historical Background," in Werner Thomas and Luc Duerloo, eds., *Albert and Isabella: Essays* (Turnhout: 1998), 343–46, 366 (plate 8).

35. Jean-François Dubost, *Marie de Médicis: la reine dévoilée* (Paris, 2009); Mark Jones, "The Image of a Queen Regent," in Tony Hackens and Ghislaine Moucharte, eds., *Proceedings of the XIth International Numismatic Congress,* 4 vols. (Louvain-la-Neuve, 1993), 4:304–5 n. 17, 308; Mark Jones, ed., *Catalogue of French Medals in the British Museum,* 2 vols. (London, 1987–88), 2:290 (#332).

36. Dubost, *Marie,* 197 (1609 engraving), 528, 774. On the famous Rubens cycle, see 651–76; the fullest discussion in English is Ronald Millen and Robert Wolf, *Heroic Deeds and Mystic Figures* (Princeton, 1989).

37. Dubost, *Marie,* 802–04.

38. *Corpus Rubeniorum Ludwig Burchard,* XIX, part 2 [Hans Vlieghe, *Rubens Portraits in Antwerp,* (London, 1987)], #109–12 (three copies exist).

39. Jean-François de Raymond, ed., *Christine, reine de Suède, Apologies* (Paris, 1994), 136.

## Chapter 5. Husbands Finessed

1. Alison Weir, *The Children of Henry VIII* (New York, 1996), 167–68; Anne Whitelock, "'Woman, Warrior, Queen?' Rethinking Mary and Elizabeth," in Alice Hunt and Anna Whitelock, eds., *Tudor Queenship: The Reigns of Mary and Elizabeth* (New York, 2010), 175–76. Mary's 1553 sovereign is reproduced in Monter, "Gendered Sovereignty," *JIH* 41 (2011), 548.

2. Charles Beem, *The Lioness Roared: The Problem of Female Rule in English History* (New York, 2006), 63–99, provided a fresh political interpretation of Mary Tudor's reign, now further enriched by Judith M. Richards, *Mary Tudor* (London, 2008), 121–81. See also Glyn Redworth, "'Matters Impertinent to Women': Male and Female Monarchy under Philip and Mary," *English Historical Review* 112 (1997), 593–613.

3. A detailed paraphrase of their prenuptial agreement appears in David Loades, *Mary Tudor: The Tragical History of the First Queen of England* (London, 2006), 109–10. Compare the generally similar articles agreed upon by France and England in 1581 for Elizabeth's marriage to Alençon: William Camden, *The History of the Most Renowned and Victorious Princess Eilzabeth, Late Queen of England,* ed. Wallace MacCaffrey (Chicago, 1970), 132–33.

4. For Spanish views of these events, see C.V. Malfatti, *The Accession, Coronation and Marriage of Mary Tudor as Related in Four Manuscripts of the Escorial* (Barcelona, 1956); for their wedding, Alexander Samson, "Changing Places: The Marriage and Royal Entry of Philip, Prince of Austria, and Mary Tudor, July-August 1554," in *Sixteenth Century Journal,* 36 (2005), 761–84. Their great seal of 1554 is reproduced in Richards, *Mary Tudor,* plate 9, and their 'floating-crown' joint coinage in Monter, "Gendered Sovereignty," 549; David Loades prints her last will in *Mary Tudor: A Life* (London, 1989), 370–83.

5. Geoffrey Parker's superb *Felipe II: La biografía definitiva* (Barcelona, 2010), 120–35, 140–54, does much to clarify Philip's role in his wife's kingdom; quote from 129.

6. Richards, *Mary Tudor,* 215–16.

7. Loades, *Tragical History,* 203; Claude Richardot, *Trois sermons funèbres* (Antwerp, 1559), 20, 23–23v.

8. Bernard Berdou d'Aas, *Jeanne III d'Albret: Chronique (1528–1572)* (Anglet, 2002), 195–204; on her coins, see François Voisin, "Les testons de Jeanne d'Albret," *Cahiers Numismatiques* #131 (1997), 38–47.

9. Berdou d'Aas, *Chronique,* 257, 262 n. 36, 298–99, 314.

10. Philippe Chareyre, "'Hasta la Muerte': La 'fermesse' de Jeanne d'Albret," in *Jeanne d'Albret et sa cour* (Paris, 2004), 82–84.

11. Pamela Ritchie, *Mary of Guise in Scotland, 1548–1560: A Political Career* (East Linton, 2002), 94–95.

12. See bibliographical essay; Thierry Wanegffelen, *Le pouvoir contesté: souveraines d'Europe à la Renaissance* (Paris, 2008), 277–8.

13. See Monter, "Gendered Sovereignty," 548–50; the counterfeits include over 350 from one location: N. M. McQ. Holmes, *Scottish Coins in the National Museums of Scotland, Edinburgh: Part I, 1526–1603* (Oxford, 2006), 4, 8, 23–25.

14. <http://commons.wikimedia.org/wiki/File:Mary_silver_rial_1566_681821.jpg>. How many 'illegal' silver *ryals* with the original inscription have been preserved is

uncertain; the British Museum holds eight "Mary and Henrys" but only one "Henry and Mary."

15. Julian Goodare, "The First Parliament of Mary Queen of Scots," *Sixteenth Century Journal* 36 (2005), 55–75.

16. Katharine Anthony, *Queen Elizabeth* (New York, 1929), 105.

17. Judith Richards, "Examples and Admonitions: What Mary Demonstrated for Elizabeth," in Hunt and Whitelock, *Tudor Queenship*, 31–45; Leah Marcus, Janel Mueller, and Mary Beth Rose, eds., *Elizabeth I: Collected Works* (Chicago, 2000), 52 n. 3; Carol Levin, *"The Heart and Stomach of a King": Elizabeth I and the Politics of Sex and Power* (Philadelphia, 1994), 121–26; also Jacqueline Broad and Karen Green, *A History of Women's Political Thought in Europe, 1400–1700* (Cambridge, 2009), 90–109. Her seal of 1584 is reproduced in Louis Montrose, *The Subject of Elizabeth* (Chicago, 2006), 96 (fig. 28).

18. Compare Cottret, *Elisabeth,* 101–2, with Camden's summary of the same problem in 1581 (MacCaffrey, *History,* 136–37). Also Frederick Chamberlin, *Sayings of Queen Elizabeth* (London, 1923), 16; Marcus et al., *Collected Works,* 79 (draft version reproduced on 78).

19. William Camden, *Annales . . . of the Reign of Elizabeth* (London, 1630), 56.

20. Chamberlin, *Sayings,* 310.

21. Marcus et al., *Collected Works,* 135–43 (quote, 141).

22. English version in ibid., 157; Spanish original in Janel Mueller and Leah Marcus, eds., *Elizabeth I: Autograph Compositions and Foreign Language Originals* (Chicago, 2003); Marcus et al., *Collected Works,* 311–21. Its frontispiece is reproduced in Linda Shenk, *Learned Queen: The Image of Elizabeth I in Politics and Poetry* (New York, 2010), 25.

23. Five early English translations of her outburst of 1597 exist: Marcus et al., *Collected Works,* 332–33 n. 1; her final harangue in *Calendar of State Papers, Venice,* 9:533 (#1134).

24. William Camden, *The True and Royall History of the famus empresse Elizabeth, Queen of England, France and Ireland* (London, 1625), 308–9; Cottret, *Elisabeth,* 229.

25. J. E. Neale, *Elizabeth I* (London, 1934), 179; Madeleine Lazard, "L'image d'Elizabeth d'Angleterre chez Brantôme," in Françoise Argod-Dutard and Anne-Marie Cocula, eds., *Brantôme et les Grands d'Europe* (Bordeaux, 2003), 99–110.

26. Meryl Bailey, "Salvatrix Mundi: Queen Elizabeth I as Christ-Type," *Studies in Iconography* 29 (2008), 176–215; *Calendar of State Papers, Venice,* 8:344–45, 379 (#640, 642, 717); Roy Strong, *Gloriana* (London, 2003), 22; Neale, *Elizabeth,* 393; Ruth Betegón Diez, *Isabel Clara Eugenia: Infanta de España y soberana de Flandes* (Barcelona, 2004), 137.

27. Strong, *Gloriana,* 22–23, 41 (quote).

28. Ibid., 20 (quote), 111 (#109); Camden, *History,* 328 (*dux foemina fecit*). For Dutch celebrations of the Armada defeat, see Edward Hawkins, *Medallic Illustrations of the History of Great Britain and Ireland, to the Death of George II,* 2 vols. (London, 1885), 1:145–48 (#111–18), 153 (#127, 128).

29. Montrose, *Subject of Elizabeth,* 249.

30. See bibliographical essay. After 1966 two smaller congresses about her have been held at Rome (1989 and 1996), where she spent most of her last thirty years, and one at Stockholm (1995).

31. Curt Weibull, *Christina of Sweden* (Stockholm, 1966), 77–78.

32. Ibid., 82–84, 88.

33. Faculty of Medicine, Montpellier, Ms. H 258, vol. 12 (*Miscellanea Politica*), fols. 28 (*il n'y avoit pas un homme en tout la Suède qui eust si hardi que d'en parler à la Reine*), 222v.

34. Kari Elisabeth Børresen, "Christina's Discourse on God and Humanity," in Marie-Louise Roden, ed., *Politics and Culture in the Age of Christina* (Stockholm, 1997), 46 nn. 24, 25; Baron Carl de Bildt, *Les Médailles romaines de Christine de Suède* (Rome, 1908), 23–32, includes 14 reproductions.

35. Veronica Buckley, *Christina, Queen of Sweden: The Restless Life of a European Eccentric* (London, 2004), 197–98, 148, 140, 164; Cavalli-Björkman, "Christina Portraits," in Roden, *Politics and Culture,* 96–102. Bernard Quilliet, *Christine de Suède* (Paris, 2005), 109–46, maintains that she was a hermaphrodite.

36. Montpellier manuscripts, vol. 10 (*Miscellanea di suo pugno*), fol. 232 (*La Regina non dice ne fa niente a caso:* a close variant on fol. 238); Michael Roberts, *Sweden as a Great Power 1611–1697* (London, 1968), 49–55. Her Polish candidacy generated 267 letters, preserved at Montpellier, of which J. Arckenholz published the most important: Waclaw Uruszczak, *Polonica w korespondencji królowej szwedzkiej Krystyny w zbiorach Bibliothèque Interuniversitaire w Montpellier* (Cracow, 2001).

37. Bildt, *Médailles,* 137–45.

38. Jean-François de Raymond, ed., *Christine, reine de Suède, Apologies* (Paris, 1994), 135, 357 (*Sentiments, #339*).

39. Swedish National Library, Stockholm, Ms. D 684, vol. 1 (marginal note in *Sentiments laconiques*); Iiro Kajanto, *Christina Heroina: Mythological and Historical Exemplification in the Latin Panegyrics on Christina Queen of Sweden* (Helsinki, 1993), 134–37; Buckley, *Christina,* 55.

40. Ludwig Lindenburg, *Leben und Schriften David Fassmanns 1683–1744, mit besonderer Berücksichtigung seiner Totengespräche* (Berlin, 1937), 88–141, esp. 103–7, 128. Fassmann wrote over 150 such dialogues by 1739.

41. Charles Beem, *The Lioness Roared* (London, 2006), 181 n. 5 and 219 nn. 6, 7.

42. Richard Doebner, ed., *Memoirs of Mary, Queen of England* (Leipzig, 1896), 10–12.

43. Ibid., 22–23, 32–33, 58–59; Rachel Weil, *Political Passions: Gender, the Family, and Political Argument in England, 1680–1714* (Manchester, 1999), 109.

44. Gregorio Leti, *Vita d'Elisabetta, Regina d'Inghilterra, detta per Sopranome la Comediante Politica,* 2 vols. (Amsterdam, 1693), 1:3–5. By 1750 this work had eleven editions in French, five in Dutch, and two in German; the Russian translation of 1795 is in the Library of Congress: Nati Krivatsy, *Bibliography of the Works of Gregorio Leti* (New Castle, Del., 1982), 7, 39–44.

## Chapter 6. Husbands Subordinated

1. Monter, "Gendered Sovereignty," 553–59; on Maria Theresa's remarkably complicated numismatic legacy, see Tassilo Eypeltauer, *Corpus Nummorum Regni*

*Maria Theresiae: Die Münzprägungen der Kaiserin Maria Theresia und ihre Mitregenten Kaiser Franz I und Josef II* (Basel, 1973),

2. Edward Gregg, *Queen Anne,* 2d ed. (New Haven, 2001), 6, 152–53.

3. See Charles Beem's sympathetic portrait in *The Lioness Roared* (London, 2006), 101–39, and Rachel Weil, *Political Passions: Gender, the Family, and Political Argument in England, 1680–1714* (Manchester, 1999), 162–86. Prince George appears on only two of the seventy-five medals from his wife's reign held in the American Numismatic Society (ANS), one because of his death in 1708; in this respect, he resembles his sister-in-law, Mary II.

4. Frances Harris, *A Passion for Government: The Life of Sarah, Duchess of Marlborough* (Oxford, 1991). Weil (*Political Passions,* 189) argues that "gender did not matter to Sarah Churchill's construction of herself as a political actor."

5. Gregg, *Queen Anne,* 53–58, 295, 297, 365. Manley's *Selected Works* (London, 1986) fill five volumes.

6. Gregg, *Queen Anne,* 82, 160–62, 330.

7. Ibid., 351. Among seventy-five different designs of medals from Anne's reign in the ANS, the phrase *Louis Magnus, Anna Maior* also appears on #0000.999. 3176 and 3177.

8. Gregg, *Queen Anne,* 143–44, 147–48, 212–13.

9. Karin Tegenborg Falkdaen, *Kungne ar en kvinna* (Umea, 2003), 207–11 (English summary).

10. English translation of the original document of 1713 in C. A. Macartney, ed., *The Habsburg and Hohenzollern Dynasties in the Seventeenth and Eighteenth Centuries* (New York, 1970), 88–91 (quote, 90); see also Karl A. Roider, "The Pragmatic Sanction," *Austrian History Yearbook* 8 (1972), 153–58.

11. Gustav Turba, ed., *Die Pragmatische Sanktion* (Vienna, 1913), 54–121, esp. 114 (quote from Macartney, *Habsburg and Hohenzollern Dynasties,* 40).

12. Turba, *Die Pragmatische Sanktion,* 138–84, 191–94; Macartney, *Habsburg and Hohenzollern Dynasties,* 86–87, 91–94. An ornately sealed copy, signed by the emperor and major Hungarian dignitaries, exists in Hungary's National Museum.

13. *Zufallige Gedanken über die Frage: Ob Ihre Majestät, die Königin von Ungarn und Böhmen, wegen der Churwürde, so der Krone Böhmen anklebet, in dem Churfürstlichen Collegio, da nun die Erb-Folge auf das Weibliche Geschlecht verfallen, Sitz und Stimme führen können?* (n.p. [Vienna], 1741).

14. See bibliographical essay; Karl Vocelka, *Glanz und Untergang der Höfischen Welt: Repräsentation, Reform und Reaktion in Habsburgischen Vielvölkerstaat* (Vienna, 2001), 28–33. During her reign, Hungarian Protestants lost about two hundred churches and schools. She began to expel the large Jewish community of Prague early in her reign but changed her mind at the last minute—and had a medal struck to celebrate her clemency.

15. Michael Yonan, "Modesty and Monarchy: Rethinking Empress Maria Theresa at Schönbrunn," *Austrian History Yearbook* 35 (2004), 25–47.

16. J. Kallbrunner, ed., *Maria Theresias Politisches Testament* (Vienna, 1952). Macartney's English translation (*Habsburg and Hohenzollern Dynasties,* 96–132) omits the second and slightly later version, which is less repetitive but also less personal (quote, 97).

17. Macartney, *Habsburg and Hohenzollern Dynasties*, 99–100, 102. Her antagonist Frederick the Great criticized himself for using faulty military tactics in his Silesian campaign of 1741: Frédéric II, *Mémoires*, ed. Boutaric and Campardon, 2 vols. (Paris, 1866), 1:93–95.

18. Frederick II, *Oeuvres*, 31 vols. (Berlin, 1846–57), 16:41; Frédéric II, *Mémoires*, 1:4. Writing for posterity, he used tactful language even about the meddlesome queen-consort of Spain, Elizabeth Farnese, who "would have wished to govern the whole world" and "marched boldly toward the fulfillment of her projects; nothing surprised her, and nothing stopped her" (ibid., 25–26).

19. R. J. W. Evans, "Maria Theresa and Hungary," in *Austria, Hungary and the Habsburgs: Essays on Central Europe, c. 1683–1867* (Oxford, 2006), 17–35; quote from von Arneth, *Geschichte Maria Theresiens*, 10:128.

20. *Schau- und Denkmünzen, welche unter der glorwürdigen Regierung des Kaiserinn Königinn Maria Thersia geprägt worden sind* (Vienna, 1782), #23. The painting, done by Sir Philip Hamilton about 1750, was shown at the exhibition *Maria Theresa als Konigin von Ungarn (1980)* and reproduced in its catalogue; Astrik Gabriel, *Les rapports dynastiques franco-hongrois au moyen-age* (Budapest, 1949), 62.

21. Olga Khayanova, "From the Theresianum in Vienna to the Theresian Academy in Buda: An Interrupted Reform of Noble Education, 1740s–1780s," in Klara Papp and Janos Barta, eds., *The First Millennium of Hungary in Europe* (Debreczen, 2002), 264–68.

22. Fullest description, with illustrations, in Gerda Mraz and Gottfried Mraz, *Maria Theresia. Ihr Leben und ihre Zeit in Bildern und Dokumenten* (Munich, 1979), 172–74.

23. Macartney, *Habsburg and Hohenzollern Dynasties*, 115.

24. Prague's Strahov Library contains no fewer than ten congratulatory tracts about her coronation in Latin and German, including the official *Actus coronationis* and a German version of her *Triumpherter Einzug* two weeks earlier.

25. Mraz and Mraz, *Bildern und Dokumenten*, 88 (*dass sie moglicherweise diese Krönung geringer einschätze als die beiden männlicher Kronen, die sie trage:* 22/8/1745); Eypeltauer, *Corpus Nummorum*, 28, 111–18, 205–07, 251–53, 339–44. After her husband's death, Maria Theresa's mints issued more than twice as many different types of thaler with her name than with that of her son and co-regent, Emperor Josef II.

26. Eypeltauer, *Corpus Nummorum*, 231, 13.

27. Emile Karafiol, "The Reforms of the Empress Maria Theresa in the Provincial Government of Lower Austria, 1740–1765" (Ph.D. diss., Cornell University, 1965), 240, 246–47, 252.

28. Vocelka, *Glanz*, 304–6.

29. Her first child died in infancy; three others, including her most talented son, Karl, died between the ages of twelve and sixteen.

30. On her Russian alliance, see the illustrated pamphlet by Emil Jettel-Ettenach, *Der Damenkrieg: ein historisches Bilderbuch* (Vienna, 1924); Georg Ludwigstorff, "Die Geschichte des Maria-Theresien-Ordens bis zum Ende des 18. Jahrh.," in H. Dikowitsch, ed., *Barock–Blütezeit der europäischen Ritterorden* (St. Polten, 2000), 27–34.

31. Christian Steeb, "Kaiser Franz I. und seine ablehende Haltung gegenüber der Stiftung des königlich ungarischen St.-Stephans-Ordens," in Dikowitsch, *Barock,* 35–40. Maria Theresa could be very cavalier about such honors; once, because "I don't know anyone who hasn't already got some honorary title," she made the fourteen-year-old granddaughter of her chief minister a knight of the Order of Malta (ibid., 63–66).

32. Alfred Ritter von Arneth, ed., *Maria Theresia und Joseph II; Ihre Correspondenz,* 3 vols. (Vienna, 1867–68), 3:277 (*Ne perdez jamais de vue: besser ein mittelmässiger Frieden als glücklicher Krieg*).

33. Michael Yonan, "Conceptualizing the *Kaiserinwitwe:* Empress Maria Theresa and Her Portraits," in Allison Levy, ed., *Widowhood and Visual Culture in Early Modern Europe* (Aldershot, 2003), 109–24.

34. The most important study remains Caetano Beirão, *D. Maria I 1777–1792,* 4th ed. (Lisbon, 1944).

35. Jenifer Roberts, *The Madness of Queen Maria* (Chippenham, 2009), 5–54; Maria do Ceu de Brito Vairinho Borrecho, "D. Maria I.: a formaçao de uma rainha" (thesis, Universidade Nova da Lisboa, 1993), esp. 9, 39–45.

36. Portugal's National Library contains thirty-two titles mentioning her in 1777 and twenty-four from the next three years. Fewer than ten of the first group came from official royal presses, which printed most of those from 1778–80.

37. Roberts, *Madness of Queen Maria,* 57–61; Do Ceu de Brito, appendix VI; *AUTO / do Levanatameno e juramento / que os grandes, titulos seculars, ecclesiasticos, e mais pessoas, que se acharão presentes, / fizerão á Muito Alta, Muito Poderosa / Rainha Fidelissima / a senhora / D. Maria I. / Nosssa Senhora / na coroa destes reinos, e senhorios de Portugal, / sendo exaltada, e coroada sobre o regio / throno juntamente com o senhor Rei / D. Pedro III. / na tarde do dia treze de maio, anno de 1777* (Lisbon, 1780), 5 (quote). A graphic portrayal of her husband's political position is provided by a contemporary joint portrait; see <http://commons.wikimedia.org/wiki/File:MariaIpedroIII.jpg>.

38. Roberts, *Madness of Queen Maria,* 64–69, 86, 111; on her letters, see Beirão, *D. Maria I,* 437–47.

39. Roberts, *Madness of Queen Maria,* 113–35.

## Chapter 7. Ruling Without Inheriting

1. Anisimov's collective biography, published in 1997, is available in English as *Five Empresses: Court Life in Eighteenth-Century Russia* (London, 2004). See the critical survey of recent Russian historians of this era (most prominently, Anisimov) by M. Mouravieva, "Figures denigrées," in Isabelle Poutrin and Marie-Karine Schaub, eds., *Femmes et pouvoir politique: Les princesses d'Europe, XVe–XVIIIe siècles* (Rosny, 2007), 312–25. For an overview from a different perspective, see John T. Alexander, "Favorites, Favoritism and Female Rule in Russia, 1725–1796," in Roger Bartlett and Janet Hartley, eds., *Russia in the Age of Enlightenment: Essays for Isabel de Madariaga* (London, 1990), 106–24.

2. Miram Yalom, *Birth of the Chess Queen* (New York, 2004), 182–87.

3. Lindsay Hughes, *Sophia, Regent of Russia 1657–1704* (New Haven, 1990), 69–70, 174.

4. Ibid., 139–45. An engraving at Amsterdam replaced the eagle with allegorical feminine virtues and translated her bombastic eulogy into Latin.

5. J. Korb, *Diary of an Austrian Secretary of Legation at the Court of Czar Peter the Great,* 2 vols. (London, 1863), 2:92 (first printed in Latin [Vienna, 1700]).

6. Gary Marker, "Godly and Pagan Women in the Coronation Sermon of 1724," in Roger Bartlett and Gabriela Lehmann-Carli, eds., *Eighteenth-Century Russia: Society, Culture, Economy* (Berlin, 2007), 207, 210, 219; and Marker, "Sacralizing Female Rule, 1725–1761," in W. Rosslyn and A. Tosi, eds., *Women in Russian Culture and Society 1700–1825* (New York, 2007), 171–90.

7. [David Fassmann], *Gespräche im Raum der Todte (129h entrevue, Band IX) zwischen der Russische Kaiserin* CATHARINA *und der weltberühmten Orientalischer Königin* ZENOBIA (Leipzig, 1729), 10–11, 13–14, 35–40, 43–45.

8. Evgenyi Anisimov's detailed biography of Anna (Moscow, 2002) remains untranslated, and his account of her reign in *Five Empresses* is extremely negative. Compare Mina Curtiss, *The Forgotten Empress: Anna Ivanovna and Her Era, 1730–1740s* (New York, 1974); also Marker, "Sacralizing Female Rule," 180–81, and Ansimov, *Five Empresses,* 95, 100.

9. Frederick II, *Mémoires,* ed.. Boutaric and Campardon, 2 vols. (Paris 1866), 1:40.

10. Catherine II, *Sochineniia,* ed. A. N. Pypin (1907; reprint, Osnabrück, 1967), 586–88.

11. Anisimov, *Five Empresses,* 81.

12. Georg Wolfgang Krafft, *Description et representation exacte de la Maison de Glace, construite à St. Petersbourg au mois de Janvier 1740, et de tous les meubles qui s'y trouvent* (St. Petersburg, 1741); Anisimov, *Five Empresses,* 91–92. On her medals, see Béatrice Coullaré, ed., *Médailles russes du Louvre, 1672–1855* (Paris, 2006); none celebrated Anna's most important foundation, the Noble Cadet Corps, or her ballet school.

13. *Gesprach in Raum der Todten zwischen Elisabetha Königin von England und Irland und Anna Ivanowna, Kaiserin und Selbsthalterin aller Russen* (Frankfurt, 1741), 111–12. Another German dialogue of the dead began with the newly arrived Anna, seated in the underworld with Catherine I, receiving a petition sent from Siberia by her favorite, Biron: *Allerwichtig Curioseste Staats-Handel im Reich der Todten: Geheim Unterredung* (Frankfurt/Leipzig, 1741), 1–20.

14. Anisimov, *Five Empresses,* 127–70. Because of her husband, the regent was also known as Anna Karlovna.

15. Francine-Dominique Lichtenhahn, *Elisabeth Ire de Russie: l'autre impératrice* (Paris, 2007). The first edition (1986) of the best modern Russian biography is available in English: Evgeny Anisimov, *Empress Elizabeth: Her Reign and Her Russia, 1741–1761* (Gulf Breeze, Fla., 1995); Anisimov's revised version of 1999 has not been translated into English.

16. Lichtenhahn, *Elisabeth,* 106–19; Anisimov, *Elizabeth,* 164–66.

17. *Krönungs-Geschichte, oder Umständliche Beschreibung des solennen Einzugs, und der hohen Salbung und Krönung Ihro Kayserl. Majest. der allerdurchlauchtigsten, grossmächtig-sten Fürstin und grossen Frau Elisabeth Petrowna Kayserin und Selbstherrscherin aller Reussen etc.* (St. Petersburg, 1745); Lichtenhahn, *Elisabeth,* 212–14, 260–61.

18. Solid diplomatic account by Francine Lichtenhahn, *La Russie entre en Europe* (Paris, 1997); also her *Elisabeth*, 38. As late as 1781 contested diplomatic protocol held up a military alliance for several months between two so-called enlightened despots of imperial rank, Catherine II and Joseph II of Austria, because Joseph refused to sign a copy that named the Russian first; Catherine finally evaded the problem through an exchange of private letters: see Isabel de Maradiaga, "The Secret Austro-Russian Treaty of 1781," in *Slavonic and East European Review* 38 (1959–60), 114–45.

19. Compare Coullaré, *Médailles russes,* with P. Ricaud de Tiregale, *Médailles sur les principaux événemens de l'Empire de Russie, depuis le règne de Pierre le Grand jusqu'à celui de Catherine II* (Potsdam, 1772), #III, 77–90.

20. Anisimov, *Elizabeth,* 67–72; Lichtenhahn, *Elisabeth,* 316–19.

21. James F. Brennan, *Enlightened Despotism in Russia: The Reign of Elisabeth, 1741–1762* (New York, 1987), 66, 163–64, 180, 182–83; Anisimov, *Elizabeth,* 59–66.

22. Lichtenhahn, *Elisabeth,* 224–33.

23. Virginia Rounding, *Catherine the Great* (New York, 2006), 110; Catherine is the ultimate source of this reported exchange, but in July 1753 the English ambassador noted, "There was nothing [Elisabeth] desired more than to be at war with that prince [Frederick II]." After both women had died, an Austrian propagandist compared the lives and government of the two empresses: *Maria Theresien und Elisabeth im Reiche der Todten: Ein Gespräch zwischen diese beeden Kaiserinnen* (Vienna, 1781).

24. Brennan, *Enlightened Despotism,* 246; Lichtenhahn, *Elisabeth,* 386; Simon Sebag Montefiore, *Prince of Princes: The Life of Potemkin* (New York, 2000), 39n.

25. Brennan, *Enlightened Despotism,* 248; Liechtenhahn, *Elisabeth,* 377–78.

26. Hélène Carrère d'Encausse, *Catherine II: Un âge d'or pour la Russie* (Paris, 2005). A pamphlet printed at Riga in 1764 called her *die allerdurchlauchtigste, grossmächtigste Kaiserin und Frau Catharina Alexiewna, Selbstherrscherin aller Reussen etc. als unserer von Gott geschenkten allerhuldreichsten Landesmutter;* one from Tallinn twenty years later extolled *der Regierungszeit der grossen Catharina der IIen.*

27. Anisimov, *Five Empresses,* 293, 316; Katherine Anthony, trans., *Memoirs of Catherine the Great* (New York, 1935), 326; on her papers, see Alexander Kamenskij's overview in Claus Scharf, ed., *Katharina II, Russland und Europa: Beiträge zur internationalen Forschung* (Mainz, 2001), 565–69.

28. Isabel de Madariaga's classic *Russia in the Age of Catherine the Great* (London, 1981) was later condensed as *Catherine the Great: A Short History* (New Haven, 1990). In addition to Scharf's volume, other published bicentennial proceedings include Eckhard Hübner, Jan Kusber und Peter Nitsche, eds., *Russland zur Zeit Katharinas II* (Cologne, 1998), and Anita Davidenkoff, ed., *Catherine II et l'Europe* (Paris, 1997), along with an exhibition catalogue: John Vrieze, ed., *Catharina, die Keizerin en de Kunsten; uit de schatzkammers van de Hermitage* (Zwolle, 1996).

29. Anisimov, *Five Empresses,* 277–83.

30. De Madariaga, *Russia,* 115–17.

31. Anisimov, *Five Empresses,* 298–300.

32. An eighty-page pamphlet commemorated him: *Histoire de la vie de George de Browne, comte du Saint-Empire, gouverneur général de Livonie et d'Esthonie, général*

*en chef des armées de Sa Majesté l'impératrice de toutes les Russies* (Riga, 1795; also in German [Vienna, 1795]).

33. Anisimov, *Five Empresses*, 295.

34. Robert Werlich, *Russian Orders, Decorations and Medals* (Washington, 1981). After the partitions of Poland, Catherine's Russia also absorbed the honorary Polish orders of the White Eagle and St. Stanislaus, founded by Stanislas Poniatowski in 1765. Grieg's commemorative pamphlet lists all his major honors: *Kanzelrede, bey der feyerlichen Beerdigung Seiner Excellenz, des hochgebohrnen Herrn Samuel Greigh, Ihro Russischkayserlichen Majestät hochbetrauten Admirals, Oberbefehlshabers der Russischen Flotte in der Ostsee, Mitglieds des Admiralitätscollegii und der Academie der Wissenschaften, Ritters des H. Andreas, des H. Alexander-Newsky, vom grossen Kreuze des Heiligen Georgs, erster Klasse des H. Wladimirs und des H. Annen Ordens, gehalten in der Ritter- und Domkirche zu Reval, den 31sten October 1788* (Reval, 1788).

35. De Madariaga, *Russia*, 267.

36. John T. Alexander, *Catherine the Great: Life and Legend* (Oxford, 1989), 180–82.

37. Paul Dukes, ed., *Catherine the Great's Instruction (Nakaz) to the Legislative Commission, 1767* (Newtonville, Mass., 1977); also see above, pp. 38–39.

38. Anisimov, *Five Empresses*, 294; De Madariaga, *Russia*, 151; Alexander, *Catherine*, 101.

39. De Madariaga, *Russia*, 277–91, 487, 586 (quote); Alexander, *Catherine*, 190–91.

40. Evgenia Shchukina, "Catherine II and Russian Metallic Art," in Magnus Olausson, ed., *Catherine the Great and Gustav III* (Stockholm, 1999), 313–19; Coullaré, *Médailles russes*. Both British medical medals are in the British Museum. The preface to Ricaud de Tiregale's *Médailles* claimed that, like the ancient Romans, his own age had perpetuated "the exploits and great deeds of illustrious men [*sic*]" in metal.

41. B. F. Brekke, *The Copper Coinage of Imperial Russia, 1700–1917* (Malmö, 1977), 109.

42. Her memoirs only recently appeared in their original language: Princess Dashkova, *Mon Histoire*, ed. Alexandre Woronzoff-Dashkova (Paris, 1999) (quote, 157).

43. C.-F.-P. Masson, *Mémoires secrets sur la Russie* (Paris, 1800), 2:116 (the Comte de Ségur tells the same story about Dashkova in his memoirs); Dashkova, *Mon Histoire*, 224, 226.

44. Marie-Liesse Pierre-Dulau, "Trois artistes lorrains à Saint-Petersbourg au XVIIIe siècle," in Davidenkoff, *Catherine II et l'Europe*, 156. St. Petersburg's Russian State Museum contains a full-size bronze model of Collot's head of Peter.

45. Quoted in Natalie Bondil, ed., *Catherine the Great: Art for Empire* (Montreal, 2007), 64.

46. Michael Raeburn, Ludmila Voronikhina, and Andrew Nurnberg, eds., *The Green Frog Service* (London/St. Petersburg, 1995).

47. Fullest discussion in Alexander, *Catherine*, 201–26.

48. On their possible marriage, see Sebag Montefiore, *Potemkin*, 138–40; de Madariaga, *Russia*, 566.

49. On her reactions to revolutionary France, see Carrère d'Encausse, *Catherine II*, 529–57 (quote, 557). The Russian National Library has nine printed lists of French men and women taking this oath after February 1793: *Rossica* 13.VIII.2. nos. 365–73.

50. *L'ombre de Catherine II aux Champs-Elysees* ("Kamchatka," 1797); an almost identical version was entitled *Conferences de Catherine II avec Louis XVI, le grand Frédéric et Pierre le Grand, aux Champs-Elysées* ("Moscow," 1797). Its author remains unidentified, but his familiarity with both Prussia and Russia suggests the Comte de Ségur.

51. Catherine II, *Sochineniia*, 583–94.

52. Alexander, *Catherine*, 97.

### Chapter 8. Female Rule After 1800

1. Charles-François-Philibert Masson*, Les Helvétiens, en huit chants, avec des notes historiques* (Paris: an VIII [=1800]; this account uses his *Mémoires secrets sur la Russie*, 2d printing, 2 vols. (Paris, 1800).

2. Masson, *Memoirs*, 1:78–83, 2:128.

3. Ibid., 1:135–36.

4. Compare epigraph with Eileen McDonagh, "Political Citizenship and Democratization: The Gender Paradox," *American Political Science Review* 96 (2002), 535–52.

5. Isabel Burdiel, *Isabel II: No se Puede Reinar Inocentemente* (Madrid, 2004); Ester de Lemos, *D. Maria II (A Rainha e a Mulher)* (Lisbon, 1954).

6. Rebecca Howard Davis, *Women and Power in Parliamentary Democracies: Cabinet Appointments in Western Europe, 1968–1992* (Lincoln, Neb., 1997), 17.

7. Blema Steinberg, *Women in Power: The Personalities and Leadership Styles of Indira Gandhi, Golda Meir, and Margaret Thatcher* (Montreal, 2008); Katharine Anthony, trans., *Memoirs of Catherine the Great* (New York, 1935), 325.

8. J. B. Almeida Garrett, "Tratado de Educação," in *Obras completas,* ed. T. Braga, 2 vols. (Lisbon, 1904), 2:310; Walter L. Arnstein, *Queen Victoria* (New York, 2003), 9.

9. Alain Lanavère, "Zénobie, personnage du XVIIe siècle?" in J. Charles-Gaffiot, H. Lafange, and J.-F. Hofman, eds., *Moi, Zénobie, Reine de Palmyre* (Milan, 2001), 139–42.

10. Mary Hamer, *Signs of Cleopatra: Reading an Icon Historically,* 2d ed. (Exeter, 2008), xiv; Hans Volkmann, *Kleopatra: Politik und Propaganda* (Munich, 1953), 222–23. G. H. Möller's *Beiträge zur Dramatischen Kleopatra-Literatur* (Schweinfurt, 1907) preceded George Bernard Shaw's play of 1913, which has influenced many subsequent adaptations.

11. See Jonathan Clements, *Wu* (Sutton, UK, 2007), 188–96. Wu also served as the centerpiece of a television series in 1984 featuring numerous Kung-Fu episodes.

12. John T. Alexander, *Catherine the Great* (Oxford, 1989), 329–41; John Vrieze, ed., *Catharina, die Keizerin en de Kunsten; uit de schatzkammers van de Hermitage* (Zwolle, 1996), 277–80.

# Bibliographical Essay

Because female rulers have been so rare throughout recorded history, they have almost always been treated as isolated individuals. To the best of my knowledge, no previous work has tried to examine the political record of every female monarch throughout Europe across several centuries and attempt to discover long-term trends of female rule in European civilization. There is a useful resource, constantly updated, for identifying all sorts of politically influential women throughout history—<www.guide2womenleaders.com>—and several recent books have discussed "queenship." However, because the academic field of gender studies rarely intersects with that of comparative politics, such works tend to collapse the political status of these women by failing to discriminate between divine-right female sovereigns and wives of kings with no formal political authority. Palgrave Macmillan offers a series entitled *Queenship and Power*, currently with ten titles either produced or announced. Half are about Elizabeth I of England; one of these—Alice Hunt and Anna Whitelock, eds., *Tudor Queenship: The Reigns of Mary and Elizabeth* (New York, 2010)—deals with Europe's only pair of autonomous old-regime female monarchs to reign consecutively. Among current feminist scholars, Sharon Jansen has provided the most ambitious recent attempts to survey female rule in early modern Europe. Both of her books, *The Monstrous Regiment of Women: Female Rulers in Early Modern Europe* (New York: Palgrave, 2002) and *Debating Women, Politics, and Power in Early Modern Europe* (New York: Palgrave, 2008), mix female sovereigns with female regents; more important, both promote a resolutely pessimistic view, which is the exact reverse of my approach.

Recent attempts by Charles Beem and the late Thierry Wanegffelen (2009) to place women rulers into broader historical contexts offer contrasting merits and defects. In *The Lioness Roared: The Problems of Female Rule in English History* (New York: Palgrave

Macmillan, 2006). Beem examined "the long view of female ruler-ship as a particular category of English kingship" from the twelfth century to the twentieth, and he also introduced the useful phrase "female kings." The greatest defect in his work is the limiting adjective "English"; insularity prevents Beem from placing any of his subjects in the context of other contemporary female rulers throughout Europe. Wanegffelen's *Le Pouvoir contesté: souveraines d'Europe à la Renaissance* (Paris: Payot, 2008) reverses both Beem's shortcomings and his virtues; it offers a more cosmopolitan approach to a period that was unusually rich in female monarchs and regents, but it lacks Beem's chronological depth. Furthermore, because Wanegffelen remains centered in France, the most important kingdom in Europe to prohibit female inheritance, he (like Jansen) paints early modern Europe's widespread experiences with female rule in essentially negative colors. For very different reasons, neither Beem nor Wanegffelen pays much attention to the most important female sovereign of this era, England's Elizabeth I.

Although abundant scholarship surrounds Europe's most successful female rulers, all of whom have useful and often superb biographies in English, these women have nearly always been treated in isolation from each other. Only one author, Katharine Anthony, ever published well-researched and well-written biographies of two extremely successful European female monarchs from different countries and centuries, and she did so over eighty years ago. Both her *Catherine the Great* (New York, 1925) and her *Queen Elizabeth* (New York, 1929) have sold more than a hundred thousand copies, and both have been reprinted within the last decade (2003 and 2004). Neither biography mentions the other woman. The remainder of this survey lists the works—overwhelmingly biographies of individual women rulers—that I have found most useful for discussing the more important women rulers featured in each chapter. This selection privileges titles in English and French, although occasional titles in Spanish and German are included when they offer invaluable information not available elsewhere.

## Chapter 1

The best study of the first truly historical female sovereign is Joyce Tyldesley's *Hatchepsut: The Female Pharaoh* (New York: Viking, 1996). Her Ptolemaic successor Cleopatra VII (r. 50–30 B.C.) ranks among the world's best known (if not necessarily best understood) female rulers, with new studies about her appearing almost annually. Two recent biographies, Duane Roller's *Cleopatra: A Biography* (Oxford: Oxford University Press, 2010) and Stacy Schiff's *Cleopatra: A Life* (Boston: Little, Brown, 2010), provide serviceable introductions, while Joyce Tyldesley's *Cleopatra: Last Queen of Egypt* (New York: Basic Books, 2008) examines her from an Egyptologist's perspective. Recent exhibitions, especially Susan Walker and Sally-Ann Ashton, eds., *Cleopatra Reassessed* (London: British Museum, 2003), also offer useful information on her reign, and Mary Hamer, *Signs of Cleopatra: Reading an Icon Historically,* 2d ed. (Exeter: Exeter University Press, 2008), is informative on her representations.

On China's only female empress, Jonathan Clements, *Wu: The Chinese Empress Who Schemed, Seduced and Murdered Her Way to Become a Living God* (Stroud: Sutton, 2007), is lively and informative, but there is more political context in R. W. L. Guisso, *Wu Tse T'ien and the Politics of Legitimation in T'ang China* (Bellingham, Wash., 1978). On Japan's early female *tennos*, see Joan R. Piggott, *The Emergence of Japanese Kingship* (Stanford: Stanford University Press, 1997). On Byzantium, Judith Herrin, *Women in Purple: Rulers of Medieval Byzantium* (Princeton: Princeton University Press, 2001), offers the best introduction. Fatima Mernissi, *The Forgotten Queens of Islam* (Cambridge: Cambridge University Press, 1993), provides a valuable introduction to women rulers in Islamic history. It must be supplemented by the essays in Gavin Hambly, ed., *Women in the Medieval Islamic World: Power, Patronage, and Piety* (New York: St. Martin's Press, 1998).

Historians of art and architecture have provided the most valuable approaches to the Christian female monarchs of the high Middle Ages. The most useful introduction to the reign of the Greek

Orthodox Tamar of Georgia is Antony Eastmond, *Royal Imagery in Medieval Georgia* (University Park: Pennsylvania State University Press, 1998). For medieval Latin Christendom, the most enlightening work is Therese Martin, *Queen as King: Politics and Architectural Propaganda in Twelfth-Century Spain* (Leiden: Brill, 2006). A small bibliography has grown up around Martin's central figure, Urraca of Castile-León, since Bernard Reilly's *The Kingdom of León-Castilla under Queen Urraca, 1109–1126* (Princeton: Princeton University Press, 1982); those who read Spanish can profit from Maria del Carmen Pallares Mendez, *La Reina Urraca* (San Sebastian, 2006).

## Chapter 2

The last author to attempt any general discussion of female rulers in Western history was Mrs. [Anna] Jameson, whose two-volume *Memoirs of Celebrated Female Sovereigns* (which she admitted might have been more properly entitled "Comparative Studies") appeared at London in 1831. It intended "to present, in a small compass, an idea of the influence which a female government has had *generally* on men and nations, and of the influence which the possession of power has had *individually* on the female character" (ix–x). After 180 years, Jameson's choice of twelve major female monarchs still seems excellent: her first volume reached from Semiramis to Elizabeth I, and her second began with Christina of Sweden and ended with Catherine II. However, Jameson's questioning how far any woman sovereign could "render [her] inseparable defects as little injurious to society, and [her] peculiar virtues as little hurtful to herself, as possible" (xiii) predicted Queen Victoria almost perfectly but seems badly outdated today. I have tried to provide a general criterion for isolating de jure female rulers in states above the level of duchies in "Gendered Sovereignty: Numismatics and Female Rule in Europe, 1300–1800," *Journal of Interdisciplinary History* 41 (2011), 533–64.

## Chapter 3

There are few useful English-language biographies of Europe's late medieval royal heiresses, although its first major female monarch, Joanna I of Naples, has been examined recently both in a readable biography by Nancy Goldstone, *The Lady Queen* (New York: Walker, 2009), and in an unpublished doctoral thesis by Elizabeth Casteen (Northwestern University, 2009). The two most notable female sovereigns to emerge shortly after Joanna I's death also possess politically oriented biographies in English: St. Jadwiga, by the well-known Polish historian Oscar Halecki, *Jadwiga of Anjou and the Rise of East Central Europe,* ed. Thaddeus Gromada (Boulder: Polish Institute of Arts and Sciences of America, 1991), and the remarkable Scandinavian ruler Margaret of Denmark, by Vivian Etting, *Queen Margrete I (1353–1412) and the Founding of the Nordic Union* (Leiden: Brill, 2004). On the two female monarchs of fifteenth-century Cyprus, see essays by Peter Edbury and Joachim G. Joachim in David Hunt and Iro Hunt, eds., *Caterina Cornaro: Queen of Cyprus* (London: Trigraph, 1989); there is a French transla-tion of the invaluable Egyptian sources on these events: M. Tahar Mansouri, *Chypre dans les sources arabes médiévales* (Nicosia, 2001).

For Isabel of Castile, the best introduction in English is Peggy Liss, *Isabel the Queen: Life and Times,* 2d ed. (Philadelphia: University of Pennsylvania Press, 2004); Barbara Weissberger, *Isabel Rules: Constructing Queenship, Wielding Power* (Minneapolis: University of Minnesota Press, 2004), also contains useful insights. These supple-ment rather than replace the thousand-page biography by a Benedictine monk writing under the name Tarsicio de Azcona: *Isabel la Católica: Estudio crítico de su vida y su reinado* (Madrid: BAC, 1993); I have used the more recent 650-page abridgment, *Isabel la Católica: Vida y reinado* (Madrid: Esfera de los Libros, 2004). The same scholar subsequently composed a lively defense of Isabel's doomed female rival: Tarsicio de Azcona, *Juana de Castilla, mal llamada La Beltraneja: vida de la hija de Enrique IV de Castilla y su exilio en Portugal (1462–1530)* (Madrid: Esfera de los Libros, 2007). Isabel's successor has a revi-sionist biography in English: Bethany Aram, *Juana the Mad: Sovereignty and Dynasty in Renaissance Europe* (Baltimore: Johns Hopkins University Press, 2005); the original Spanish edition, published in 2001, has a better preface. A fine study of joint rule in Navarre is Alvaro Adot Lerga, *Juan de Albret y Catalina de Foix, o la defensa del Estado navarro (1483–1517)* (Pamplona: Pamiela, 2005).

## Chapter 4

Apart from Catherine de Medici, the major female regents of early modern Europe lack recent biographies in English. The great sixteenth-century Netherlands regents have occasionally been treated together; chapters 3–7 of Helmut G. Koenigsberger, *Monarchies, States Generals and Parliaments: The Netherlands in the Fifteenth and Sixteenth Centuries* (Cambridge: Cambridge University Press, 2001), provides a useful assessment of their political roles. Both Margaret of Austria and Mary of Hungary have had biographies by the same author: an earlier set in French by Ghislaine de Boom, published in 1936 and 1951, and later in Dutch by Jane de Iongh, with revised versions appearing in 1966 and 1981 (only the earlier versions of de Iongh's biographies have been translated into English, in 1953 and 1958, respectively). Margaret's most recent biographers are Austrian and French: Ursula Tamussino, *Margarete von Österreich: Diplomatin der Renaissance* (Graz, 1995), and Jean-Pierre Soisson, *Marguerite, Princesse de Bourgogne* (Paris, 2002), while the outstanding modern biography of Mary of Hungary by Laetitia Gorter-van Royen is in Dutch. Recent international congresses devoted to each woman have generated some literature in English: Dagmar Eichberger, ed., *Women of Distinction: Margaret of York/Margaret of Austria* (Louvain: Brepols, 2005), and Orsolya Rethelyi, ed., *Mary of Hungary: The Queen and Her Court 1521–1531* (Budapest: Budapest History Museum, 2005).

Spain's young mid-sixteenth-century female regent has a good biographer in Antonio Villacorta Baños-Garcia, *La Jesuita* (Barcelona: Planeta, 2005). Among the later Low Countries regents, useful biographies of Margaret of Parma exist in Dutch, Italian, and French, but not in English, while no English-language study of the long-serving archduchess and governor general Infanta Isabel Clara Eugenia has appeared since 1910. Matters are very different with the prominent French female regents. There are a dozen serviceable biographies of Catherine de Medici in French, and an almost equal number in English. Among the former, that by Ivan Cloulas (Paris: Fayard, 1979) still ranks among the best, although it lacks footnotes; among the latter, that by R. J. Knecht, *Catherine de' Medici* (London: Longman, 1998), is most recommendable. No equally recommendable modern life of Marie de Medici exists in English; the recent thousand-page effort by Jean-François Dubost, *Marie de Medicis: la reine dévoilée* (Paris: Payot, 2009), supersedes all its predecessors.

## Chapter 5

Good Queen Bess seems an inexhaustible topic. English-language biographies of Elizabeth I continue to appear almost annually, but one should still begin with the classic life by Sir John Neale, first published in 1934 and never equipped with footnotes. Katharine Anthony's biography is even older (1929) but still worth reading. For purposes of studying female rule, the two outstanding recent explorations are Carole Levin, *The Heart and Stomach of a King: Elizabeth I and the Politics of Sex and Power* (Philadelphia: University of Pennsylvania Press, 1994), and Louis Montrose, *The Subject of Elizabeth* (Chicago: University of Chicago Press, 2006). No less indispensable is the magnificent critical edition by Leah Marcus, Janel Mueller, and Mary Beth Rose, eds., *Elizabeth I: Collected Works* (Chicago: University of Chicago Press, 2000); three additional volumes have since appeared from the same publisher, providing the foreign-language originals of Elizabeth's original compositions (2003) and two volumes of her own translations (both in 2009). She has been relatively little studied outside England and America, although a satisfactory French biography, Bernard Cottret, *La monarchie au féminin: Elisabeth Ire d'Angleterre* (Paris: Fayard, 2009), has recently appeared alongside two German theses: Ursula Machoczek, *Die regierende Königin-Elizabeth I. von England: Aspekte weiblicher Herrschaft im 16. Jahrhundert* (Pfaffenweiler, 1996), and Robert Valerius, *Weibliche Herrschaft im 16. Jahrhundert: Die Regentschaft Elisabeths I. zwischen Realpolitik, Querelle des femmes und Kult der Virgin Queen* (Herbolzheim, 2002).

Among Europe's other mid-sixteenth-century female rulers, Elizabeth's predecessor Mary Tudor remains politically incorrect and consequently has received relatively little attention until recently. The useful brief study by Judith M. Richards, *Mary Tudor*

(New York: Routledge, 2008), updates the classic biography by David Loades, *Mary Tudor: A Life* (Oxford: Blackwell, 1989), later abridged and updated by Loades himself as *Mary Tudor: The Tragical History of the First Queen of England* (Kew: National Archives, 2006). For Scotland's Mary Stuart, the classic biography by Antonia Fraser, first published in 1969, still dominates the field through thirty reprints—although the resolutely negative portrait by Jenny Wormald, *Mary Queen of Scots: A Study in Failure* (London: G. Philip, 1988), updated as *Mary, Queen of Scots: Politics, Passion and a Kingdom Lost* (New York: St. Martin's, 2001), is also worth reading. The last female monarch of Navarre is still best approached through the classic biography by Nancy L. Roelker, *Queen of Navarre: Jeanne d'Albret, 1528–1572* (Cambridge: Harvard University Press, 1968), although additional useful material has appeared subsequently in French.

In complete contrast to the erudite but insular Elizabeth I, biographies of Europe's next female monarch, Sweden's Queen Christina, have, like their subject, always been remarkably cosmopolitan. Even modern expositions about her have been unusually international; the organizing committee for a major exposition at Sweden's National Museum in 1966 represented ten European governments, including Vatican City-State. Since 1800 approximately equal numbers of biographies of Christina have appeared in German, English, and Swedish, followed closely by Italian and French. This trend persists into the twenty-first century. Verena von der Heyden-Rynsch, *Christina von Schweden: Die rätselhafte monarchin* (Weimar, 2000), has been translated into French (2001) and Spanish (2001), while other recent biographies have also appeared in Flemish (2001), Italian (2004), and Norwegian (2005). Her most notable recent biography, by Veronica Buckley, *Christina Queen of Sweden: The Restless Life of a European Eccentric* (London: Fourth Estate, 2004), has already been translated into Swedish (2004), German (2005), and Italian (2006). The most provocative title remains Bernard Quilliet, *Christine de Suède: un roi exceptionnel* (Paris, 1982). All these biographies rely on an eighteenth-century Swedish scholar who collected information on her throughout Europe: J. Arckenholz, *Mémoires concernant Christine, reine de Suède,*

4 vols. (Amsterdam/Leipzig, 1751–60). The bulk of her personal papers, many still unpublished, gather dust in the library of the Medical Faculty of the University of Montpellier, where they must be consulted through a nineteenth-century manuscript inventory (H 587); a copy exists in Stockholm's National Library (Ms. U 205).

The few biographies of Mary II—none of them recent—present Europe's last female figurehead as a mere auxiliary to her husband: in English, Lady Hamilton, *William's Mary* (London, 1928); in Dutch, Jacqueline Doom, *Die vrouw van de Stadhouder-Koenig, Mary Stuart II* (Zaltbommel, 1968). Her recapitulatory memoir for 1688, in French, was found in the Netherlands and printed in Mary II, *Lettres et Mémoires* (The Hague, 1880). Those from 1689–93, in English, were printed from copies in the Hanoverian archives: Richard Doebner, ed., *Memoirs of Mary, Queen of England* (Leipzig, 1896).

## Chapter 6

Both old and new scholarship on the greatest female monarch of Mitteleuropa, Austria's Maria Theresa, is predominantly in German. Still fundamental to any biographer is the unbelievably detailed ten-volume study of Alfred Ritter von Arneth, *Geschichte Maria Theresiens* (Vienna, 1863–79). Von Arneth also edited four volumes of Maria Theresa's letters to children and friends (Vienna, 1881); three volumes of her correspondence with her oldest son and successor, Joseph II (Vienna, 1867–68); and, in conjunction with the French scholar M. Geoffrey, three volumes of secret correspondence between Maria Theresa and the French court during Marie Antoinette's residence (Paris, 1874). New works about Maria Theresa, usually in German, appear almost annually, although none has yet emerged from von Arneth's shadow into international prominence. Meanwhile, the best available biographies in English, by Edward Crankshaw (New York: Viking, 1970) and the short study by C. A. Macartney in a series called "Men and Their Times" (London, 1969), are beginning to show their age alongside a solid French biography by Jean-Paul Bled (Paris: Fayard, 2001).

Among Europe's other eighteenth-century royal heiresses, England's last female monarch of the old regime has only one important biographer, Edward Gregg, whose *Queen Anne* (London: Routledge, 1980) was revised and reissued by Yale University Press in 2001. Sweden's Ulrika Eleanora remains mysterious to anyone unable to read Swedish; very few of her forty entries in Stockholm's National Library are genuine biographies, and only two brief funeral orations are in foreign languages. A recent work in English offers some information about Europe's final female monarch of the old regime: Jenifer Roberts, *The Madness of Queen Maria: The Remarkable Life of Maria I of Portugal* (Chippenham: Templeton Press, 2009).

## Chapter 7

The French have traditionally been interested in Catherine II, including the recent biography by a female academician, Hélène Carrère d'Encausse, *Catherine II: un âge d'or pour la Russie* (Paris: Fayard, 2002), but the outstanding living expert on her writes in English. Isabel de Madariaga's exemplary life-and-times study, *Russia in the Age of Catherine the Great* (London: Weidenfeld and Nicholson, 1981), preceded her brief sketch, *Catherine the Great: A Short History* (New Haven: Yale University Press, 1990). Also valuable is John T. Alexander, *Catherine the Great: Life and Legend* (Oxford: Oxford University Press, 1989). Simon Sebag Montefiore, *Prince of Princes: The Life of Potemkin* (London: Weidenfeld and Nicolson, 2000), provides a major contribution toward understanding the last two decades of her reign.

Russia's other women rulers have also been well served in English. Its first female autocrat has an excellent biography in English: Lindsay Hughes, *Sophia: Regent of Russia 1657–1704* (New Haven: Yale University Press, 1990). In 1997 Russia's leading eighteenth-century expert, Evgeny Anisimov, wrote a five-part collective biography in Russian, available in English as *Five Empresses: Court Life in Eighteenth-Century Russia* (Westport, Conn.: Praeger, 2004). Anisimov's earlier study of Catherine II's immediate predecessor, published in 1986, is also available in English as *Empress Elizabeth: Her Reign and Her Russia, 1741–1761* (Gulf Breeze, Fla.: Academic International Press, 1995), but Anisimov's revised version remains in

Russian. Those who read French will enjoy Francine Lichtenhahn, *Elisabeth Ire: l'autre impératrice* (Paris: Fayard, 2007).

## Chapter 8

Because so few women have become heads of state in recent times, collective studies of them are still unusual; a welcome exception is Blema Steinberg, *Women in Power: The Personalities and Leadership Styles of Indira Gandhi, Golda Meir, and Margaret Thatcher* (Montreal: McGill-Queen's University Press, 2008). For an introduction to twentieth-century American cinematic portrayals of women sovereigns, see Elizabeth Ford and Deborah Mitchell, *Royal Portraits in Hollywood: Filming the Lives of Queens* (Lexington: University Press of Kentucky, 2007).

# Index

Page numbers in boldface indicate principal treatment of a subject; references to illustrations are in italics